GW00809296

(o'br
wine off-l

Three yea[...]
cuit, I dec[...]
Brendan O[...]
to upgrac[...]
family company. I was excited enough to put on the proverbial old boots again and to take the position of Director of Wine.

Already in my short review of their portfolio of wines, it is apparent that O'Briens have some outstanding suppliers from both the New World and from Europe. Their range of Fine Bordeaux and Vintage Port is exceptional.

During my sojourn in my new role I have overseen a significant enhancement of the product range and have been delighted to introduce the wines of Rust en Vrede, Los Boldos, Beau Rivage and Reynolds. These wines are exclusive to the O'Briens Group and meet the stringent quality and value criteria that I have set in place for the group.

I am committed to tracking down the most exciting and best quality wines from all the wine producing Continents and have identified many new wines to stock which you will encounter on your forthcoming visits to one of our outlets or our website.

Experience the difference at O'Briens.

T. P. Whelehan

T.P. Whelehan
Director of Wine

Exclusive stockists of these highly recommended award winning wines

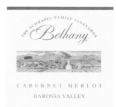

Visit our web site www.obrienswines.ie

Blackrock • Bray • Dalkey • Donnybrook • Dun Laoghaire
Greystones • Glasnevin • Malahide • Navan Rd • Rathgar • Rathmines
• Sandymount • Stillorgan • Templeogue • Vevay

The Best of Wine in Ireland 2001

Editorial Director: Anna Farmar
Production and Design Director: Tony Farmar

Wine Editor: Liam Campbell
Associate Editor: Pat Carroll
with Barbara Boyle and Kate Barrett

Contributions by: Barbara Boyle, Pat Carroll
Alan Crowley, Kathy Farmar, Sandy O'Byrne

Market Research: Clíodhna Foley
Cover design: Liam Furlong at Space
Text design: A. & A. Farmar
Typesetting: A. & A. Farmar
Sales and Promotion: Siobhán Mullet
Distribution: Columba Mercier Distribution

Printed and Bound by Cahills

The publishers would like to
thank the management and
staff of Findlater Wine Merchants for the use of their
premises for the tastings.

A. & A. Farmar's
Best of Wine in
Ireland 2001

Edited by
Liam Campbell

A. & A. Farmar

British Library Cataloguing in Publication Data
A CIP catalogue record for this book is available from the
British Library

ISBN 1-899047-67-0

Published by
A. & A. Farmar
Beech House
78 Ranelagh Village
Dublin 6
Ireland
Tel: (01) 496 3625
Fax: (01) 497 0107
E-mail: afarmar@iol.ie
Web: www.farmarbooks.ie

Printed by Cahills

Contents

An Invitation

To Readers

Tell us what you think about this book—especially how you think it could better, to enable you to get more out wine. The ten best suggestions will get a free copy of the next edition!

To Importers

We are always happy to welcome new suppliers of interesting wines. If you would like to participate in the next edition, please contact Anna or Tony Farmar at the address below.

A. & A. Farmar
Beech House
78 Ranelagh Village
Dublin 6
Ireland
Tel: (01) 496 3625
Fax: (01) 497 0107
E-mail: afarmar@iol.ie

Introduction

For the sixth edition of the *Best of Wine in Ireland* we have become more selective in our approach. There are now so many decent, acceptable wines available in Ireland that we decided that to qualify for inclusion this year a wine must have something extra; it must be a particularly good example of its style, or very good value, or represent an area or style that would not otherwise appear. We have also included a number of good reliable, widely available, sip-in-front-of-the-television wines. Our approach was to list fewer wines, but with more information about the recommendations. The tasters approached the wines with this in mind, and scored accordingly. We also decided that for the blind tastings we would concentrate on wines costing up to £25.

Because the enjoyment of wine is such a personal experience we have introduced two new features this year. We invited each member of the tasting panel to choose some of his or her personal favourite wines tasted within the past year. The only restrictions were that the wine must be available in Ireland, and tasters employed by a particular wine importer may not choose any of that firm's wines. In some cases, this posed a genuine difficulty: there were a few heartfelt cries of regret: 'But that means I can't choose my all-time favourite Meursault!'

We also invited the participating suppliers, all those importers who appreciate what we are doing in helping Irish consumers to get even more enjoyment out of their wine, to nominate some of their more expensive wines in the 'Money No Object' category.

Reflecting the way people choose wine we have presented the wines slightly differently this year: wines from the Old World by region and appellation; wines from the New World by grape variety and country. Inside these categories, as usual, the wines are presented in ascending price order.

We hope that these innovations will help you to find more examples of the style of wine you enjoy and will encourage you to experiment, to try out new styles and regions.

As before we wish to thank the tasters for giving so freely of their time and experience to evaluate the wines. The book would not be possible without the generous contributions of the wine importers who submit wines for tasting and patiently answer our requests for further information.

Sniff, sip, savour, write your own tasting note, but above all, enjoy!

Anna and Tony Farmar
November 2000

The tastings

For *The Best of Wine in Ireland 2001* we conducted tasting sessions between May and October 2000, handling nearly 1,300 wines submitted by importers, of which some 850 were regarded by the panel as worth recommending as good buys. Some of the wines included this year were also in previous editions, with the same or different vintages. However, every single wine included in the book is *re-tasted* each year.

As before, each of the wines was blind tasted by two members of our expert tasting panel tasting on their own and then comparing notes. We agree with Robert Parker that judging wines by committee can penalise wines of individuality and character. Critical to the fairness of the process is the fact that all wines were tasted blind, that is, with their labels hidden. Without this precaution tasters (faced with say a poor wine from a prestigious Burgundian house) might allow pre-knowledge to cloud the judgement.

Each wine was assessed for:

nose — aroma, intensity, complexity

taste — balance, structure, extract, complexity, length

value — price/quality ratio.

Only those wines gaining at least 60 per cent of the available marks qualified for inclusion. As a result, *every wine listed is recommended as well-made and of reasonable value for money.*

WHAT THE AWARDS MEAN

☆☆☆ — exceptional wines of considerable complexity and classic balance from a very good vintage which reward serious tasting. Such wines show a classic balance and are some of the best examples of their type and origin. They are wines to drink, taste and enjoy for themselves. For this year's edition twenty wines were short-listed for three stars. They were retasted blind by three members of the tasting panel. Ten were finally awarded three stars, and one was further selected as Wine of the Year 2001 — see page 5.

☆☆ — elegant wines which show character and complexity above expectations, with balance, subtlety and 'typicité'; ideal to accompany carefully prepared food at a special dinner party.

☆ — wines which show character and style and are particularly good examples of their region and winemaking. The quality of these wines generally exceeds the expectations of the label and the price.

We have indicated the approximate retail price of each wine listed. However, wine prices are not fixed, so please regard these as guide-lines only.

The tasting panel

Members of the tasting panel hold the Wine & Spirit Education Trust (WSET) Diploma.

Kate Barrett works for Wines Direct.

Niamh Boylan is a food and wine lecturer and consultant.

Barbara Boyle, having previously worked as a financial consultant, is now concentrating on wine and wine web sites. She gained a distinction in the WSET Diploma.

Brian Brady is catering manager at a leading private club in Dublin.

Liam Campbell lectures on wine for the Wine Development Board and for off-licences and wine clubs.

Patricia Carroll is a food and wine editor, Secretary of Premier Cru Wine Club, and joint co-ordinator of the WSET Diploma tasting group on Dublin's north side.

Tony Cleary, who has worked for over twenty years in the wine trade, is with Barry & Fitzwilliam, specialising in Central and South Eastern Europe.

Colm Conaty is Sales Representative for TDL, Chairman of the WSET Diploma Students and Graduates Wine Club.

Fiona Conway works with Findlater Wine Merchants, Dublin.

Alan Crowley, MW, is Business Development Director of Edward Dillon & Co. Ltd.

Willie Dardis is Regional Manager for TDL and joint co-ordinator of the WSET Diploma tasting group on Dublin's north side.

Martina Delaney has been sommelier at L'Écrivain Restaurant since 1993.

Fergal Downey works for Gilbeys.

Des Drumm is Managing Director of C & C Wholesale Ltd. He gained a distinction in the WSET Diploma.

Alison Gallagher is a member of the Irish Guild of Sommeliers.

Evelyn Jones is the proprietor of The Vintry wine shop, winner of the Gilbey/NOffLA Dublin Off-licence of the Year Award, 1996 and 2000. She is a member of the Champagne Academy.

Simon Keegan, who worked at the K Club, is a member of the Irish Guild of Sommeliers.

Jacinta Kennedy is manager of the Crowe Supervalu Off-licence Group.

Ian Lacey works for Bacchus.

David Lonergan is the manager of The Vintry wine shop in Rathgar, Dublin 6. He lectures for The Vintry Wine Club where his particular forte is the Rhône Valley.

Canice McCarthy is an off-licence manager for O'Brien's Wine Off-Licence Malahide branch.

Julie Martin is a sommelier and wine consultant. She holds Amabassadeur Diplome membership of the Commanderie du Chardonnay d'Or and is a member of the Champagne Academy.

Anne Mullin is co-founder of WineOnline and council member of the Irish Guild of Sommeliers.

Monica Murphy of Febvre is a wine and cheese consultant, lecturer and writer.

Mary O'Callaghan is a trained chef, wine consultant and lecturer for the Wine Development Board. Winner of the Ruinart Trophy Meilleur Sommelier d'Irlande 1996, 1998 and 2000.

Maureen O'Hara is a manager with Findlater Wine Merchants, Dublin.

Carly Ptashnick works in the Creative Sales Department of Gleesons Wines & Spirits and contributes on wine to *The Big Issues*.

Peter Roycroft is developing the new wine web site www.Irelandonwine.com.

David Whelehan is Marketing Manager of O'Briens Wine Off-Licence.

WINE COURSES

"Knowledge of wine enhances its enjoyment!"

The Wine Development Board offers wine training courses countrywide. Our programme includes the following courses:

Wine Appreciation Course
Wine Appreciation Varietal Course
Wine & Food Course
W.S.E.T. Certificate Course
W.S.E.T. Higher Certificate Course

Gift Vouchers Available

For Information Brochure
Tel: (01) 280-4666; Fax: (01) 280 7566
email: info@wineboard.com
website: www.wineboard.com

WINE DEVELOPMENT BOARD OF IRELAND

Best of Wine in Ireland 2001

Three-Star Wines

WINE OF THE YEAR

DO Costers del Segre Castell del Remei Gotim Bru 97 £9–£10
Searsons

Chosen for its excellence, value for money, interesting provenance and reasonable availability (this is not an 'allocation' or special edition wine). It scored very highly in successive blind tastings.

THREE-STAR WINES

Lawson's Dry Hills Marlborough Sauvignon Blanc 99
£12–£13 *Febvre*

Clos La Chance Santa Cruz Mountains Chardonnay 97
£20–£21 *Oddbins*

AC Margaux Ch. La Tour de Mons Cru Bourgeois 95 £24–£25
Gilbeys

Pedroncelli Mother Clone Dry Creek Valley Zinfandel 97
£11–£12 *Dunnes Stores*

Saint Clair Rapaura Reserve Merlot 99 £12–£13 *Greenhills*

Montes Alpha Cabernet Sauvignon 97 £12–£13 *Grants*

Barossa Valley Estate Ebenezer Cabernet Sauvignon 96
£18–19 *Allied Drinks*

Royal Tokaji Tokaji Aszú 5 Puttonyos 93 £11–£12 *Findlaters*

De Bortoli Noble One Botrytis Semillon 95 £20–£21 *Febvre*

Grape varieties

Pat Carroll

What determines the character of a wine?

The country, the soil and the climate are all very important. And let's not forget the winemaker. But the grape variety is crucial. We all know the names of the most popular varieties — Cabernet Sauvignon, Chardonnay, Shiraz, Sauvignon Blanc — but wine is made from around a thousand European grape varieties. Portugal, for example, has hundreds of grape varieties, including the highly acidic Esgana Cão, or 'Dog Strangler'.

Sometimes the name of a grape variety is shown on the label, which makes it simple to identify, but wines are often blends of different varieties. When you buy Valpolicella, you may not realise that it is made from Corvina, Rondinella and Molinara grapes. And up to thirteen varieties may go into red Châteauneuf-du-Pape. The fact that a wine is a blend of different varieties doesn't make it inferior — some of the most expensive wines in the world are blends. Bordeaux clarets, such as premier cru Château Margaux, are made from Cabernet Sauvignon, Cabernet Franc, Merlot and Petit Verdot, while sweet French Sauternes, for examples, the fabulously expensive premier cru Château d'Yquem, is made from a blend of Sémillon, Sauvignon Blanc and Muscadelle.

The listings below provide a short guide to what some of the most popular grape varieties have to offer, where they come from and some of the wines to which they contribute.

Red

Barbera (Piedmont, NW Italy)
Deep ruby, fruity, full bodied, not very tannic; for early drinking
Barbera d'Alba, Barbera d'Asti, Barbera del Monferrato

Bonarda (Argentina, N Italy)
Dense, fruity, plummy, full bodied
Rising star in Argentina; Oltrepò Pavese

Brunello (Tuscany, central Italy)
Relative of Sangiovese, but with more flavour and body; plums, prunes and spices, fair bit of tannin; ages well
Brunello di Montalcino

Cabernet Franc (Bordeaux, Loire)
Fragrant, lighter in colour and less tannic than its relative, Cabernet Sauvignon; redcurrant fruit, medium body
Blended in Bordeaux, playing a more important role on the right bank of the Gironde in the St Émilion/Pomerol area; on its own or blended in Loire reds – Saumur-Champigny, Bourgeuil, Chinon, Anjou-Villages

Cabernet Sauvignon (originally from Bordeaux but now planted world wide)
Deep ruby with a purple tinge, blackcurrants, chocolate, violets, green peppers, cigar-box aromas when mature, firm tannins; capable of very long ageing; good affinity with oak cask maturing
Blended in Bordeaux clarets, ranging in quality from AC Bordeaux through crus bourgeois to crus classés; on its own or blended in Australia (with Shiraz), California (with Merlot etc.), Chile, Italy (Supertuscans), South Africa, Spain, Romania, Bulgaria – everywhere

Carignan/Cariñena/Mazuelo (S France (most widely planted grape variety in France), Rioja, Sardinia)
Lots of colour, tannin, alcohol and bitterness, but little fruit or aroma; some good examples from old vines in S France, but mostly blended with Cinsault and Grenache
Part of the blend in many Languedoc-Roussillon wines such as Corbières, Costières de Nîmes, Coteaux du Languedoc, Côtes du Roussillon, Faugères, Fitou, Minervois, St Chinian; Carignano del Sulcis from Sardinia; some Riojas from Spain

Carmenère (Chile, Bordeaux)
Deep ruby, red berry fruit aromas, soft red fruit flavours, hint of chocolate, full bodied, similar to Merlot but less ageing potential
Now being produced as a varietal in its own right in Chile, but confused with Merlot in Chile for many years (70–90% of Chilean 'Merlot' is Carmenère); permitted ingredient of red Bordeaux but rarely used

Cinsault/Cinsaut/Hermitage (S France, Lebanon, South Africa)
Pale, soft, light, quite perfumed and fruity; used a lot for rosé in France
Blended in Languedoc-Roussillon wines such as Corbières, Costières de Nîmes, Côtes du Roussillon, Faugères, St Chinian; blended with Cabernet Sauvignon and Syrah in Ch. Musar (Lebanon); crossed with Pinot Noir in South Africa to produce the Pinotage grape

Dolcetto (Piedmont, NW Italy)
Deep purple-ruby colour, soft, gentle wine with a touch of

liquorice; drink young
Dolcetto DOCs from Italy, e.g. Dolcetto d'Alba
Gamay (Beaujolais, Loire)
Pale in colour with a bluish tinge, light wine with juicy red fruit
aromas; some people find bananas and boiled sweets there
too; drink very young
*Beaujolais, Beaujolais crus (Brouilly, Chénas, Chiroubles, Côte de
Brouilly, Fleurie, Juliénas, Morgon, Moulin-à-Vent, Regnié, St
Amour), Cheverny, St Pourçain*

Grenache/Garnacha/Cannonau (Rhône, S France, Spain,
Sardinia, Australia, California)
Fairly light colour, fruity, juicy, slightly sweet raspberry fruit,
lowish tannin and acidity, high alcohol; can be spicy if not
overcropped; huge variation in quality
*One of the ingredients in Châteauneuf-du-Pape; Côtes du Rhône; S
France rosés, Vins Doux Naturels such as Rivesaltes and Banyuls
(great with chocolate desserts), Spanish Priorato and Rioja;
Cannonau di Sardegna; blended into mass-market wines in Aus-
tralia and California*

Malbec/Cot (Argentina, Cahors, SW France)
Dark-coloured, ripe, tannic wines with good concentration and
blackberry flavour; can be austere, peppery, spicy; wines age
well
*Treated properly, capable of great things in Argentinian varietals –
similar to Bordeaux in flavour but not as firm in structure; in
France, part of the blend in AC Cahors and other wines from SW
France*

Merlot (Bordeaux, S/SW France, Italy, California, Washington,
South America, Bulgaria, Romania, Australia, New Zealand)
Deep ruby, smooth, plummy, maturing to rich fruit cake
flavours – velvety texture, with less colour, tannin and acidity
than Cabernet Sauvignon; softer and earlier maturing
*Generic AC Bordeaux, St Émilion, Pomerol, Buzet, Cahors, Vins de
Pays from S France, N Italian Merlots, US varietals or Meritage (a
blend of Cabernet Sauvignon, Merlot, Cabernet Franc, Malbec and
Petit Verdot), varietal in South America (though much Chilean
Merlot is really Carmenère, a Bordeaux variety now little used in
France); Bulgarian, Romanian, Australian and New Zealand
varietals*

Montepulciano (Central Italy, mainly Abruzzo)
Deeply coloured, rich, brambles, cherries, pepper, spice, zesty
acidity, firm tannins, best can age well
*Montepulciano d'Abruzzo, Rosso Conero, Biferno, Rosso Piceno
(just to confuse everyone, Vino Nobile di Montepulciano is made*

with sangiovese, not Montepulciano)

Mourvèdre/Monastrell/Mataro (S France, S Rhône,
Languedoc-Roussillon, Spain, Australia, California)
Lots of blackberry fruit, fleshy, high in alcohol and tannin,
slightly meaty flavour in youth; blends well with Grenache or
Cinsault, giving structure
*Blended in Bandol, Côtes du Rhône, Côtes du Ventoux, Vacqueyras,
Costières de Nîmes, Côtes du Roussillon, Faugères, Fitou,
Minervois, St Chinian; used in many Spanish DOs, e.g. Alicante,
Almansa, Jumilla, Valencia, Yecla; Australian varietals from the
Barossa Valley; fashionable in California in the 1990s as part of the
Rhône Ranger movement to make Rhône-style wines (e.g. Bonny
Doon's 100% Mourvèdre Old Telegram)*

Nebbiolo (Piedmont, NW Italy)
Not very deep colour, but powerful truffle, raspberry, liquorice, chocolate and prune aromas — even violets; high acidity,
very firm tannins; usually needs long ageing
Barolo, Barbaresco, Gattinara, Nebbiolo d'Alba, Valtellina

Negroamaro (Puglia, S Italy)
Deep colour, high alcohol, rich, robust red wines, some of
which can age well
Salice Salentino, Rosso di Cerognola

Petit Verdot (Bordeaux, California)
Rich colour, hint of violets on the nose, concentrated tannic
wines with a touch of spice
*Used as a small part of the blend in Bordeaux clarets and Californian
Meritage wines*

Petite Sirah (California, South America)
Inky, quite tannic, firm, robust, full-bodied wines
*Unrelated to the Syrah of the Rhône; traditionally blended with
Zinfandel in California, now offered as a varietal as well*

Pinot Meunier (Champagne, Australia, California)
Gives freshness, fruitiness and crisp acidity to sparkling wines
Champagne, sparkling wines from Australia and California

Pinot Noir/Pinot Nero/Blauer Spätburgunder (Burgundy,
Champagne, Loire, Alsace, Germany, Italy, California, Oregon,
Australia, New Zealand, South Africa, Romania)

Much lighter in colour and less tannic than, say, Cabernet
Sauvignon, quite high acidity, magical sweet aromas of
strawberries or cherries, turning to mushrooms, truffles and
even farmyards as it ages; velvety texture; long ageing; used
in sparkling wines to give body and fruit
*Red Burgundy from basic AC Bourgogne to Grand Cru, blended in
Champagne, used in sparkling wines from the New World; red
Menetou-Salon, red Sancerre; varietal in Alsace, Germany, Italy,
California, Oregon, Australia, New Zealand, South Africa, Romania;
best in cool, marginal climates*

Pinotage (South Africa)
South African crossing of Pinot Noir and Cinsault, deep colour,
can have good body and juicy berry fruit, but there can be a
certain paint-like or 'hospital' aroma (isoamyl acetate) in some
wines
South African varietal

Sangiovese (central Italy, especially Tuscany)
Slightly pale colour, very dry, cherry and possibly farmyard
aromas, cherry and plum flavours, high acidity, robust
tannins, slightly bitter finish; good for ageing, can be austere
in youth
*Part of the blend in Chianti, Carmignano, Vino Nobile di
Montepulciano, Torgiano and the Supertuscan Tignanello*

Syrah/Shiraz (Rhône, Languedoc-Roussillon, Australia)
Deep colour, intense blackberries, raspberries, earthy, spicy,
pepper, burnt rubber, tannic, rich, needs time to soften
*Hermitage, Crozes-Hermitage, St Joseph, Châteauneuf-du-Pape,
Vins de Pays from Languedoc-Roussillon; on its own or blended
with Cabernet Sauvignon in Australia*

Tannat (SW France, Uruguay)
Very dark, very tannic, raspberry aromas, needs time in
bottle; can age well
Part of the blend in Madiran and Cahors; as a varietal in Uruguay

Tempranillo (Spain)
Deep colour, strawberry and tobacco aromas, low acidity and
tannin, good for early drinking or ageing
*Blended in Rioja, Costers del Segre, Navarra, Penedès, Ribera del
Duero, Somontano, Valdepeñas; as Tinto Roriz, part of the blend in
port*

Touriga Nacional (Portugal, Australia)
Deep colour, mulberry aromas, concentrated fruit, high
tannins; in port, very long ageing potential
Part of the blend in port, Douro and Dão wines; Australian port

Zinfandel (California)
Varies in style from very dark, alcoholic, bramble-flavoured

reds to mass-produced sweetish 'blush' wines; can make excellent reds in the right hands
Zinfandels in all shades from palest pink to deepest red

White

Chardonnay (originally from Burgundy but now grown everywhere)
Chameleon — ranges from very dry, light, minerally, high-acid, citrus-dominated wines from cooler climates to dryish oaked heavyweights full of butterscotch, peaches, melons and pineapples from hotter regions; affinity with oak cask ageing
Champagne, white Burgundy, including Chablis, Mâcon, Marsannay, Meursault, Montagny, Montrachet, Pouilly-Fuissé and Rully; varietal from Argentina, Bulgaria, California, Chile, New Zealand, South Africa, Australia

Chenin Blanc/Pineau/Steen (Loire, South Africa, California)
Dry to sweet, pale lemon in youth maturing to pale gold in older sweet wines, honey, wet wool and damp straw flavours, possibly nuts and marmalade in mature sweet wines; high acidity ensures that Loire sweet wines will age for decades
Dry *Savennières, South African varietals, mass-produced Californian blends*
Dry/medium dry/sweet *Vouvray*
Sweet *Bonnezeaux, Coteaux du Layon, Montlouis, Quarts de Chaume* Sparkling: *Saumur Mousseux*

Cortese (Piedmont, NW Italy)
Dry, crisp wines with fresh acidity, slightly floral, lemony aromas and steely lemon fruit
Gavi

Garganega (Veneto, NE Italy)
Dry, aromas of lemon and almonds in the best wines, fresh and fruity; drink very young
Soave (with Trebbiano — dry), Recioto di Soave (sweet)

Gewurztraminer/Gewürztraminer (Alsace, Germany, Austria, New Zealand, Australia)
Medium dry to sweet, colour can be deep; very characteristic perfumed aromas of lychees, roses and spice, flowery flavour but lacking the acidity of Riesling; classic accompaniment to spicy food
Try a dry Gewurztraminer from Alsace for pure flavour; available as a varietal from Germany, Austria and the New World; occasionally blended with Riesling in Australia

Macabeo/Viura/Maccabeu (Spain, S France)
Dry, floral aromas, not much acidity, quite fruity; most wines

should be drunk young
Blended in white Rioja, Cava, Rueda, white Côtes du Roussillon

Malvasia/Malmsey (Friuli, central Italy, Sardinia, Madeira)
Ancient grape, making dry to sweet styles, pale lemon (dry) to
deep amber (dessert), nuts, cream and apricots, slightly spicy;
early drinking or long ageing
*Collio, Isonzo, blended with Trebbiano in Frascati and central Italian
whites; sweet wines in Sardinia; Madeira*

Marsanne (Rhône, Australia — Victoria)
Dry, deep coloured, full bodied, peach, honeysuckle and
almond aromas (melons and mangos in Australia), quite
heavy, usually matured in oak, often blended with Roussanne
*White Coteaux du Tricastin, white Côtes du Rhône, white Crozes-
Hermitage, white Hermitage, white St Joseph, St Péray; varietal in
Australia, e.g. Ch. Tahbilk*

Melon de Bourgogne/Muscadet (Loire)
Very dry, light, fresh, crisp, some green apple flavours but
often fairly neutral; best examples are 'sur lie' (matured in
barrels containing yeast sediment); classic seafood wine
*In ascending order of quality — Muscadet, Muscadet de Sèvre et
Maine, Muscadet de Sèvre et Maine sur lie*

Müller-Thurgau (Germany)
Usually off-dry to medium-sweet wines, light in colour, not
much aroma or acidity; not a quality grape; drink young
Liebfraumilch, e.g. Black Tower, Blue Nun

Muscat (Alsace, Rhône, Italy, Australia, Greece)
Dry to very sweet, pale lemon (dry) to deep amber (sweet),
marked grape and musk aromas, scented fruity flavours,
touch of spice, moderate acidity
Dry *Muscat d'Alsace Sparkling*
Medium sweet *Asti Spumante*
Sweet *Vins Doux Naturels from France, e.g. Muscat de Beaumes de
Venise, liqueur Muscats from Australia and Greece*

Palomino (Spain (Jerez), South Africa, Australia, California)
Low acidity, low sugar levels and its tendency to oxidise make
Palomino the perfect grape for dry, medium or sweet sherry
All styles of sherry — fino, amontillado, oloroso, palo cortado

Parellada (Spain)
Dry, lemon and flower aromas, zesty acidity, apple fruit; drink
very young
*Blended in Spanish sparkling wine Cava and white Costers del
Segre; 100% in Torres' Viña Sol*

Pinot Blanc/Pinot Bianco/Weissburgunder (Alsace, Italy,
Germany, Austria)

Mostly dry, some apple aromas, almonds in Austria, soft, quite full bodied, moderate/high acidity; usually for early drinking
Alsace varietal, Italian varietal or blend, e.g. Colli Orientale del Friuli, Collio; Italian sparkling wine; dry wines from Pfalz and Baden; sweet and dry wines from Austria

Pinot Gris (formerly Tokay d'Alsace)/Pinot Grigio/Ruländer (Alsace, NE Italy)

In Alsace styles range from dry to sweet, with fairly deep colour and quite full body, slightly spicy, perfumed aromas, peach fruit that develops buttery flavours with age—rich and spicy wine; drier, lighter, crisper and not so aromatic in Italy
Varietal in Alsace, varietal in Italy or part of the blend in Collio

Riesling (Germany, Alsace, Austria, Australia, New Zealand, USA, South Africa)

Dry to sweet, pale straw with green hints to deep gold in older sweet wines, floral and honey aromas when young, developing petrol-like notes on ageing; apple or peach flavours in Europe (depending on sweetness), limes in New World, piercing acidity, rich fruit on the palate; can age for decades
Made usually as a 100% varietal, from dry to sweet, in Germany (Mosel-Saar-Ruwer, Rheingau, Pfalz, Nahe), Alsace, Austria (Wachau), Australia (Clare Valley, Eden Valley), New Zealand (Marlborough), California, Oregon, Washington State, South Africa

Roussanne (Rhône)

Dry, aromatic, herbal aromas, elegant, good acidity, often blended with Marsanne
White Châteauneuf-du-Pape, white Coteaux du Tricastin, white Côtes du Rhône, white Crozes-Hermitage, white Hermitage, white St Joseph, St Péray

Sauvignon Blanc (Loire, Bordeaux, New Zealand, Chile, California, South Africa)

Dry or sweet, grassy, herbaceous, gooseberries, green apples, even cat's pee aromas, with citrus and green apple flavours, steely acidity; mostly for early drinking
Sancerre, Pouilly-Fumé, part of the blend in white Bordeaux and Sauternes; varietal from New Zealand (especially Marlborough), Chile, California (oaked), South Africa

Sémillon/Semillon (Bordeaux, Australia)

Dry to sweet, light in colour to deep gold, not much aroma when young, perhaps some toast or wax, lowish acidity, but matures to nutty, waxy, honeyed aromas in Australia and honey and marmalade in Sauternes and Barsac wines; citrus and nuts on the palate in drier wines, marmalade and honey in sweet wines; very long-lived wines

Most important grape in Sauternes, Barsac and white Bordeaux;
varietal in the Hunter and Barossa valleys; often blended with
Chardonnay in Australian mass-market wines

Torrontés (Argentina)
Dry, with distinctive flowery, Muscat-like fragrant nose, zesty
acidity, rich fruit; early drinking
Blended or varietal from Argentina

Trebbiano/Ugni Blanc (Italy, SW France)
Dry, light, high acidity, quite neutral flavour, medium body,
workaday grape; early drinking
Found in Trebbiano d'Abruzzo, Trebbiano di Romagna, Orvieto,
Frascati, Soave, Lugana, Galestro, Vin de Pays des Côtes de
Gascogne; base wine for French Cognac and Armagnac

Verdelho (Portugal, Australia, Madeira)
Fresh, lively, lemony wines of good quality; good ageing
potential
Dry whites from the Douro Valley and Australia; Madeira

Verdicchio (Marches, central Italy)
Dry, pale straw with green tinge, crisp, lemony acidity, nutty
flavour with a mineral, salty edge, slight bitter almond finish;
drink young, though best can age for five years; good with
seafood; semi-sweet and sweet wines also made
Verdicchio dei Castelli di Jesi, Verdicchio di Matelica (white and
sparkling)

Viognier (Rhône, Languedoc-Roussillon, California)
Dry, pale straw developing to pale gold, apricot, peach and
spring blossom aromas becoming honeyed with maturity,
deep, rich palate with apricot and peach flavours, quite high
alcohol; drink young, less than eight years old; moderate to
low acidity
Condrieu (vast majority dry, but a few producers make demi-sec
wines), Ch. Grillet; can appear in red Côte Rôtie; increasingly used
in white Côtes du Rhône; Vins de Pays from Languedoc-Roussillon;
varietal in California

Click on wine — wine web sites reviewed

Barbara Boyle

Wine is nearly as popular on the World Wide Web as music and books. More and more retailers are providing wine-buying services, and there are numerous sites where information about wine can be accessed.

The great advantages of web-shopping are convenience — 'the comfort of your own home', as the advertisers put it — price comparison and greater choice. The possibility of price comparison in the fine wine market, where prices do vary widely, is a great advantage: is £950 too much to pay for a bottle of Château Petrus 1990, or is it a bargain? The internet will make it easier to make price comparisons and there are a number of sites that specifically address this (e.g. winesearcher.com)

Another advantage is the saving of that all too precious commodity — time.

The greatest disadvantage — apart from missing out on the chat — is probably the lack of immediate gratification that comes with visiting a wine store. Wine is a 'high touch' product i.e. a product which we generally like to see and feel and even occasionally taste in advance of buying. The Net may work better initially for replacement or repeat buys than it does for new purchases. It should also work well for well-known brands that are familiar to, and trusted by, consumers. The same applies to existing and reputable retailers.

The real problem with Web-retailing is fulfilling the orders. The delivery of wine (and other foodstuffs or large bulky items) needs to be considerably improved if the retail aspect of the Web is really to take off. The bigger players, larger supermarkets or retailers with a number of stores, have an advantage as they are more widely based and meeting your order should theoretically be easier. At the moment most companies use carrier companies or the An Post service for delivery. This poses problems if you are not there to receive your order — the timing of deliveries is usually pretty vague. Your package will then be delivered to a central warehouse for you to pick it up. Some companies will deliver to your work address during office hours but not all bosses think this is an appropriate use of their premises, and you still have to transport the wine home.

In the early days of e-commerce there was a lot of concern about the security of giving credit card information over the web. Most sites now use encryption software so that your information is secure — certainly much more secure than giving your details over the phone, or allowing someone to take your card away. When buying from a web site it goes without saying that you should check that the site uses encryption.

What makes a good site

A good web site is dependent on good content, quickly delivered. How many times have you visited a site and got bored with it really quickly or quit without really investigating what it has to offer? We can happily spend an hour browsing in a good wine shop but get impatient after a very short time online.

The design and interactivity of the site (as well as the content) should keep you enthralled. Some good features on websites include: questionnaires on style preferences; competitions and promotions; good information, encyclopaedias or wine reference books accessible on line, such as the *Oxford Companion to Wine* on Winepros.com and the *Oz Clarke World Atlas of Wine* on winetoday.com; online tastings (see wine.co.za), organised wine clubs, a permanent profile of what you have ordered — this allows for suggestions to be put forward of similar wines to try; and finally, live customer queries through online chat not unlike talking to a shop assistant.

The sites

In choosing the following sites I scored the two hundred or more I visited by five criteria:
  • speed
  • ease of navigation
  • how up to date they are
  • good design and content
  • having something unique or different to offer.

(Of course, endorsement of the site is not an endorsement of the products.)

The sites are listed according to their primary function (selling, information etc) and in order of achievement against the five criteria.

Irish selling sites

www.chateauonline.ie Recently launched in Ireland giving access to a wide and new range of wines. Check out the wine forums, link of the week, and the news sections.

www.oddbins.com Straightforward site launched first in Ireland, very much in keeping with the ethos of Oddbins, can't search for a specific wine but must follow a series of questions which can lead to interesting results or try their recommendations for different situations

www.bubblebrothers.com Specialist site, principally for Champagnes, offering a wide and comprehensive choice. Lots of information, but it helps if you know a bit about Champagne.

www.liquorstore.ie Completely revamped and up to date site, good content and design, very special offers. Run by Molloys.

www.wineonline.ie Wine by the case or selected cases. Wide range of wines. Very fast and easy to navigate. Hasn't changed much since its original launch.

www.frontpagewines.com Five Irish restaurants offering wine for sale online. The site is reasonably fast and easy to navigate. It offers a wine course which is still in development. Other features include a wine of the week, an ideal cellar, featured wines and featured vineyards.

www.karwig-wines.com Straightforward e-commerce site with a large selection of wines. Features include special offers, competitions, focus on regions. A very friendly, well run site and a good example for independent retailers.

www.onthegrapevine.com The site is a good resource for buying wines on the net. An easy-to-use wine search and informative wine information. The speed of connection is consistently slow compared with other sites.

www.Buy4now.ie is a new super mall online with a selection of large Irish stores. The food and wine section is to be provided by Superquinn supermarkets.

www.jnwine.co.uk The site was in redevelopment for some time and the result is a very professional and easy to use site which brings this Northern Irish merchant to a wider Irish audience.

The following site is to be launched at the end of 2000:

www.irelandonwine.com It aims to provide even more choice to Irish consumers with new and some branded wines online. Wine will be available by the bottle and by the case. Straightforward ecommerce in the beginning, with further developments as the site is established.

International selling sites

There are so many great sites out there but because they do not deliver to Ireland it is just frustrating to visit them (unless you want to send a gift to an international destination). So the sites below all deliver internationally. It can be difficult to determine if you are getting good value so it would be interesting to use the price comparison web sites if in any doubt.

www.wine.co.za A very comprehensive site for South African wine. You can buy online and the delivery costs are not too unreasonable, if you can wait a bit. They host online tastings over the Internet each month which are interesting if you stay up late (usually about 1 am, our time).

www.bbr.co.uk Although a UK based site, because there is a Berry Brothers & Rudd store in Dublin, the site is of interest to Irish consumers. Wide range of personalised services. The pronunciation guide is a good example of how sites can be more interesting and educational. With sound-playing software, you can hear how some major Bordeaux wine names should be pronounced.

www.seckfordwines.co.uk A rare and fine wine merchant. A lot of
stock is in bond so duty and VAT needs to be added to the
prices. Also the sterling currency exposure shouldn't be for-
gotten. Delivery is charged at cost price

www.madaboutwine.com A very down to earth and appealing UK
site. There is a freight converter to work out the price of a
delivery and the charges are not cheap. Can look at the site
in euros exclusive of VAT.

www.la-cle-de-la-cave.com A French site which delivers worldwide.
Set the site to English and then select Ireland as a destination.
The prices are in euros.

www.winesmart.com focuses on New World wines. It delivers to
Ireland with a delivery charge using UPS, a variety of
offers including a wine of the day, case of the week and
information on their top ten sellers.

Ezines

www.winetoday.com Up to date news and articles freely available,
comprehensive links to wineries and travel sites, access to *Oz
Clarke World Atlas of Wine*, interesting forums, using new technology e.g. with RealPlayer software (which can be down-
loaded free from www.real.com), you can look at video clips
online.

www.decanter.com Daily wine news and views, must register and
pay a subscription to use the fine wine tracker. The online
information is for the more serious wine collector or hobbyist.

www.winezine.com The site works on two levels — some things
are free but a subscription is required for full access. Features
include forums, a wine library, links to wineries, weekly wine
picks by four different tasters.

www.italianwinereview.com Very specific to Italian wines with vintage reports, details of producers, extracts from the hard
copy magazine. Site is still under development. A comprehensive, well thought-out and appealing site.

www.wineenthusiastmag.com Extracts from the hard copy US
magazine are given online. The buying guides can be interesting and are done Robert Parker style.

www.winexwired.com A wine magazine aimed at the younger
market, which is interesting in itself. The site gives little away
but may be of interest to those who are looking for a different type of wine magazine which isn't 'black tie'.

www.foodmad.com is an Irish site which has a wine section.
Weekly wine review and competition with a growing list of
tasting notes.

Wine finders and price comparisons

www.winesearcher.com Find any wine from a growing worldwide
selection of retailers and wholesalers, currently including six

Irish suppliers. Really useful for price comparisons. Nicely designed and easy to use site.

www.infowines.com A search engine for fine wines and details of prices. Similar size database to winesearcher but a lot slower and not as easy to use.

Wine Auctions and brokers

www.uvine.com Wine exchange, currently only for wine still in bond. Aimed at the fine wine market. Currently a UK based site but international sellers are sought. International buyers can avail of the site.

www.winebid.com A premier auction site with locations in Australia, USA and the UK. If you are comfortable with participating in auctions either as a buyer or seller then this is a great site. Need to read the terms and conditions carefully as there are the usual auction charges — buyer and seller premiums, VAT and duties. All transactions are done in US dollars so be aware of the currency difference. A site for serious wine owners or enthusiasts.

www.wine-owners.com Still in its early days. Register your wine portfolio. As a member you can buy and sell wine, share tasting notes, ratings and valuations. Originating in the UK, it will need a critical mass to sustain itself. Very professional looking site.

Directories

www.vinosearch.com Search for a wine web site by keyword. Better than a regular search engine or directory as you will only hit on wine web sites. Can also search for information and wineries by region.

www.wine.about.com Very comprehensive website listings. Keeps up to date with new sites.

www.allaboutwine.com Easy to use and reasonably detailed directory to wine sites. Divided into categories and by country location. Can't do a general word search which would make it even more useful.

Education

www.wineandco.com Although this is an e-commerce site there is a lot of learning on it. (Originally a French site, it has been extended to six countries, but not Ireland yet.) With shockwave animation software you can access tutorials on a range of wine topics, good encyclopaedia, maps and web addresses for wineries.

www.winepros.com Access the *Oxford Companion to Wine* by Jancis Robinson online. Go to authors and click on Clive Coates for access to extracts from the monthly fine wine bible *The Vine*. A host of wine information, reviews and news. Strong Australian focus. It is also an e-commerce site but international delivery is not a key feature of the site.

www.evinopolis.com The site for the London-based World of Wine experience. Whereas the tour is very interactive the site is more promotional. Lots of details of what is happening at Vinopolis—you can arrange to book tickets online and can request booking for their wine tastings. If you haven't been already, go the next time you are in London!

www.wineplanet.co.uk An australian ecommerce site that launched in the UK, there is a lot of reference material, a good food and wine matcher, Ask Oz, and most interestingly Wine TV with tutorials and shows on wine topics – it shows how the web is developing.

Personality homepages

www.wineanorak.com A UK site with a distinctive personality. Fronted by 32-year-old Jamie Goode with a genuinely fun and refreshing approach to wine. Some nice sections if you are very new to wine. Lots of information for the serious wine lovers as well.

www.ozclarke.com Changes weekly with extracts from his many wine books. Effectively short soundbites covering grape profiles, words on wine, wine of the week, producer profiles. A good way to pick up a little bit of knowledge each week. Reasonably good listing of food and wine web addresses.

www.wine-pages.com A guide with a bit of everything by Tom Canavan. The news is very UK orientated. Most interesting bit for Irish consumers are the what's new and the wine forum which is a very active chat group.

www.wine-lovers-page.com A bit overwhelming on the information stakes as this is a huge unfiltered site. However, you just might find what you are looking for. Really like the 30 second wine advisor. Very comprehensive tasting notes by Robin Garr.

Comments or feedback are welcome. Contact me at
barbaraboyle@eircom.net

Glossary

Compiled by Kathy Farmar

AC: Appellation Contrôlée, a French wine classification system that certifies a wine as coming from a particular region, area or even vineyard. Rules of inclusion differ from AC to AC, but they may prescribe any or all of the following over and above the wine's place of origin — grape varieties, density of planting, yield, alcohol level. Not all good French wines are AC wines. Some excellent varieties are grown under the Vin Délimité de Qualité Supérieure (VDQS) or Vin de Pays (VdP) schemes. A wine designated as Vin de Table (VdT) has no guarantee of origin.

acidity: all wines contain acids of various kinds, including malic, lactic, tartaric, citric (fixed acids) and acetic (the acid found in vinegar). The fixed acids give wines a crispness to the taste and contribute to the ageing process, but too much acetic or ethanoic acid makes a wine taste unpleasantly of vinegar.

American oak: see **oak**.

aroma: a somewhat imprecise term, sometimes applied to the entire **nose**, sometimes only to specific simple and easily distinguishable smells.

balance: a term of praise when applied to a wine, indicating that its **tannins**, **acidity**, alcohol and sugar blend well and complement each other, without any one element dominating.

barrique: an **oak** barrel with a capacity of 225 litres.

big wine: a full-bodied wine with an exceptionally rich flavour.

black fruits: tasters' term used to refer to dark berry **fruits** such as blackberries, blackcurrants, black cherries, blueberries, etc.

blend: a wine made from more than one grape variety, as opposed to a **varietal**.

blind tasting: a tasting in which the identities of the wines are unknown to the taster until after tasting notes have been made and scores assigned. All competitive tastings are blind, as are all tastings for *The Best of Wine in Ireland*.

body: the combination of **fruit** extract and alcoholic strength that gives the impression of weight in the mouth.

botrytis: properly *botrytis cinerea* (noble rot), a fungus that attacks grapes on vines. Depending on weather conditions and the ripeness of the grapes, it will either spoil the harvest completely (in which case it is known as grey rot) or concentrate the sugars in the **fruit** to produce a high-quality, sweet, and very long-lived wine.

bottle: the standard bottle size is 75 centilitres or three-quarters of a litre. A magnum contains two bottles or 1.5 litres. See also **maturation**.

bouquet: strictly speaking, this refers only to those mature aromas that develop as the wine ages in the **bottle**, but it is often used to refer to all characteristics of the grape variety on the **nose**.

buttery: a rich, fat and delicious character found in some Chardonnay wines, particularly if produced in a good **vintage** year or warm climate.

carbonic maceration: see **maceration**.

claret: an English term for a red Bordeaux wine. It comes from the French 'clairet', which refers to a wine between a dark rosé and a light red.

classic: word used by wine tasters to indicate that a wine is of high quality, showing the correct characteristics for its type and origin, and possesses great style.

cold stabilisation: the removal of tartrates in a young wine by refrigeration and cold filtration. Refrigeration precipitates the soluble tartaric acids with which young wines may be saturated into crystals that are then filtered out to leave the wine clear.

corked: a wine is corked when it has been spoiled by contact with a contaminated cork. This is the most common cause of wine spoilage and can be identified by the wine's stale, woody, mould-like smell. (The presence of little pieces of cork floating in the wine does not indicate that the wine is corked — it merely means that the cork broke slightly on being pulled out.)

cru: literally means 'growth', but on a French wine label refers to the status of the vineyard in which the vines were cultivated; the cru classification is in addition to the **AC**. The system is rather complicated and varies from region to region. In the Médoc region of Bordeaux, there are five *Grand Cru Classé* divisions, beginning with *Premier Cru* (1st Growth), *Deuxième Cru* (2nd Growth), and so on down to the *Cinquième Cru* (5th Growth). In St Émilion, there are three levels — *Premier Grand Cru Classé* at the top, then *Grand Cru Classé* and *Grand Cru*. In Burgundy the top vineyards are *Grands Crus* and *Premier Cru* comes below them. *Grand Cru* is also used in Alsace and Champagne to distinguish particularly good vineyard sites.

crust: sediment that forms in **bottle**-aged port.

DO/DOC: Denominación de Origen (DO), a Spanish wine classification. Denominación de Origen Calificada (DOC) applies only to wines from the Rioja region.

DOC: In Portugal the highest quality classification is Denominaçoa de Origem Controlada. Next is Indicação de Proveniência Regulamentada (IPR); then Vinho Regional (VR) a classification akin to France's Vin de Pays. Vinho de Mesa (VdM) is the equivalent of Vin de Table.

DOC/G: In Italy the category Denominazione di Origine Controllata e Garantita (DOCG) is applied to the highest grade of wine, with Denominazione di Origine Controllata (DOC) coming next, followed by a relatively new classification, Indicazione Geografica Tipica (IGT), which has almost completely absorbed the old Vino da Tavola (VdT). In Italy, even more than in France, there are fine wines available that do not fall under the DOCG or DOC classification system.

fermentation: the chemical process whereby the sugar in grapes turns into alcohol. Some wines undergo a second fermentation, called 'malolactic fermentation' because it involves transforming crisp malic acid into lactic (milky) acid. This creates a smoother, softer taste.

fining: the process of adding substances such as egg whites, gelatine or clay to a wine, which causes microscopic suspended solids to fall to the bottom, so that after being racked (transferred to another barrel) or bottled, there will be a minimum of **sediment** or cloudiness in the wine.

finish: the last flavours a wine leaves in the mouth, especially after being swallowed or (in a tasting) spat out.

French oak: see **oak**.

fruit: the fruity flavour of a wine made from grapes with the correct combination of ripeness and **acidity**.

grip: word applied to a firm wine with a positive **finish**. Grip on the finish indicates a certain bite of **acidity**, or, if red, **tannin** sensed on the teeth and gums.

IGT *see* **DOC/G**

IPR *see* **DOC**

lees: sediment that falls to the bottom of a vat of wine after **fermentation** and **maturation**. Most wines are transferred to another container when the lees form; others, especially Muscadet and sparkling wines, are aged on the lees (*sur lie*).

length: the length of time a wine's flavours linger in the mouth after sipping. Long length is one of the markers of a quality wine.

maceration: the period of **fermentation** of a red wine during which the **must** has contact with grape skins. It is during this process that red wines derive their colour and **tannin**. Rosé wines undergo a very short maceration period of one or two days. Red wines intended to be drunk young sometimes undergo carbonic maceration, in which uncrushed grapes are fermented under a layer of carbon dioxide. This results in a wine light in colour and low in tannin, but high in **fruit** and **aroma**.

malolactic fermentation: see **fermentation**.

maturation: the ageing process by which wines develop character and complexity. Maturation is good only up to a point, beyond which the wine will start to decline, but that point differs for each type of wine. A Beaujolais Nouveau will spend only a few months maturing, while tawny port may be aged in **oak** for as long as twenty years. The larger the **bottle**, the slower the maturation — half-bottles of wine mature and decline more quickly than whole bottles.

mousse: the bubbles in a sparkling wine. Ideally these should be very small and long lasting.

mouthfeel: specifically refers to the texture of a wine, as opposed to the **palate**, which also refers to the flavour.

must: unfermented grape juice.

noble rot: see **botrytis**.

nose: the combined smells of a wine's grape varieties' **aromas** and **bottle**-matured **bouquet**.

oak: maturation in new oak adds flavours to wine — the smaller the barrel, the greater the effect. Old oak does not have this effect, but it does allow for controlled **oxidation**. Oak barrels vary, depending on the species of tree (French or American) or the location of the forest (Allier, Tronçais, Nevers, Limousin, all French), and have different effects on the wine. See also **barrique**.

oxidation: a chemical reaction that takes place when wine is exposed to air. Barrel **maturation** allows for slow, controlled oxidation, improving the flavour of the wine. However, if this happens too fast or if the process is allowed to go too far, it transforms the alcohol into acetic acid. Wine that is too oxidised tastes unpleasant and may look brown and smell of vinegar.

palate: the flavour and texture of the wine in the mouth; see also **mouthfeel**.

QbA/QmP Germany has two categories for its quality wines — QbA (Qualitätswein bestimmter Anbaugebiete), the first entry into the two-tier quality system, and QmP (Qualitätswein mit Prädikat), the higher level. QmP has six sub-categories, each determined by the ripeness of the grapes at harvest time.

reserve: in Italy, Portugal, Spain and Bulgaria, a wine labelled 'riserva' or 'reserva' must by law be of very high quality and, in the case of Italy and Spain, have undergone a certain minimum ageing, with at least some of it in **oak** barrels. Anywhere else, the word 'reserve' or 'réserve' just means that the winemakers think it is one of their best.

sediment: solid debris that falls to the bottom of a wine barrel or, in the case of an unfiltered wine, the **bottle**. Wines undergo **fining** or filtration to reduce the amount of sediment left after bottling, but some winemakers prefer not to handle their wine too much lest they spoil its flavour.

stainless steel vats: vessels used in **fermentation** and **maturation**. The use of stainless steel vats, rather than wood or concrete, makes it easier to control the wine's maturation, but it also rules out certain maturation processes that can occur in **oak**.

structure: the sum of the component parts that shape a wine, including **fruit**, **alcohol**, and **acidity**, and, in reds, **tannin**.

sur lie: see **lees**.

tannin: a chemical substance found in grape skins and hence in red wines but not white. The ability of a red wine to improve as it matures depends very much on its tannins, but a wine that is too tannic will taste dry and hard; red wines intended to be drunk young will sometimes undergo carbonic **maceration**, which minimises tannin. Tannins can also be derived from **oak**, stalks and pips. Tannin from pips is the harshest of all.

terroir: the complete growing environment of soil, aspect, altitude, climate and any other factor affecting the life of the vine.

vanilla: often used to describe the **nose** and sometimes the **palate** of an **oak**-aged wine, especially a Rioja.

varietal: a wine made entirely, or almost entirely, from a single grape variety, as opposed to a **blend**.

VdP: *see* **AC**.

VDQS: *see* **AC**

VdT: *see* **AC**, **DOC**

VdM: *see* **DO**

VR: *see* **DO**

vintage: the year the grapes were harvested. In the EU, up to 15% of the grapes in a wine labelled as one vintage may come from another year's harvest. Champagnes and sparkling wines, unlike plain reds and whites, are more often than not made from **blends** of grapes harvested in several different years ('non-vintage'). A vintage Champagne — one made from grapes harvested in a single season — is rare and expensive, although not necessarily better than a non-vintage.

Matching wine and food

Sandy O'Byrne

The old rules of 'red wine for red meat and game; white wine for white meat and fish' are generally accurate though very limited advice. It is more a question of the weight or balance of a wine than its colour. Many red wines are more robust, full-bodied and structured than many whites and therefore suit more textured, substantial foods which meat and game usually are. White wines are usually lighter and better with fish and delicate meats such as chicken or veal. The theory falls down however, with textured fish like tuna or with a very light red wine. A less traditional method of cooking, such as a stir-fry of beef, changes the texture and introduces spices which are less happy with full-bodied red, while roasting cod can make it meaty and substantial enough for a middle-weight red like Pinot Noir or Chinon.

It is therefore the balance of weights between wine and food that is most important. To enjoy both, one must be able to taste both, and neither should overpower the other in weight (body) or intensity of flavour.

Apart from weight and body, other aspects of wine affect food in particular ways. Acidity is essential to all wine, it keeps it fresh, makes it appetising and produces the bouquet. Acid stimulates the palate and so cuts through fat and richness in food. A crisp fresh white wine acts like a squeeze of lemon on a buttery fish. Tannin which comes from the skins and stalks of grapes in red wine making, helps the wine to age and gives it bite. High tannin has a drying effect on the palate like cold, strong tea; in very young wines it can be quite astringent. Tannin interacts with protein and tough young reds are softened by rare lean meat which protects the palate. More moderate tannin is dry and appetising and an excellent foil to rich foods like game, casseroles and many classically cooked dishes.

Certain combinations of wine and food clash either because of something in the food, which reacts with wine, or something which affects the ability to taste.

Hot spices burn so that tasting anything is impossible. Mild spices can work with light fruity wines, but hot chilli, lots of ginger or crushed pepper are better with beer or water. Beware of horseradish and mustard which can be very hot and really spoil a fine red wine intended for the beef.

Some foods are difficult because of texture. Chocolate is notorious for coating the palate with a layer of fat which dulls all other flavours. High alcohol and sweetness in a fortified dessert wine such as Port, Banyuls, or Liqueur Muscat usually do the trick. Egg yolks in sauces like mayonnaise, have a similar effect, so can a lot of oil. For these, oak and high acidity work.

Acids are less a problem than might be thought. While I cannot think of any wine which would benefit from being drunk with grapefruit, it is principally fine and mature wines which suffer from vinaigrette sauce or the sweet sour effect of tomatoes. Such foods are best with wines which have lots of lively fruit.

Artichokes and, to a lesser extent asparagus can make wine taste metallic, while vegetable-based dishes in general need rather fresh, lively whites or soft, rich, red wines with little oak.

Sweet food is often just too sweet for even the most luscious wine. Natural fruit ripeness together with the acidity of a dessert wine are no match for a pudding based on refined sugar. The wine must be as sweet or preferably sweeter than the food it accompanies which means serving simple, fruit or nut-based puddings with the best dessert wines.

The taste of wine comes from the grape, soil, climate, winemaking, vintage and age. When considering wine and food combinations it often helps to start with the grape variety, then to decide which style of that grape might suit a particular dish or vice versa. (See the chart of major grape varieties on pages 28–9 below).

Varietals tend to have fairly direct fruit flavours, which are good with strongly flavoured dishes and relatively complex foods. Where soil and terroir dominate the grape variety, the wine is often drier and more austere and will suit more integrated flavours and richer foods and cooking methods. Hot climates give very ripe, rich flavours and plenty of alcohol as well as less obvious acidity. Such wines will go with strong flavours but with food that is less rich, less protein and dairy-based, and it can tolerate spices.

Oak-ageing adds to the structure of the wine therefore needs more substantial food. Its drying effect is also good with rich and creamy sauces. Strong oak flavours respond best to char-gilled or barbecued foods. Maturity makes a wine more complex in flavour, but more fragile. An old Bordeaux will need quite simple meat with a carefully made sauce and subtle flavours. Old Burgundy is rather more robust but will still benefit from classically cooked food.

Further reading: Sandy O'Byrne goes into more detail on the principles and practice of *Matching Food and Wine* in her book of that name.

Whites	Characteristics	Food Matches
Riesling	Dry to sweet, high acidity, light to medium body, fine and aromatic, ages well	Delicate foods like fish, richness in sauces, cooking methods and ingredients. Off-dry versions with spices, light aromatic fruit with rich sauces
Chardonnay	Balanced acidity, medium to full body, usually oaked though amount of oak varies, apple to peach or melon-type fruit, creamy and buttery flavours with toasted influence ripeness, medium to high alcohol level	Depends on style and amount of oak influence. Main course foods, fish with sauces, chicken and light meats, smoked foods, fruit-influenced savoury dishes, pasta with cream sauces, creamy cheeses
Sémillon	Dry or sweet and botrytized full-bodied, waxy, honeyed character with citrus-type fruit acidity when young	Dry—with textured fish, chicken and light meats, spices and many Chinese dishes Sweet—nutty puddings, light cakes and pastries, blue cheese, foie gras and similar rich pâtés
Sauvignon Blanc	Dry, crisp acidity, medium body, very aromatic and intense, from gooseberry to green apple, citrus type fruit to limes, green peppers and grassy influences. Classically minerally, flinty overtones	Well-flavoured fish, some chicken and light meats, vegetable and tomato based pasta, smoked salmon, spicy and herb flavoured food, goats' cheese, some blue cheese and strong cheeses in general
Chenin Blanc	Dry to sweet, high acidity, medium to full-bodied, aromatic citrus, apple, floral and honeyed fruit, ages well	Dry—rich food especially fish with sauces, pâté and charcuterie, salads and some spices Sweet—depending on sweetness, some spicy savoury food, goats' cheese and strong cheeses; also fruit-based puddings

Picture The Possibilities

ESTABLISHED IN 1883, WENTE VINEYARDS
IS THE OLDEST FAMILY OWNED WINERY IN
CALIFORNIA. TODAY THE FOURTH GENERATION
OF WENTES MANAGE FOUR HISTORIC
WINERIES, AN ELEGANT AWARD-WINNING
RESTAURANT, A GREG NORMAN DESIGNED
CHAMPIONSHIP GOLF COURSE, A SUMMER
CONCERT SERIES AND OVER 3,000 ACRES OF
ESTATE OWNED VINEYARDS IN MONTEREY
AND THE LIVERMORE VALLEY.

WENTE
VINEYARDS
CALIFORNIA

Picture Perfect California Wines

GILBEYS

NATIONAL OFF-LICENCE ASSOCIATION

OFF LICENCE AWARDS 2001

The final of the Gilbeys/NOffLA Off-Licence of the Year Awards will take place at the RDS in Dublin on Monday 15 January 2001. There are nine awards in total: the top award of *National Off-Licence of the Year*, four *Regional Awards* (Dublin, Leinster, Connaught/Ulster and Munster), three *Specialist Awards* (Spirits, Wine, Beer) and one *Certificate of Merit* to the Best Mixed Trader Specialist.

The twenty-five finalists are:

Callan's Off-Licence, 40 Park Street, Dundalk, Co. Louth

Deveney's Off-Licence, 382 South Circular Road, Dublin 8

Fahy's Off-Licence, Teeling Street, Ballina, Co. Mayo

Galvins Wines & Spirits, 37 Bandon Road, Cork

Jus de Vine, Unit 10, Portmarnock S.C., Co. Dublin

Lonergan Off-Licence, O'Connell Street, Clonmel, Co. Tipperary

Mac's Off-Licence, Ennis Road, Limerick

McCabe's Off-Licence, 51–5 Mount Merrion Avenue, Blackrock, Co. Dublin

McHugh's Off-Licence, 57 Kilbarrick Road, Dublin 5

Molloy's Liquor Stores, Clonsilla Mall, Clonsilla, Dublin 15

Molloy's Liquor Stores, Nutgrove Shopping Centre, Rathfarnham, Dublin 16

Next Door, Main Street, Enfield, Co. Meath

O'Briens Wine Off-Licence, 30 Donnybrook Road, Donnybrook, Dublin 4

O'Briens Wine Off-Licence 1 Main Street, Malahide, Co. Dublin

O'Briens Wine Off-Licence, 149 Upper Rathmines Road, Dublin 6

O'Briens Wine Off-Licence, Templeogue Village, Dublin 6W

O'Briens Wine Off-Licence, 19 Quinsboro Road, Bray, Co. Wicklow

O'Donovans Wines & Spirits, Riversdale, Midleton, Co. Cork

Redmond's of Ranelagh, 25 Ranelagh, Dublin 6

Sweeney's Off-Licence, 20 Lower Dorset Street, Dublin 1

The Mill Wine Cellar, Mill Street, Maynooth, Co. Kildare

The Ryan Vine Wine Shop & Off-Licence, Trimgate St, Navan, Co. Meath

The Vintry, 102 Rathgar Road, Dublin 6

The Wine Centre, John Street, Kilkenny

Vineyard Off-Licence, 14 Mainguard Street, Galway

NOffLA, the National Off-Licence Association,
1-3 Sandford Road, Ranelagh, Dublin 6
Tel: 01 497 9286 Fax: 01 491 0172 Email: awards@noffla.ie
Website: www.noffla.ie

Reds	Characteristics	Food Matches
Cabernet Sauvignon	Tannin, medium acidity, full body, typically blackcurrant-type fruit with mint, cedar and cigar-like aromas, ages well	Protein, especially red meat, matches rich meats like lamb and duck, rich meat sauces and game like widgeon
Pinot Noir	Medium tannin, medium to upper acidity, elegant body, rich fruit, typically strawberry type with spicy overtones, develops gamey vegetal character, moderate to long ageing	Red meat and some cheeses, typically game or beef, also casseroles and wine-based sauces. Lighter, fruity styles with textured fish, some spices and mushroom pasta or risotto
Syrah	Tannin, acidity, high alcohol, full body, can be firm and dense in structure or rich and fruit driven, dark fruit character of brambles, dark plums, violets with very spicy peppery overtones, ages well	Depends on structure and tannin, red meat, grilled and barbecued meats, game, casseroles, substantial pasta and grain-based dishes which include meat; richer styles can match spicy food
Merlot	Low to moderate tannin, higher alcohol, medium to full body, ripe, rich fruit character typically raspberries, plums and chocolate, can be fruity and simple or layered, rich and complex, ageing depends on style, generally moderate	Depends on tannin and oak influence, meats like beef, game like quail, pasta dishes and vegetarian food if not too oaky. Sausages, salamis and pâtés with fruity versions, some cheeses

The mystery of vintages

Alan Crowley, Master of Wine

A great part of the mystique of wine is the importance of the 'vintage', and which are the better or lesser years. Unfortunately, to many consumers the concept of a vintage represents yet another unknown in the wine maze.

Put simply, a vintage is the year in which the grapes were picked and the wine was made. It is therefore an indication of how old the wine is. However, as with other agricultural products, the critical importance of the vintage lies in the variability from year to year of weather conditions during the growing season. In some regions, notably in Europe, the effect is of a particular importance on the potential quality of the final wine. Thus, in good vintage years, when there have been sufficient rainy and dry periods, with sufficient sunshine and warm temperatures at the right time, grapes can be produced of a better quality to make a superior wine, as opposed to those in lesser years when the weather is not so right for quality grape production.

The effect of the weather, and hence the reputation of the vintage, is usually more important in wine regions whose climate is more marginal for the growing of grapes. Generally such regions are in Europe — in Germany, in Burgundy and Bordeaux in France, in Spain and Italy. Wine regions with more or less regular weather conditions produce wines where vintages year to year assume less importance. Such wine regions include the New World vineyards of South Africa, California, Australia and Chile. In these cases the vintage serves the consumer simply as a reminder of how old the wine is, and hence when it should be drunk. Of course, even in these regions knowledge of the vintage and wine style is important to ensure the optimum time for drinking the wine.

Because European wines in particular are so dependent for their quality on the weather conditions of any one year, for many wine lovers the vintage is one of the keys to the quality of any particular wine. As such there is a benefit in having vintage knowledge, as it will assist in:

- selecting wines from better years rather than lesser years.
- ensuring a wine which is meant to be drunk young, or is better after a few years ageing, is at the correct age at the time of drinking.

Some wines are best consumed while still young. For example, Muscadet and Valpolicella are best consumed up to three

Region	97	96	95	94	93	92	91	90	89	88	87	86	85	Classic vintages
Bordeaux red	7	8	8	7	6	4	4	10	10	9	5	8	9	82, 78, 70, 61
Sauternes	8	8	8	5	5	4	3	10	10	8	5	9	7	80
Burgundy red	7	8	8	6	8	6	7	10	9	9	7	7	9	83, 78
Burgundy white	8	9	8	6	7	7	5	9	9	8	5	8	9	83, 78
Rhône	8	7	8	7	5	5	7	10	9	8	7	8	8	78, 67, 61
Champagne	8	–	8	–	7	7	6	8	8	–	–	8	9	79
Germany	8	7	8	8	8	7	6	10	8	7	6	6	8	76, 75
Spain	8	7	9	10	4	6	8	6	6	5	7	6	6	82, 64
Italy	8	8	7	8	8	4	5	9	7	8	6	7	9	78, 71
Port	8	–	7	10	–	8	8	–	–	–	–	–	9	77, 70, 66, 63
Australia	7	8	7	8	7	7	8	7	6	7	7	8	8	82, 79
California	6	6	7	8	7	8	9	8	7	7	8	7	8	74

According to *Hugh Johnson's Pocket Wine Book 2000*, the 98 vintage was as follows:

Bordeaux red: good–very good; Sauternes: good; Burgundy red: average–good; Burgundy white: good–very good except Chablis: average–fair; Rhône very good–excellent; Champagne: mostly non-vintage; Germany very good–excellent; Spain: average–good; Italy: excellent in Piedmonte, average–good in Tuscany; Australia: good–very good; California: poor–average.

years after their production or vintage as their charm lies in their fresh, youthful character.

On the other hand some wines, while generally not changing much in quality from vintage to vintage, benefit from two to three years' bottle maturation before consumption, for example, Australian Shiraz or Californian Cabernet Sauvignon.

As a very general guide, it can be said that most New World quality red wines benefit from having two to three years' maturation from the date of vintage before consumption, while most New World whites do not benefit from long maturation and are best consumed within three to four years after their vintage.

Identifying which European wines and which vintages have produced wine of superior quality depends more on detailed knowledge of the wine region than on general country classification. This can only be gained by wine education and experience. However, many regions are historically famous for producing fine 'vintage' wines such as Bordeaux, Burgundy, Barolo and Rioja, to name a few.

As a guide to the reputation of each year's vintage since 1985, a quick reference vintage chart is attached. Of course, any vintage chart is only a general guide—the best producers can make a good wine in 'off' years, and in some years a winemaker, or part of a wine region, can experience local problems resulting in quite ordinary or inferior wines in an otherwise good year.

Old World White

Austria

Polz Grassnitzberg Grauburgunder 98 £10–£11
This Grauburgunder (Pinot Gris) shows a lot of complex,
white-fleshed, vegetal fruit wound into oak. The wine finishes
with a full-flavoured and balanced length. It will continue to
improve over the next three years.
Oddbins

Polz Grassnitzberg Weissburgunder 98 £10–£11
Weissburgunder (Pinot Blanc) has some of the full-bodied
character of Chardonnay. Here it has spicy aromas with fresh
tropical fruits and complex, creamy, spicy flavours on the
palate. It's nicely reserved with some grape-skin contact and
oak influence showing at the end. A well-made, pricey wine, it
will gain complexity over the next three years.
Oddbins

Hungary

Chapel Hill South Balaton Irsai Olivér 97 £5–£6
Originally developed as a table grape, Irsai Olivér produces
intensely aromatic wines. This example has ripe melon, roses,
ginger and spice aromas. Dry, with flavours of intense apricot,
peach and pear, it finishes with a crisp, crunchy, green-apple
freshness. Drink it over the next two years.
Barry & Fitzwilliam

Disznókö Tokaji Dry Furmint 97 £6–£7
A most unusual wine that needs food, this Furmint has pears
and spearmint on the nose, followed on the palate by assertive
and contrasting melon and citrus fruits, with marked crisp
acidity dominating on the finish. Drink it before 2003.
Barry & Fitzwilliam

Bulgaria

Bulgarian Vintners' Reserve Chardonnay 95 £4–£5
The Rousse area of the Balkan Mountains, where this wine is
made, produces quality white wines. This classy Chardonnay's
apple fruit flavours are enlivened with lemon peel on the
palate. It has a long, minty finish. An honest, straightforward
wine it is very good value.
Irish Distillers

France — Alsace

Alsace, in France's sheltered north-east corner, is well suited to growing vines, with a wide range of different soil types, very low rainfall and long sunny autumns. It offers a range of varieties and dry styles matched by few other regions. Even the late-harvest over-ripe wines are off-dry rather than sweet. Alsace produces predominantly white wines, most of them excellent partners for food, and is one of the regions in France that may specify the grape variety in the AC.

In this section the wines are listed by
- grape variety
- price

AC Alsace Gewurztraminer Tesco Gewurztraminer 98 £8–£9
With a heady perfume of old rose petals, this is a classic pungent and aromatic Alsace Gewurztraminer. Powerful flavours dance on the palate — rosewater infused with freshly chopped root ginger and ripe white-fleshed exotic fruits. The acidity is moderate and the wine finishes warm and long with a Turkish Delight aftertaste. Serve it as an aperitif or with pungent cheeses, smoked fish or fresh salmon.
Tesco

AC Alsace Gewurztraminer Dietrich 98 £9–£10
Wines made from the pink-skinned Gewurztraminer are naturally higher in alcohol than those made from other varietals found in Alsace, due to the grape's natural ability to create abundant sugars when ripening. Gewurztraminer wines produced in this region are heady, with a perfume and flavour so full that the wines often give an impression of sweetness, although they are quite dry. This example from Dietrich has all the expected varietal characteristics — it's spicy with oriental lychee flavours and a must with your Chinese takeaway.
TDL

> The term **Vieilles Vignes** (old vines) on a label is a signal of higher quality, as old vines produce fewer but more intensely flavoured and concentrated grapes than younger vines. As the vines age, their roots penetrate deeper into the subsoil and absorb the really interesting minerals and trace elements that produce the extra flavours and aromatics.

AC Alsace Gewurztraminer Vieilles Vignes Sipp Mack 98 £9–£10

The extra dimension given by old vines can be tasted in this off-dry Gewurztraminer, which is laden with ripe, spicy, juicy fruit. Big on the palate with luscious mouthfilling flavours, it has a long, ripe, fruity finish and would go well with lightly spiced dishes and rich sauces.

Mitchells

AC Alsace Gewurztraminer St Hippolyte Charles Koehly & Fils 98 £10–£11

Charles Koehly keeps a tight rein on this Gewurztraminer, a grape that can be a little over the top and blowsy if not disciplined. His other varietal wines are typified by their austerity and are reserved, lean and elegant in style, but this Gewurz is very assertive on the tastebuds. The attack of Oriental spices and ginger spiking the ripe exotic fruitiness is softened with rosewater essence. It's excellent value and a good partner for goose pâté.

Irish Distillers

AC Alsace Gewurztraminer Trimbach 98 £12–£13

Here is a textbook Gewurztraminer from the famous Alsace house of Trimbach, which has been making wine since 1626. An oriental meal in a glass! Think of fragrant rosewater infused with Chinese lychees, fleshy nuggets of fruit and an added grating of root ginger to excite the tastebuds. Finishing deep and long, it will improve for two more years. It goes well with duckling, fish in creamy sauces, Chinese or Cajun dishes, or fruit and strong cheeses.

Gilbeys

AC Alsace Cuvée des Seigneurs de Ribeaupierre Trimbach 88 £18–£19

One of Trimbach's top-of-the-range dry Gewurzttaminers, this wine delivers a rainbow of sensations from ripe melon fruit to gingery spice with an intriguing and atypical sage-like herbal tone adding complexity. There was a remarkable vintage in Alsace in 88 and this wine will be very long lived – it's good for another two years at least – but it's pricey. Try it with sweet and sour oriental dishes and pungent cheeses.

Gilbeys

AC Alsace Gewurztraminer Herrenweg de Turckheim Dom. Zind-Humbrecht 97 £21–£22

This Gewurztraminer from Humbrecht offers all the rich aromas and taste expected from the grape. Exotically perfumed, it's dry but luscious, with flavours of sticky honeycomb, vanilla, pepper and elderflower — not for the fainthearted! It will keep for another two years. Try it with spiced guinea fowl.
United Beverages

AC Alsace Muscat Herrenweg de Turckheim Dom. Zind-Humbrecht 97 £15–£16

Muscats in Alsace are always dry and have a musky, grapey character. The Humbrechts succeed in finding a depth of flavour in this varietal seldom achieved elsewhere, as shown in this rich classic with its layered palate of soft ginger, honey, white pepper and rose hips. It's full bodied, offering a good round mouthful with an elegant balance of ripe, warm fruits and spices and will hold for another two years.
United Beverages

AC Alsace Pinot Blanc Dopff & Irion 98 £8–£9

Pinot Blanc tends to have a delicate bouquet with well-balanced fruit, acidity and alcohol. It's a versatile wine, going well with most foods, apart from cheese and desserts, and makes a good house wine for restaurants. This example, from the long-established Dopff & Irion, is very refreshing and lively with more personality than most Pinot Blancs. Its mouth-watering green apple fruit flavours are cut with a squeeze of lemon and finish with an attractive mineral tone. Enjoy it on its own as an aperitif or with a light fish soufflé for a delicious lunch.
Bacchus

AC Alsace Tokay Pinot Gris Réserve Sipp Mack 98 £10–£11

Pinot Gris is a white grape derived from the black Pinot Noir variety. It can make a golden, rich and powerful wine with heady aromatics. This example is a delicious, refreshing, zippy wine, laden with spicy, ripe, grapey fruit. Big and mouthfilling, it has a crisp, dry, fruity finish and is just the drink to accompany spicy food and Chinese meals — try it with quail marinated in honey and five spice.
Mitchells

AC Alsace Pinot Gris Réserve Trimbach 97 £12–£13

Trimbach's Réserve and Sélection wines are intended to be
richer and longer lived than the regular wines named after the
varietal only. They make a lovely change for those who like
oaked Chardonnay, for although new oak is never used in
Alsace, mature Pinot Gris can acquire a grilled nuttiness
reminiscent of Burgundy's Meursault. This 97 Réserve has
fleshy white fruit flavours with a streak of spice adding
interest and complexity. It is rich and seductive, if a little
pricey, and will drink well for another two years. It's a good
partner for fish, especially salmon, as well as chicken and light
meat dishes.
Gilbeys

AC Alsace Riesling Dietrich 99 £7–£8

Despite their Germanic heritage, Alsace wines are typically
dry. This good-value youthful Riesling displays an attractive
style for the price, with lots of apple and custard flavours
intermingling on the palate. Drink it on its own or with oily
fish and shellfish.
TDL

AC Alsace Riesling Sipp Mack 97 £8–£9

Riesling is the prince of grapes in Alsace. It produces dry,
fruity and firm wines with a subtle aroma, with the best
examples capable of distinction and long ageing. This example
from the very reliable producer Sipp Mack is a refreshing,
mouthfilling wine laden with ripe juicy Muscatels, with a long,
delicious finish. It's excellent value and is capable of ageing and
developing for some time — try it with mousseline of fish with
butter sauce.
Mitchells

AC Alsace Riesling Mader 97 £8–£9

Originally from Germany, Riesling found a new identity in
Alsace when it crossed the Rhine border. The exceptionally dry
and sunny local climate produces grapes with added ripeness,
high sugar levels and ensuing high alcohol. Jean-Luc Mader
has produced a very pleasant Riesling from his 6.5 hectares of
vines in the village of Hunawihr, famous for its church and
fortified cemetery. It has good soft apple and quince fruit,
giving a full fat mouthfeel. Drink it now or keep it for up to
two years. It's good on its own or with fish dishes.
Wines Direct

AC Alsace Riesling Tradition Kuentz-Bas 98 £10–£11

Top-quality grower and négociant/wine merchant Kuentz-Bas
was founded in 1795. The Réserve Personnelle wines are estate
bottled from their 12 hectares of vineyards and are made to be

kept for ten to fifteen years. Here we have their other label, Cuvée Tradition, made to be drunk within three to four years of the vintage. It has a delicate floral aroma with a good weight of apple and apricot fruit, balanced nicely with crisp and steely acidity.
Cana

AC Alsace Riesling Pierre Frick 98 £11–£12

Pierre Frick is a rare breed in Alsace. He does not use herbicides or pesticides in his bio-dynamic vineyards and his winery does not engage in chaptalisation (enriching the grape juice with sugar to boost the alcohol level). The wines can be slow to reveal their full potential, but are worth the wait. This one is very immature, but has lots of promise. Its shy aromas are followed by intense yellow citrus fruit flavours — zesty, crisp grapefruit, lemon and kumquats. Give it two or three years to reach its potential.
Bubble Brothers

> Just fifty vineyards on the steep slopes of the Vosges Mountains in Alsace are classified as **Grand Cru**. They can offer excellent value, as the jump in quality is not reflected proportionately in the price.

AC Alsace Grand Cru Riesling Rosacker Sipp Mack 97 £13–£14

This Grand Cru from the Rosacker vineyard is deliciously refreshing and zippy with an excellent weight of lemon and lime fruits and ripe, sun-drenched raisins. The lovely mouthfilling fruity finish and flavours linger on forever. It will drink well for another two years, and is just the wine to serve with brill in cream sauce.
Mitchells

AC Alsace Riesling Gueberschwihr Dom. Zind-Humbrecht 98 £15–£16

There are many different soil types in the Alsace rift valley, which explains why a number of varietals flourish here. Father and son winemaking team Leonard and Olivier Humbrecht match soil type with grape variety and produce wines that are legendary for their drama and concentration. The Riesling profiled here is crisp and perfectly dry with a citrus-centred palate showing pink grapefruit, vanilla and a bittersweet finish. It's fruitier than the average Alsace Riesling and is good for another two years. Traditional Quiche Lorraine is the perfect match.
United Beverages

☆ ☆

AC Alsace Riesling Clos Häuserer Wintzenheim Dom. Zind-Humbrecht 96 £19–£20

White wines are usually fermented at cool temperatures to preserve their floral and fruity aromas. However, the Humbrechts ferment their whites at exceptionally high temperatures, which neutralises the varietal character but gives an added layer of complexity as the long-lived wines mature. Their 96 Riesling has a gorgeous nose of caramel, apple and honey and a huge, concentrated fruit centre of kumquats, tangerine and lemon curd. Still going strong, it's rich, rich, rich—a super example of concentrated ripe Riesling with lovely mellow, mature flavours. Enjoy it now or cellar it with confidence for three years or more.

United Beverages

France — Bordeaux

Traditionally, white Bordeaux was made from a blend of Sémillon and Sauvignon Blanc. Nowadays the proportion of Sauvignon in the blend is often increased; sometimes to 100%, in which case this is stated on the label. White AC Bordeaux are at their best when they are young and fresh.

In this section the wines are listed by price.

AC Bordeaux Dourthe No. 1 Bordeaux 99 £7–£8
A modern-style Bordeaux from a good vintage for whites, this is excellent value for money. Its very intense aroma of green leafy gooseberries indicates that Sauvignon Blanc is the dominant grape in the blend, unlike more traditional styles where Sémillon dominates. The flavours are very tasty, too — fresh green gooseberries with a twist of lemon and nettle freshness. Try it with creamy chicken risotto.
Oddbins

AC Bordeaux Marquis de Chasse 98 £8–£9
A typically ripe wine from this excellent vintage (despite El Niño), this is a very decent offering. Honeyed fruits from those ripe grapes result in a full-flavoured wine, yet with freshness and crispness from a balancing tart note. It will keep for a year or two. This would be ideal as an aperitif or with seafood.
Bacchus

AC Bordeaux Signatures en Bordeaux 97 £8–£9
The crisp and refreshing style of Sauvignon Blanc is very evident in this wine from the 97 vintage, when summer rain challenged winemakers. The aromas of grass and lemons show the typically herbaceous character of the Sauvignon Blanc. A lively attack on the palate of citrus fruits evolves into gooseberries and semi-ripe peach fruitiness. Partner this crisp wine with white meats and poultry.
O'Briens

AC Bordeaux Ch. Timberlay 99 £9–£10
Ch. Timberlay's vineyards are planted with Sauvignon Blanc (40%) and Sémillon (60%) and the wines are vinified at low temperatures to accentuate their fresh and aromatic appeal. This 99 is a lovely light white with a decent concentration of fruit. Refreshing lemon and lime with some spice fan over the palate, making it a nice match for fish, seafood or poultry dishes.
Maxxium

France — Burgundy

Most white Burgundies are produced from 100% Chardonnay, either oaked or unoaked. A small proportion is produced from 100% Aligoté, a local variety, rarely seen outside the region.

In this section the wines are listed by
• Appellation Contrôlée
• price

> **AC Bourgogne** is the most basic AC in Burgundy, but is by no means to be despised. It often offers very good quality and value.

AC Bourgogne Louis Jadot Couvent des Jacobins 98 £9–£10

Louis Jadot is a very important négociant (wine merchant) in Burgundy. For this Couvent des Jacobins 98 — a good-value wine — the Chardonnay grapes are crushed and fermented in oak barrels and aged for 12–18 months. The wine's attractive buttery apple aroma is followed by plenty of green apple, melon and clove-studded lemon fruit with a peppery finish. It has another two years to go and would be a good partner for light fish or a cheese soufflé.
Grants

AC Bourgogne Antonin Rodet Chardonnay de Vieilles Vignes 97 £12–£13

Antonin Rodet is now being managed by Bertrand Devillard with great dynamism. Its vineyards are in the Côte Chalonnaise district/Région de Mercurey, south of the heart of Burgundy's Côte d'Or, where the wines tend to mature earlier. This wine is made from Chardonnay grown on old vines, which give an added dimension of aroma and flavour. The riper fruit is evident in this wine from the excellent 97 vintage. Luscious Galia melon aromas waft from the glass. There are decent fruity flavours of ripe melons with a mineral edge and an earthy note to add interest. Drink it over the next two years and partner it with roast white meats, vegetarian nut risotto.
Febvre

AC Bourgogne Hautes Côtes de Nuits Dom. Henri Naudin-Ferrand 97 £11–£12

This domaine is one of the best sources in the Hautes Côtes for well-crafted and charming wines. Henri Naudin is ably assisted by his two qualified oenologist daughters Claire and Anne, who have seasoned this pleasant wine with careful and subtle use of new oak. Plenty of ripe fruits appear on the nose,

followed by a dry, slightly creamy palate, with citrus fruit flavours. Have it with a light lunch of brill in butter sauce.
Wines Direct

> **Aligoté** is a lesser-known white grape variety grown in Burgundy. While it shares the same broad structure as Chardonnay, it is not as highly regarded. Its very high acidity makes it the ideal base for Kir, a local aperitif, which is made with Aligoté and a little Crème de Cassis.

AC Bouzeron Aligoté A. et P. de Villaine 98 £10–£11

De Villaine's mastery of Aligoté makes the grape's acidity seem less like meanness and more like an attractive, nervy quality. His recipe for success is healthy vines, gobelet pruned to restrict yields, and pressing the grapes in a pneumatic press to give a very clear juice. After a light sulphuring to purify the juice ('must'), he uses local yeasts in the fermentation. In Burgundy 1998 was a better year for whites than reds. This 98 has a sherbet-like scent, which is intensified on the palate as an abundance of zesty lemons, limes and crunchy Granny Smith apples. The tingling acidity is very refreshing without being tart. Partner it with light creamy pasta dishes, oily fish, tapas or goats' cheese.
Wines Direct

> **Chablis** is one of France's classic white wines, characteristically steely and fresh. Made from Chardonnay, much of its character comes from the limestone subsoil with its high content of marine fossils and chalk. There are three quality levels of Chablis: **AC Chablis**, made from grapes from anywhere in the region, is flinty and minerally with crunchy green apple flavours; the wines should be drunk about two to three years from the vintage. The best vineyards are classified as **Premier Cru** or **Grand Cru** and the name of the vineyard will appear on the bottle. Premier Cru wines require at least five years' bottle ageing. The wines are more intense and concentrated than AC Chablis, with pure citrus fruit flavours. Grand Cru wines are richer and fatter and should be aged for ten years. Fish and white meat are good matches for both Premier and Grand Cru. Unlike other fine Chardonnay wines from Burgundy, Chablis is not always oaked; in maturity, some unoaked Chablis can take on nutty qualities, leading unwary tasters to detect an oak influence that is not there.

AC Chablis Dom. Séguinet-Bordet 98 £10–£11

It will be interesting to see whether this producer's style changes in the future. A young winemaker, he has just taken over from his grandfather and has worked on some vintages in the New World. Here he has produced a very typical Chablis with all the characteristics you'd expect—clean, crisp and dry with citrus fruit flavours and a mineral note (what the French call 'gunflint'). The balance between acidity, alcohol and fruit is just right and the wine feels satisfyingly fat in the mouth.

Wines Direct

AC Chablis Ropiteau 99 £11–£12

Ropiteau is a well-respected négociant house in Meursault. It was founded in 1848 by Jean Ropiteau, who was convinced that the arrival of the railway in that year would help to spread the fame of Burgundian wines. Their AC Chablis 99 is a classic, with concentrated clean fresh fruit—lively green apples and lemons—and would be ideal as an aperitif or with simple fish dishes.

TDL

AC Chablis Barton & Guestier Tradition 97 £12–£13

This is a fine example of Chablis from Barton & Guestier, part of the huge Seagram group. As 97 was a fine vintage, this wine may mature more quickly than the 96. It has subtle elderflower and spearmint aromas and intense, zesty mineral and green fruit flavours. The crisp acidity is very refreshing and a charge of alcohol warms the throat on the finish. Try it with seafood, poultry or white meat.

Dillons

> **Négociants** (wine merchants) buy grapes, juice or wine and then complete the winemaking process, blending the final individual wines from the same AC and selling it under their own label. **Domaine-bottled** wines are grown, vinified and bottled by a single winemaker or family.

AC Chablis Laroche 98 £12–£13

An excellent example of Chablis from the Laroche family, who have owned vineyards in Burgundy since 1850, and are also dynamic négociants. Their 98, a reasonable vintage in this area, which will age for up to two years, has moderate acidity and is fruit-driven with mineral tones and great concentration. It would be a good wine with food, say chicken escalopes in a light sauce.

Allied Drinks

AC Chablis Alain Geoffroy Dom. Le Verger 99 £13–£14

A very reliable producer, Geoffroy is a traditionalist and his wines need bottle age to develop. With nicely focused, youthful fruity flavours, his Dom. Le Verger is atypically ripe for Chablis, yet it maintains the trademark steely crisp austerity that sets this expression of Chardonnay apart. Just the thing with oysters.
Febvre

AC Chablis Joseph Drouhin 98 £13–£14

Drouhin is one of Burgundy's leading houses, excellent and reliable, and this is a wonderful example of their Chablis. They like to use wood and the resulting wines are rich and fat, so keep well in bottle. This Chablis is strong, dry and intense with good mineral tones. For a delicious light lunch serve it with fish simply cooked in butter.
Gilbeys

AC Chablis Dom. Laroche St Martin 99 £13–£14

Laroche uses the most modern winemaking techniques, with limited use of oak and then only for the Grands Crus. The St Martin 99 is an excellent AC Chablis — very concentrated and well made with good balance between the crisp, grassy fruit and the fuller apple fruit on the mid-palate. The steely, mineral bite on the finish is delicious. This wine would be good with chicken escalopes in a light sauce.
Allied Drinks

AC Chablis Berrys' Own Selection Chablis 98 £14–£15

Berry Bros & Rudd can trace its origins back to 1698, when the Widow Bourne established her shop opposite St James's Palace in London. Their Chablis is made by Guy Mothe and his sons Jean-Louis and Thierry at Dom. du Colombier. Unoaked, it has aromas of butter and green apple. Nettle-like acidity awakens the tastebuds to the grapefruit and green apple flavours competing for attention. Try it with grilled chicken or white fish.
Fields

AC Chablis William Fèvre Champs Royaux 97 £14–£15

This is a wine of character from the very important William Fèvre domaine, which was recently acquired by Bouchard Pere & Fils, which is in turn owned by Champagne Henriot. William Fèvre's wines have elegance and panache, with the creamy texture from ageing in new barrels found in the best wines. This Chablis is beautifully mature, with an earthy minerally bouquet and classic flinty flavours asserting them-

selves over crisp lively citrus fruit. Well integrated and harmonious, it has a long, lingering finish. Try it with mussel stew.
Febvre

AC Chablis 1er Cru Jaffelin 98 £18–£19

Jaffelin was sold to the enormous Boisset group in the early
1990s. This wine, made from a selection of 1er Cru vineyards,
couples oily, honeyed aromas with tangy lemon and lime fruit.
The minerally citrus flavours will develop well over time. It's a
good, well-made wine but at a price.
Cassidy

AC Chablis 1er Cru 'Fourchaume' Jean Durup Père et Fils Dom. de la Paulière 98 £16–£17

The Durup family has been making wine for five centuries.
They do not use oak and produce floral wines, rarely deep in
flavour but always elegant. This 1er Cru is a classic example of
Chablis — light, fresh and fruity with a good concentration of
lemon, limes and apples complemented by a mineral note. It is
a really well-made wine with all the elements beautifully
integrated and balanced and a lovely, lingering finish. If you
are patient, this wine will improve even more over the next
five years or so .
Ecock

AC Chablis 1er Cru 'Les Vaillons' Dom. Long-Depaquit 98 £16–£17

This is a very well-run famous old estate now backed by
Bichot of Beaune. Their Vaillons 98 is an elegant, harmonious,
balanced wine with good, rich, concentrated fruit, mainly
lemons, but without the tartness occasionally present with
citric fruit flavours. Integrated and stylish, it will reward
keeping until at least 2003. A delicious match with this Chablis
would be brill with prawn sauce.
Irish Distillers

AC Chablis 1er Cru 'Montmains' Chanson Père et Fils 98 £18–£19

Established in 1750, Chanson — one of whose customers was
Voltaire — is both an important négociant and owner of some
excellent vineyards. This 1er Cru is one of the négociant wines
made from grapes bought in from different suppliers. Shy
aromas are no preparation for the intense minerally and zesty
flavours. You can taste the terroir — the site's unique combination of soil, climate and topography — in the fruity flavours
and the way the minerally soil transposes itself into a remarkably long finish. Another five years will see this wine improve
even more.
O'Briens

Mâcon whites, from Burgundy's most southerly wine
district, are fast maturing with softer acidity. The
Chardonnay grape is used. In the south of the district
43 villages may add their names to the wine. AC Mâcon
Villages is made from a blend of the listed villages.

AC Mâcon Uchizy Champy Père et Cie 98 £9–£10

Established in 1720, Champy is acknowledged as the oldest
négociant in Burgundy. It was sold to Jadot and is now owned
by Henri Meurgey and his son Pierre. This 98 from the
commune of Uchizy is aromatic with lovely, light, grapey fruit
flavours. It's a frank and open-faced wine — perfect for summer lunch.
Allied Drinks

AC Mâcon-Villages Chanson Père et Fils 98 £7–£8

Here is an honest straightforward Mâcon from a vintage that
favoured whites more than reds. Simple fruitiness and earthiness give the wine interest and the price adds to the appeal.
O'Briens

AC Mâcon-Villages Béatrice & Jean-Michel Drouin Dom. des Gerbeaux Mâcon-Solutré 99 £8–£9

Jean-Michel Drouin is a passionate winemaker and it shows in
the noticeable progress he has made since 88. He presses his
Chardonnay grapes slowly and gently, uses various yeast
cultures and stirs the lees regularly to make soft and lovely
wines which are charming in youth. This one is dry with citrus
and tropical fruit on the nose and palate. It's drinking nicely
now and has very good, quite rich fruit and a long spicy finish.
Excellent value, it will cellar for another two years.
Burgundy Direct

Meursault is a commune in the Côte de Beaune, the
best area for Burgundy whites. Showing another side
to the Chardonnay grape, the wines are full bodied,
rich, ripe and nutty.

AC Meursault Ropiteau 94 £24–£25

Ropiteau has been owned by Boisset since 1994. As a vintage,
94 was variable for whites, many of which should be drunk
during 2001, like this Meursault. It has a very pronounced
bouquet of mature stewed fruits with a smoky note. On the
palate creamy caramel flavours are followed by delicious
warm apple pie, cashew nuts and a whisper of toffee. Gloriously rich and concentrated with very good length, this is a
real treat.
TDL

AC Meursault Louis Jadot 96 £24–£25

The skilled and passionate Jacques Lardière has been
winemaker with Jadot since 1970. The firm was bought in the
mid-eighties by its American distributor Kobrand and benefited from the new investment by extending its domaines
and building new winemaking facilities. This Meursault 96 is a
lovely, full-bodied, elegant, concentrated wine from a great
vintage for whites. Ripe and bursting at the seams, it's full and
fat on the palate with classic grilled nutty tones. Powerful, with
a kick of alcohol on the finish, it's really good, but should be
drunk with food, perhaps lobster or Christmas turkey or
goose.
Grants

> **Montagny** is located in the Côte Chalonnaise. The AC
> is for white wine only, from four villages. The wines
> usually have a subtle peppery tone from some oak
> maturation, yet they maintain a fresh crispness and an
> expression of the soil.

AC Montagny 1er Cru Louis Latour 'La Grande Roche' 98 £12–£13

Latour is a family-run house, founded two hundred years ago.
It was among the first to sell varietal Burgundian wines and
expand outside Burgundy, notably in the south of France. This
subtle Montagny 1er Cru is a lovely, well-balanced wine,
which doesn't shout, but has very good fruit and length and
gentle nuances.
Gilbeys

> **Pernand-Vergelesses** is in the Côte de Beaune district,
> producing mainly red wines. The whites are typically
> soft and good quality, best drunk within three to four
> years of the vintage.

AC Pernand-Vergelesses 1er Cru Chanson Père et Fils 'Les Caradeux' 98 £20–£21

El Niño prevented 98 from being a great vintage. A hot
August with very ripe grapes was followed by September rain
at harvest time. However, good winemakers can still make
excellent wine in these adverse circumstance, as Chanson has
succeeded in doing here. A delicious concentration of fruit
explodes on the tastebuds, expressed as fresh-cut lemon and
zest, green apples, melons, all finishing in unison on a very
long and minerally ending. It's a very refined wine with a nice
touch of oak that will drink well for another three to four
years.
O'Briens

The vines producing **Pouilly-Fuissé** wines are grown in a number of amphitheatre-like slopes that trap the sun's rays. The resulting wines are amongst the richest in Burgundy, often achieving up to 13% alcohol.

AC Pouilly-Fuissé Dom. Saumaize-Michelin 'Clos sur la Roche' 98 £15–£16

Talented winemakers Roger and Christine Saumaize have captured their single vineyard's limestone rock in this elegant wine. It has a fresh and lively mouthfeel of lemon sherbet and limes with rich, ripe apple and tropical fruit flavours that linger on the palate, ending in a spicy ginger finish. For a Burgundy it's surprisingly ripe. It's very well made — a joy to drink now, and for another four years, with chicken cooked in white wine or John Dory.
Wines Direct

Rully was the first village appellation in the Côte Chalonnaise or the Région de Mercurey. White Rullys do not have the weight and concentration of their neighbours, but they have delicacy and elegance. They are one of the best-value white Burgundies.

AC Rully Jaffelin 96 £12–£13

This Rully has complex, spicy burnt citrus aromas. It's very concentrated with lots of fruit — apples, peaches and melons, all beautifully integrated, with lovely length. It's good on its own or would go well with grilled fish.
Cassidy

AC Rully A. et P. de Villaine 'Les Saint Jacques' 98 £14–£15

This domaine is owned by one of the co-directors of the superlative Domaine de la Romanée-Conti, Burgundy's rarest and finest. Aubert and his American wife Pamela tend their vineyard using organic methods. The 98 has lovely ripe citrus fruits with a floral character on both nose and palate and great balance between fruit and acidity. The oak is evident in the pleasing smoky finish.
Wines Direct

St Véran often represents the best value in the whites of the Mâconnais and — when very good — can rival its neighbour Pouilly Fuissé. They are soft and mature quickly, so are best drunk young.

AC St Véran Dom. Saumaize-Michelin 'Les Crèches' 98 £10– £11
This St Véran has quite an intense floral character. It's elegant, with crisp, tightly knitted flavours of back garden crab apples, lemon curd and toasted pecans and a long, warm finish. It will age well for another two years. Savour it with freshly roasted turkey or butter-basted chicken.
Wines Direct

AC St Véran Joseph Drouhin 98 £10–£11
Joseph Drouhin is a négociant established in 1880. Having purchased an old Beaune house founded in 1756, he quickly acquired the cellars of the kings of France, the dukes of Burgundy and the Collégiale of Beaune. The St Véran 98 is crisp and attractive. It has a good attack of lemon peel, followed quickly by long, lingering green apple and melon fruit with a hint of apricot on the finish. Drinking well now, it will age for another two years. Try it with blanquette of veal.
Gilbeys

France — Loire

In this section the wines are listed by
- Appellation Contrôlée
- price

> **Menetou-Salon,** made from Sauvignon Blanc, is not as well known as its neighbour Sancerre, also made from Sauvignon Blanc, so it tends to be cheaper. It also tends to be slightly more floral. The vineyards are based on the same Kimmeridgian type subsoil as Chablis, which grows Chardonnay.

AC Menetou-Salon Dom. de Chatenoy 99 £12–£13
The floral note of Menetou-Salon can be discerned in the lovely aromatic nose of nettles, grass and spring blossom in this wine. Made by the Clément family, one of the best known in Menetou, who have been making wine here since the 17th century, it is bone dry, with mouth-tingling acidity and green apple fruit. It's ready to drink now — delicious with fish in cream — and will keep for two years.
Febvre

> **Muscadet de Sèvre et Maine sur lie** is made from the Muscadet grape. It is the only wine in France to have a maximum alcohol level — 12%. 'Sur lie' ('on the lees') means that the wine has been aged on the sediment left behind after fermentation, which gives it a creamy, yeasty flavour and even perhaps a slight spritz. These wines are made to be drunk young and are traditionally partnered with seafood.

AC Muscadet de Sèvre et Maine sur lie Ch. La Noë 98 £7–£8
Here's a reasonably priced Muscadet with aromas of fresh citrus fruit and a hint of mineral. It's fresh and lively on the palate with crisp citrus flavours showing a mineral edge. The finish is good and the wine will hold for a year or so. Try it with moules marinières–or any other mussels, for that matter.
Irish Distillers

AC Muscadet de Sèvre et Maine sur lie Marquise de Goulaine Cuvée du Millénaire 99 £9–£10
A decent Muscadet, with a concentration of flavour that justifies its price, this is crisp without any tartness. The mineral flavours and fresh citrus fruits linger on the finish. Not for ageing, this classic seafood partner should be drunk by the end of 2001.
Gilbeys

Pouilly-Fumé is made from Sauvignon Blanc grapes
grown on chalky, stony and flinty soil. The flint produces characteristic smoky ('fumé'), flinty aromas,
hence the name of this appellation — Pouilly-Fumé.

AC Pouilly-Fumé Dom. du Petit Soumard 98 £11–£12
The grassy, herbaceous aromas of this delicious crisp wine lead
on to a palate packed with gooseberries with a mineral edge
to give it structure. It has a pleasant finish and should age for
two years. Try it with trout cooked in butter.
Irish Distillers

AC Pouilly-Fumé Ch. de Tracy 98 £16–£17
Descended from Scottish soldiers who fought for Charles VII
of France against the English, the d'Estutt d'Assay family has
been making wine here since the 16th century. They currently
own 24 hectares of land and their investment in modern
equipment has resulted in some excellent Pouilly-Fumé. This
98 has aromas of gooseberries and green apples with a
mineral note. The palate is fruity and full, with ripe apples,
some citrus fruit and good length. It's drinking well now and
will hold for up to two years. Good with brill or turbot with a
herb sauce.
Febvre

AC Pouilly-Fumé Pascal Jolivet 'Les Griottes' 96 £17–£18
Pascal Jolivet is one of the best young winemakers in the
Loire. He prefers natural techniques as far as possible, using
natural yeasts instead of the commercial variety to give his
wines a unique flavour. His painstaking methods are rewarded in this unusual and quirky Pouilly-Fumé. It has
minerally and honeyed lemon fruit, which settles on the palate
and stays quite flinty — smoky terroir in a glass. Drink by
Christmas 2001; perhaps with salmon trout in pastry with
herb butter sauce.
Maxxium

Sancerre wines, which include some of the finest in the
Loire, are made from Sauvignon Blanc. The wines have
a distinctly herbaceous taste and tend to be high in
acidity. They are best drunk young.

AC Sancerre Dom. Masson-Blondelet Thauvenay 99 £11–£12
This couldn't be anything but Sauvignon Blanc — the aromas
alone tell the tale. A well-made wine, it has a pungent nettle
nose, green fruit flavours and decent length. It will keep for
about two years, and is a good match for goats' cheese.
Wines Direct

AC Sancerre Dom. Michel Brock Le Coteau 98 £11–£12
New Zealand, eat your heart out! France fights back with gooseberries all the way — green gooseberry aromas and ripe, concentrated gooseberry flavours with grassy hints. The zesty acidity and long, clean finish make for a very satisfying wine that will drink well over the next two years. It is equally good without food, before a meal, or with fish, shellfish or lighter meat dishes.
Irish Distillers

AC Sancerre Fournier 98 £12–£13
The Sauvignon Blanc vines for this Fournier wine are 15–20 years old; they grow on limestone soil, which suits Sauvignon Blanc well. Fermented in stainless steel vats, the wine is matured without removing the yeast sediment ('lees'), which adds extra flavour. There is good ripe gooseberry fruit here, almost like a gooseberry fool, and it has a medium-long finish. Ready to drink now, it will last for up to two years and goes well with smoked salmon or sashimi.
TDL

AC Sancerre Jean-Max Roger Cuvée C.M. 99 £12–£13
The Roger family's domaine in the village of Bué covers 24 hectares in the AC of Sancerre. All the vineyards are 'lieu-dits', individual sites with excellent terroir of stony Jurassic lime-stone. This cuvée is from the vineyard Chêne Marchand. After fermentation and extended lees contact the wine is racked (transferred from one barrel to another) before bottling in the spring following the vintage. It is dry, with zesty acidity and citrus and greengage fruit flavours on the palate. The wine will drink well for another year. Serve it with grilled white fish or sole meunière.
Findlaters

AC Sancerre Les Celliers St Romble 98 £13–£14
The limestone soils around the beautiful hilltop town of Sancerre produce this classic appealing wine, fresh and floral with citrus and grassy aromas. The acidity marries very well with the green apple and citrus fruit flavours. With a lovely long, lingering finish, it would stand up to mildly spiced oriental dishes. Drink it over the next year or two.
Fields

AC Sancerre Dom. Jean-Paul Balland 99 £13–£14
Jean-Paul Balland produces this wine in Bué, just south of the town of Sancerre, on chalky soil — ideal terroir for Sauvignon Blanc. Sancerre isn't always nettles and gooseberries — this one has wonderful peachy, floral aromas, following through on

the palate with weighty fruit flavours and a good long finish.
Sole, simply grilled or with a light, not too rich, sauce, would
be an ideal match. Drink it over the next two years.
Taserra

AC Sancerre Dom. Vacheron 98 £14–£15

From a family-owned estate, this is an elegant, classic blend of
gooseberries and grassy flavours. It has floral and green apple
aromas with a creamy edge. The acidity is high but not
challenging — and there is a soft creaminess to the citrus and
apple fruit. It has a long, persistent finish. Drink it by the end
of 2001. It would make a classy partner for fried fish.
Febvre

AC Sancerre Fournier Vieilles Vignes 97 £14–£15

'Vieilles Vignes' means 'old vines' — the older a vine, the more
concentrated the flavour. Here the combination of forty-year-
old vines and low yields gives a pronounced aroma of green
fruit, a little oily, with a honeyed sweetness. The palate is dry,
with apples, lemons and very ripe gooseberries accompanied
by a touch of minerals, all held together by a balanced acidity.
Extra value comes in the long finish in this wine of promise. It
will be at its best in the next year and will last for two years.
Serve it with river fish with a rich herb sauce.
TDL

AC Sancerre Comte Lafond 98 £15–£16

Produced by Baron Patrick de Ladoucette, one of the best
producers of Sancerre, this is a full and rich wine with earthy
and minerally aromas. It has a deep concentration of lemony
fruit and an added weight of gooseberries suggesting terroir.
A great match for goats' cheese.
Gilbeys

AC Sancerre Pascal Jolivet 'Les Caillottes' 98 £16–£17

Pascal Jolivet, one of the stars of the Loire, brings his natural
approach to bear on this assertive and pushy Sancerre that
demands all your attention and tastebuds. Lemon zest excites
the palate and minerally fruit satisfies the mid-palate, finishing
with a sting of nettles as a memorable souvenir. With a very
long finish, it's an ideal partner for white fish with a creamy
sauce. Drink it over the next year or two.
Maxxium

AC Sancerre Fournier 'La Chaudouillonne' Grande Cuvée 97 £17–£18

The Fournier family began with a single hectare in 1950. They
now own 60 hectares in the Loire, basing their success on

adopting new techniques without abandoning tradition. This example, their top Sancerre, has a combination of citrus, honey and nutmeg aromas. The palate is dominated by the citrus influence, but there is a lovely concentration of underlying sweeter fruits. Acidity is refreshing and the wine delivers a nice lengthy finish with some spiciness. It's drinking well now and will continue to do so for two years.
TDL

> **Savennières** is one of the smallest ACs in the Anjou region of the Loire district. Made from Chenin Blanc grapes, it can take up to seven years to reach maturity. Roche-aux-Moines is a cru ('growth' — area of exceptional quality) of Savennières and is entitled to its own AC.

AC Savennières Roche-aux-Moines Ch. de Chamboureau 97 £18–£19

This 97 is from Ch. de Chamboureau, which was founded in the 15th century, and is worth visiting for its architecture as much as its wine. The wine's toffee apple and butterscotch aromas suggest a sweet wine, but it is bone dry with concentrated baked apple and honey fruit on the palate and a very long finish. It will continue to improve and mature for ten years. Try it with lobster.
Febvre

> White wines from **Touraine** are made from Sauvignon Blanc or Chenin Blanc. A good example of each is given below.

AC Touraine Pineau de la Loire 98 £6–£7

Lively and refreshing, this is a very good typical Loire Chenin Blanc. It has peppermint, lemon and grass aromas and lovely crisp lemony freshness, with gooseberries and blackcurrants on the mid-palate. This would be a good match for salads or shellfish.
River

AC Touraine Sauvignon Ch. de la Roche 99 £7–£8

Well-made Touraine from Sauvignon Blanc grapes can be hard to distinguish from Sancerre — but it's much cheaper. This one has a great lift of grassiness and green fruits on the nose with strong gooseberry flavours of good intensity and a fairly long finish. Overall, it's a very good wine and great value. Drink it over the next year, especially with seafood, fish or goats' cheese.
Bacchus

France — Rhône

In this section the wines are all from the southern Rhône. They are listed by
- Appellation Contrôlée (AC)
- price

> **Côtes du Lubéron,** from the far south of the Rhône region, was awarded AC status in 1988. These wines are light in style but offer great value.

AC Côtes du Lubéron La Vieille Ferme 98 £7–£8
There is a good mélange of flavours here — delicious ripe fruits with a haunting note of lychees. Acidity is firm, making this a very attractive offering at the price. Drink it within two years with simply cooked salmon.
Allied Drinks

> **White Côtes du Rhône** is usually made from a blend of white grapes — Clairette, Roussanne and Bourboulenc, although it may also be made from other grapes, for example Viognier.

AC Côtes du Rhône Ch. de Ruth 98 £7–£8
The ripeness of fruit in the 98 vintage shows through in the intensity of fresh water melon and mango aromas of this delicious wine. Some apricot and tropical fruit comes through on the fairly long, dry finish. This well-made wine should drink nicely over the next year.
Dillons

AC Côtes du Rhône Berrys' Own Selection 98 £8–£9
A robust wine with aromas of apricots and honeysuckle, followed by apricots and nuts on the palate, this is a well-structured wine. It has nicely balanced acidity and integrated flavours. Great on its own or with bean casserole, it should be drunk within the next two years.
Fields

AC Côtes du Rhône Ch. du Trignon 98 £11–£12
Made with 100% Viognier, a lovely aromatic grape, this is an unusual white Côtes du Rhône. Oak slightly dominates the peach and apricot fruit, but the overall effect is toasty and nutty with a creamy buttery texture. Rich and complex with lots of warm, vibrant spice, this wine will age for up to two years.
River

France — South

In this section the wines are listed by
- region
- price

Languedoc-Roussillon

The vineyards of **Languedoc-Roussillon** lie to the west
of the Rhône's marshy Camargue delta, and together
they produce more wine than Australia. The good
consistent Mediterranean climate ensures ripe fruit,
especially in the superb 98 vintage. There are many
bargains to be had in this region.

**VdP des Côtes de Thongue Chardonnay Dom. Val St Jean 99
£6–£7**
Here's a very reasonably priced, well-made and pleasing wine.
Pineapple, lemon and apple appear on the nose. Tropical fruits
and zesty lemon and pear drops dominate the palate.
Mitchells

**VdP des Côtes de Thongue Sauvignon Dom. Val St Jean 99
£6–£7**
A light, fruit-driven wine with an abundance of lemon, apples
and pear drops, this Sauvignon is bone dry. It is well-made
and very drinkable, especially at this price. Drink it on its own,
with canapés or at a barbecue.
Mitchells

VdP de l'Hérault Moulin de Gassac Guilhem 99 £6–£7
This refreshing wine has aromas of pear drops and apples,
followed by clean citrus fruit flavours. Well balanced by fresh
acidity, it has a nice long finish and would make a fine aperitif.
O'Briens

VdP d'Oc Marsanne-Viognier Dom. de la Cessane 99 £6–£7
This winemaker is producing good-value, quality wines from
grape varieties from all over Europe. Viognier and Marsanne
are classically found in the luscious wines of the Rhône Valley.
Here the blend produces a lovely, dry, light wine with deep
floral and apricot fruit aromas that follow through on the
palate with great intensity and lead to a long, flavoursome
finish.
WineOnline

AC Costières de Nîmes Mas des Bressades 99 £7–£8
Costières de Nîmes is fast making a name for itself as one of
the areas to watch in the South of France. Mas des Bressades is
no exception — it's full of summer fruits on the nose, with
more of the same on the palate and hints of peaches and
honey with a touch of vanilla.
Bubble Brothers

VdP d'Oc Chardonnay DLC Chevalière 98 £7–£8
Combining Old World terroir with New World technology,
this wine is indicative of the winemaking techniques often
used in the South of France to produce tasty and affordable
wines for everyday drinking. Matured in oak, it has lots of
tropical fruits on the nose turning to hints of pineapple on the
palate, with oaky tones and great length. Drink it within three
years of the vintage with roast chicken or pork or brill with a
light ginger sauce.
Allied Drinks

VdP d'Oc Chardonnay Michel Picard 97 £7–£8
Made from 100% Chardonnay, this wine was aged in small oak
barrels. It has inviting tropical fruit and apple aromas and
quite concentrated apple fruit flavours with nicely integrated
oak. It has good length and would go well with chicken dishes.
TDL

VdP de l'Hérault Moulin de Gassac Eraus 99 £8–£9
An inviting nose of fruit and flowers leads to powerful
flavours on the palate — orchard fruits with lovely lemon
undertones. It's a well-made, fairly complex wine nicely
balanced by zippy acidity, finishing with style. Serve it with a
salad for a light summer lunch.
O'Briens

**VdP du Val de Montferrand Bergerie de L'Hortus Classique
99 £8–£9**
Pic St Loup, the micro-climate where this wine is produced, is
as beautiful as it is exciting for wines. Here, a delicious blend of
Chardonnay, Sauvignon Blanc and Viognier makes an intriguing wine. Lovely hints of lemon and apricots follow through in
the mouth with a delicious, crisp, citrus acidity and a long,
honeyed finish.
Wines Direct

AC Coteaux du Languedoc Ch. Pech Redon La Clape 98 £9–£10

This property is situated beside the beautiful Mediterranean town of Narbonne, an area more usually known for its reds. The wine has an attractive floral nose, followed by peaches and a little marzipan on the palate. Ripe fruits finish with good length.

Bubble Brothers

VdP de l'Aude Chardonnay Dom. de Brau 98 £10–£11

Dom. de Brau is an organic estate 5 km from Carcassonne. It's obviously a friendly place — the back label on this 100% Chardonnay says 'Come and visit us'! The wine's perfumed aromas promise enjoyment and the palate delivers. The lovely concentrated medley of flavours of ripe Galia melon and mango, with melted butter and a twist of white pepper, will appeal to those who like a touch of oak with their Chardonnay. This 98 will develop into a beauty in two to three years if you can wait until then. It wouold be good with roast turkey or pork.

On The Case

VdP de l'Hérault Mas de Daumas Gassac 98 £20–£21

Long before most people had realised the potential of the south of France, Aimé Guibert was producing reds and whites that showed the region's huge promise. This wine, made from Chardonnay, Petit Manseng (more normally seen in South-West France), and Viognier has set the standard for the region. The 98, so worthy of its star status, reflects the wonderful vintage in Languedoc-Roussillon — it was the first time that better quality came together with climatic conditions to prove that the region as a whole has to be taken very seriously winewise. This is a seriously rich wine with its layers of complex flavours. The intense nose of ripe tropical fruit with citrus hints is followed by wonderful flavours of honey and apricots in the mouth that just keep on going.

O'Briens

VdP de l'Hérault Mas de Daumas Gassac 99 £20–£21

The 99 from this superb producer is another top-quality wine from the South of France. It has an attractive nose of honeyed melon with a little touch of sherbet. Fresh, lively flavours on the palate of vanilla and some tropical fruit are underpinned with a twist of lemon. This is a very well-made wine with interesting complexity that will keep for a few years to come.

O'Briens

South-West

The **South-West** region is influenced by the style and grape varieties of its northern neighbour, Bordeaux. The Atlantic helps to moderate and cool the climate.

VdP des Landes Dom. d'Espérance 99 £4–£5
A light, fresh and fruity wine with a nice lively zesty palate of pear drops, lemon and apple, this is ideal for a party. Try it with quiche with spinach and feta cheese.
Mitchells

AC Montravel Ch. Pique-Sègue 98 £6–£7
Made in a traditional Bordeaux style, but with Sémillon taking the lead, this wine has aromas of blackcurrant leaf, with semi-ripe peach and green apple flavours. It has a lovely oily texture, and a stylish citrus finish. The wine would go well with baked white fish.
United Beverages

VdP des Landes Dom. d'Espérance Cuvée d'Or 99 £6–£7
Another crowd pleaser, this wine has fresh and lively flavours of lemon and green apples, with gentle hints of grassiness and honeydew. Zesty and lightweight, but with good concentration, it would be great on a hot day for the barbecue or just to keep in the fridge for everyday drinking.
Mitchells

VdP des Côtes de Gascogne Dom. du Rey 99 £6–£7
A fresh and youthful wine, this has very zippy citrus acidity. Good zingy fruit flavours make it the perfect accompaniment to a light lunch.
Searsons

> **Jurançon**, in the foothills of the Pyrenees, is best known for its sweet wines, but the 'sec' style — vinified to complete dryness — is also very attractive.

AC Jurançon Sec Grain Sauvage 99 £7–£8
This Jurançon Sec is still quite young, but it is showing promise with attractive citrus peel and spice on the nose and palate. The lovely warm fruit flavours should evolve to show honeyed tones.
Searsons

AC Jurançon Sec Ch. Jolys 98 £7–£8
Heather and herbs are followed on the nose by intense grapefruit flavours with pink peppercorns. This refreshing, fruity wine has a long finish and would be good with a cheese soufflé or barbecued chicken.
Wines Direct

Germany

Germany has two categories for its quality wines—QbA (Qualitätswein bestimmter Anbaugebiete), the first entry into the two-tier quality system, and QmP (Qualitätswein mit Prädikat), the higher level. QmP has six sub-categories, each determined by the ripeness of the grapes at harvest time.

Kendermanns Dry Riesling QbA 98 £7–£8

Liebfraumilch is one of the most famous German QbA wines. This wine, however, has a completely different and drier style. A herbaceous and zany bouquet of tropical fruit invites interest. On the slightly oily palate there is greengage fruit with lemon and limes generating a crisp acidity. The level of alcohol is light, as expected from a cool climate where sugar levels are low. The citrus fruit finishes pleasantly dry and long. Partner it with simple lunches of Cheddar cheese and crusty bread.
Gilbeys

Hessische Bergstrasse, lying to the east of the river Rhine between Darmstadt and Heidelberg, is one of Germany's smallest wine regions in terms of production, with a predominance of Riesling being grown. Rainfall is high in the mild climate, but the rain runs off the well-drained soils of the steep vineyard slopes. This accounts for the more moderate acidity levels in the region's wines.

Hessische Bergstrasse Weisser Riesling Trocken QbA 98 £7–£8

This Riesling is a very refreshing and zesty wine with solid fruit flavours of zippy lemon tart, gooseberry and rhubarb. It has a nice, crisp, light finish and is a lovely summery wine. Try it with salads, grilled fish or chicken.
Classic

Hessische Bergstrasse Heppenheimer Schlossberg Kerner Kabinett Halbtrocken QmP 98 £7–£8

Kabinett on a label indicates that the grapes were harvested at normal harvest time. It's the lightest and most delicate of styles in the QmP category. This Kabinett is made from Kerner, an individualistic white grape variety. It was made by crossing a red grape, Trollinger, with a white grape, Riesling. The wine's shy aromas in this halbtrocken (medium-dry) wine do not prepare you for the gigantic flavours of pure sweet apricots and juicy blood oranges that descend on the palate. The finish is quite long.
Classic

Spätlese (late-harvested) grapes are often, but not always, medium sweet. However, following the fashion for drier styles, some Spätlese wines are fermented to full dryness, giving more body, concentration of fruit and fullness.

Hessische Bergstrasse Heppenheimer Steinkopf Riesling Spätlese 99 QmP £8–£9

This Spätlese (late-harvested) wine from the state domaine vineyards at Heppenheim impresses with a gorgeous nose and leads on to a medium-dry palate of orchard apples, peach and lemon curd. The finish is exceptionally fruity and long. The full benefit of the wine's potential won't be evident until 2003.
Classic

Hessische Bergstrasse Heppenheimer Maiburg Riesling Spätlese QmP 99 £10–£11

Riesling has a wonderful ability to maintain its fresh acidity levels, even when super-ripe with high sugar levels. In medium-sweet or dessert wines the acidity counterbalances the honeyed sweetness and refreshes the palate. This late-harvested Riesling delivers intense apple flavours that explode all over the palate. Medium sweetness persists on to a very long finish.
Classic

Weingut Schumacher Riesling Spätlese Trocken QmP 98 £13–£14

The climate is normally quite warm in the Pfalz, where this wine comes from, and the grapes are usually riper than those from more northerly neighbouring regions. 1998 was an excellent year for ripening the grapes, resulting in wines with richness and balance, especially the late-harvested Spätlesen. This is an example of the drier ('trocken') style. It's crisp, with a floral and apple character on the palate and good crisp acidity that keeps it fresh. The wine ends with a good finish.
Mitchells

Greece

Traditional styles of Greek wines have been adapted for the export market.

In this section the wines are listed by price.

'Achaia' Clauss, one of Greece's largest producers, has been making wine since 1861.

'Achaia' Clauss Belle Hélène Vin de Table £4–£5
Achaia Clauss is a good example of an appealing, modern-style Greek winemaker. This wine offers freshly crushed, fruity grapes in an aromatic, easy-drinking style, delicious and unpretentious. Its simple and honest fruit is ideal for aperitifs, poultry, fish and cheeses. It's also great for parties and very good value for money.
Taserra

'Achaia' Clauss Pelponnesiakos Topikos Oenos 99 £4–£5
Much of Greece's wine is produced in the mountainous Peloponnese region. This one is a blend of the French Chardonnay and Ugni Blanc grapes with the native Roditis. It's an interesting, easy-drinking, aromatic wine, with a mélange of fruit cocktail flavours with a floral-infused liquor. It's great value and would be ideal for a garden party.
Taserra

'Achaia' Clauss Patras 99 £6–£7
The pink-skinned Roditis grapes are grown around Patras in the Peloponnese region, producing relatively delicate and prized wines. If you're looking for a lively refreshing wine to go with a wide range of food, this is it. With its grassy and herbal flavours it's reminiscent of Sauvignon Blanc with an oily texture and a decent concentration of lemon and olive oil flavours. It's so versatile that it would be a great restaurant house wine. Try it with kebabs, baked aubergines, roasted fish or summer barbecues.
Taserra

Tsantali Chromitsa 99 £9–£10
From the Agioritikos region on Mount Athos (not to be confused with the red grape Agiorgitiko), this is rather like Australian Chardonnay. Very ripe, buttery and peppery flavours combine with butterscotch and pineapple, but not in an overblown style. It's not at all over the top and has a refreshing twist of lemon on the finish.
Oddbins

Italy

Italy produces and exports more wines than any other country. It has an enormous range of grape varieties and styles.

In this section the wines are listed by
- region
- Denominazione de Origine Controllata (e Garantita) (DOC/DOCG), Indicazione Geografica Tipica (IGT) Vino da Tavolo (VdT)
- price

Calabria

DOC Sannio Falanghina Feudo di San Gregorio 99 £8–£9
From the volcanic Campania region surrounding Naples in south-west Italy, Sannio is made from the ancient native variety Falanghina. The grapes for this wine were hand picked and fermented slowly for 28 days at cool temperatures to preserve the floral aromatics. Distinctive and different, this herby floral wine has an intriguing peppermint and apple palate. Balanced acidity shies the wine away from too-creamy foods. The peppermint lingers on the finish. Good as an aperitif or with leafy salads, it should last for three years.
Oddbins

Friuli-Venezia Giulia

DOC Friuli Chardonnay Collavini dei Sassi Cavi 99 £8–£9
Chardonnay is given DOC status in a number of zones in the north-eastern Friuli region. The style, however, varies more among the producers than between the zones. This one is a refined and elegant wine, showing Chardonnay fatness of texture in a subtle way. Full flavoured, crisp and zesty, with long length, it is a good food wine, especially with seafood.
Ecock

DOC Friuli Pinot Grigio Collavini Villa del Canlungo 99 £9–£10
A stunning north-eastern Italian white with amplified elegant flavour, this is a lovely example of a classic well-crafted Pinot Grigio. Full bodied with savoury flavours, it has a good smooth texture and long length with a clean, crisp, elegant finish with an aromatic twist. A wine with the style to handle any authentic Italian dish of seafood or poultry, it is to be savoured over the next three to four years.
Ecock

DOC Colli Orientali del Friuli Ribolla Gialla Collavini Turian 99 £12–£13

The Ribolla grape is grown mainly in the Friuli-Venezia Giulia region, producing soft wines with citrus fruit and medium body. This is a good example—an easy, well made wine with a complex combination of fruity and savoury flavours, finishing with lovely length. It's a zippy, interesting, characterful white in a fresh and elegant style, but at a price. Drink it by 2003.
Ecock

Latium

The Latium or Lazio region surrounding Rome is white wine country. This is home to **Frascati**—pale, fresh, crisp wines. The more characterful Frascatis, like the one below, have a higher proportion of the flavour-some and nutty Malvasia than the neutral Trebbiano (Ugni Blanc).

DOC Frascati Fontana Candida 98 £6–£7

Fontana Candida is considered to be one of the best producers of Frascati. This wine doesn't disappoint—it has heady, fresh floral aromas, green apple tingling acidity, citrus fruit and a slightly nutty character leading to a long, dry finish. Try it with Chinese food or a seafood salad.
Dillons

Lombardy

The two wines from Lombardy described below are both from Lugana on the Lombardy/Veneto border in the north of Italy near the southern shores of Lake Garda. Although the wines are made with a local version of the often neutral **Trebbiano**, the variety finds an elegant, attractive expression here, making one of the region's finest whites.

DOC Lugana Fabiano Argillaia 98 £6–£7

A light, fresh wine for enjoying on summer days, this has a deep vanilla bouquet with an oily lanolin undertone. Sweet honeyed fruit flavours follow on the dry palate with a touch of oak.
WineOnline

DOC Lugana Zenato San Benedetto 99 £8–£9

Zenato is one of the best producers of Lugana. This wine is fresh and dry with lovely green aromas and good complexity—and elegant weight. Tasting of biscuits and cloves, it's stylish and well integrated with refreshing acidity on the finish.
Searsons

Marches

The two unusual delicious **Verdicchios** described below are from the Marches region along the Adriatic Sea. Gaining recognition as one of Italy's most promising white wines from a native variety, the Verdicchio is sometimes blended with small amounts of Malvasia and Trebbiano — up to 20% maximum. The style ranges from light and crisp with a hint of lime to a full and richly textured wine with a golden hue. Verdicchio's high acidity, salty character and nuttiness make it a good partner with seafood. Watch out for the 'Gina Lollobrigida'-shaped bottle.

DOC Verdicchio dei Castelli di Jesi Classico Vignetti Mancini 99 £7–£8

Bright lemon/gold in colour, this appealing wine has an attractive nuttiness on the nose. There's lots of satisfaction with each mouthful, with ripe, ripe pineapple and citrus fruits with a topping of nuts. Drink it over the next couple of years.
Ecock

DOC Verdicchio dei Castelli di Jesi Classico Riserva Fazi-Battaglia San Sisto 95 £10–£11

Full and richly textured with a crisp and refreshing style this wine, is full of character. The pronounced nose of ripe pear with a hint of vanilla is full of complexity, matched on the full-bodied palate with mouthfilling stewed pear, banana and hints of oak. It would be a good match for fish, pork, ham, wild boar or any oily or fatty meats.
Select

Piedmont

Piedmont, Italy's most north-westerly region, is renowned for some of the country's most serious reds and, surprisingly, its most frivolous and frothy white — sweet, sparkling Asti Spumante. It also produces some delicious dry whites, as described in this section.

VdT Piemonte Muscaté Sec Alasia 99 £6–£7

The grape used for Asti Spumante, Muscat, is also used in this still, dry version and shows no error. Because it is non-traditional, it is declassified as simple table wine. But there is nothing simple about this wine, with its floral, perfumed nose and palate of pears and fruit gums with a touch of goose-berries. Flavours are light, floral and delicate with a clean fresh finish. It never fails to please, and it makes a lovely aperitif.
Findlaters

DOC Piemonte Cortese Giribaldi 99 £8–£9

Regarded as one of the prime grapes for dry whites in the
north-west, the Cortese produces delicately scented fresh
wines with an oily texture and a twist of acidity on the finish.
This wine offers a little more, with its greengage nose and
crisp pears and apples on the palate. A nice honest style with
good crisp fruity flavours, it should be enjoyed while still
young and fresh.
Cana

DOC Roero Arneis Alasia Sorilaria 99 £10–£11

The DOC of Roero lies south-east of Turin near Alba. The hills
have sandy calcareous soils which favour the Arneis vine,
yielding fruity styles of wines. This new estate wine was
partially barrel fermented and has a youthful fragrant nose of
apples and marzipan. It's delicious and original with a lovely,
rich, fruity nuttiness. Almond paste flavours coat the palate,
well balanced by acidity and finish beautifully. Any pasta or
risotto with rich nutty flavours will taste wonderful with this
rare wine. Drink it over the next three years.
Findlaters

> Viticulture has been noted in the hills around the town
> of **Gavi** since 972. Gavi received its DOC in 1974 and
> has enjoyed a designer label following in Italy —
> sometimes with prices to match. It must be made from
> the **Cortese** grape, whose vines excel in the beige-
> coloured calcareous clays and thrive in Piedmont's hot
> dry summers. Gavi is typically dry and neutral with an
> oily texture cut with refreshing acidity.

DOC Gavi Giribaldi 99 £11–£12

This Gavi has a hint of nutty fruit flavours — apricot kernels
and crisp apple. It's a good match for any understated foods
with a creamy or oily texture requiring Gavi's fresh acidity to
cleanse the palate.
Cana

DOC Gavi Villa Lanata 97 £12–£13

A subtle and elegant wine with typically understated notes of
minerally fruit, this Gavi's oily texture is counterbalanced by
fresh acidity. Good for food partnering or as an aperitif, it's a
versatile wine — but not cheap!
Irish Distillers

Trentino-Alto Adige

Trentino-Alto Adige (or Südtirol), a cool region in the
Alpine foothills, is strongly influenced by German
language and culture, having been ruled by the
Hapsburg dynasty until shortly after the First World
War. German and French grapes are both grown.

DOC Valdadige Pinot Grigio della Luna 99 £7–£8
France's Pinot Gris, Italianised to Pinot Grigio, is usually less
oily, smoky and intense when grown in the crisp mountain air
of the Italian hillsides. Here there are white hedgerow flowers
on the nose and nectarines on the palate. It's an attractively
fruity, medium-bodied quaffing wine, clean with good acidity.
Very easy-drinking, it has good length and would go well with
creamy pasta dishes, possibly seafood based. It should keep
for up to two years.
TDL

DOC Trentino La Vis 98 £9–£10
This Pinot Grigio has wonderful complex aromas of honey
and pear tart. Acidity and fruit are well balanced, with ripe
pears and apples leading to a rounded, long, appealing finish.
Definitely for those looking for a change from Chardonnay, it
should be enjoyed over the next couple of years.
Febvre

DOC Alto Adige/Südtirol Eisacktaler Gewürztraminer della Valle Isarco 99 £11–£12
The Valle Isarco or Eisacktaler has some of the highest vine-
yards in Italy. The soil is gravelly and the cool, moist conditions suit white varietals, which need less heat and sun to ripen
than black grapes. This very typical Gewürztraminer has an
attractive floral and exotic fruit-driven palate with fine crisp
acidity that is so often lacking in this varietal. It's ideal for
fatty, heavy, traditional food, having the acidity to cut through
it. Drink up to 2003.
Select

DOC Alto Adige Pinot Grigio Kettmeir 99 £12–£13
Kettmeir is a respected house, now
owned by Vinicola Santa Margherita,
but still run by Franco Kettmeir. It has a
full range of regional wines, including

this delicious Pinot Grigio. Complex, subtle aromas of roses and smoke lead to flavours of figs, peaches and nuts fanning over the palate. Full-bodied with loads of intense sensations, acidity, fruit character and typicity, this wine is well worth the money. It will drink well until 2003.
Select

DOC Alto Adige/Südtirol Pinot Grigio Alois Lageder 99 £12–£13

Alois Lageder founded this large family winery in 1855. Today his great-grandson and namesake has made it a leader in modern winemaking in the region. This Pinot Grigio has a fragrant perfume of freesia and lemon aromas, followed by lovely concentrated flavours of ripe, mouth-watering melon, lychee, lemon and pear drops, which linger through to a dry and assertive finish. It should be drunk before 2003.
Febvre

DOC Valdadige Pinot Grigio Santa Margherita 99 £12–£13

Pinot Grigios from this northern region of Italy tend to belong to one of two styles, either simple and fresh or more full bodied and richly textured like this one. Fragrant flower petals and musky spices on the nose are mirrored on the palate by an attractive textured mouthfeel balanced by crisp acidity with lots of peachy fruit lasting to the end of a long finish. A full and flavoursome wine, enjoy it before 2003.
Select

DOC Alto Adige/Südtirol Alois Lageder Lehenhof 97 £18–£19

Alois Lageder's Sauvignon Blanc has pungent and attractive aromas of blackcurrant leaf and tom cat on the nose. Bone dry on the palate, its assertive citrus fruit assails the tastebuds. Once the acidity subdues, minerally and semi-ripe gooseberry fruit evolves on the palate with nettles and green fruit flavours. Very long on the finish, it will be delicious until 2003.
Febvre

Tuscany

DOC Pomino Marchesi de' Frescobaldi Castello di Pomino Bianco 99 £9–£10

The illustrious Frescobaldi family has been in the wine trade since 1300. They have estates in Rufina and Pomino totalling more than 500 hectares. This generous wine shows a myriad of firm fruit flavours, good weight and length and a nicely buttery, toasty finish. A remarkably polished wine, it is well

crafted and superbly made. It will keep beautifully over the
next three years.
Allied Drinks

**DOCG Vernaccia di San Gimignano Melini Le Grillaie 98 £9–
£10**
This is Tuscany's only white DOCG wine. The vineyards
surrounding the medieval town of San Gimignano, just west
of the Chianti Classico area, produce dry, full-flavoured and
nutty wines from the Vernaccia grape. This one is a big wine in
a modern idiom, having been fermented in new oak
barriques. A delicious offering, with a profusion of fruit
flavour supported by enchanting toasty notes, it will drink
even better from 2002. Serve it as an aperitif or with seafood.
Gilbeys

Umbria

Umbria, half way down the leg of Italy, land-locked
between the knee and the calf, is gently hilly and
forested, with landscapes straight out of a medieval
religious painting. The DOC area of **Orvieto** shares the
name of the beautiful town it surrounds. Traditionally
the style was abboccato (medium sweet), but the drier
style is becoming more popular.

DOC Orvieto Falorni 99 £4–£5
The dry style of Orvieto is beautifully expressed here in a very
pale, light and pretty wine. It has a limy spritz and a lovely
range of flavours — apples spiked with nutmeg, pear drops
and honey — and finishes with a delicate almond nuttiness
typical of the style. Great value for money, it's a good party
wine.
SuperValu-Centra

DOC Orvieto Classico Secco Bigi Torricella 99 £7–£8
One of the best Orvietos currently available is this one from
Luigi Bigi's Torricella vineyards. Aromas of pear drops with a
floral touch are followed by citrus, apples and herbs on the
palate and a good finish. This delicately flavoured wine is light
and easy to drink. A great partner for salads or grilled chicken,
it should be drunk by the end of 2002.
Findlaters

Veneto

The **Soave** district lies east of the medieval city of Verona in the north-east Veneto region. Made mostly from the delicate almondy Garganega and blended with Trebbiano, Soave wines are subtle and have a wide appeal.

DOC Soave Fabiano Le Coste 99 £7–£8

This example shows the big improvement in white winemaking in the Veneto. It's a flavoursome, well-made wine, with good almond flavours, a nice weight and texture, and a lovely salted almond nuttiness on the finish. And it's deliciously crisp. Altogether a wine of character.
WineOnline

Classico on an Italian wine label indicates that the wine's source is the heartland of the original centre of a DOC quality region, making the most typical styles of wine.

DOC Soave Classico Bolla 98 £7–£8

Bolla is considered one of the top producers of Soave, with bitter almonds on the nose, a good weight of flavours and long, clean length. This wine has a savoury character. Crisp and stylish, this classic Soave would go well with seafood risotto.
Dillons

DOC Soave Classico Costeggiola Guerrieri Rizzardi 98 £9–£10

This Soave has good depth of flavour for a usually neutral-tasting wine. With its slightly oily texture and almond nutty flavours, it's subtle and undemanding. It will drink well for two years.
Irish Distillers

IGT (Indicazione Geografica Tipica) is a new quality category in Italy. Designed to encourage better-quality wines, the producer is allowed to specify the region, as in French Vins de Pays. IGT encourages experimentation with non-traditional winemaking practices and non-Italian grape varieties.

IGT del Veneto Serègo Alighieri Bianco di Garganega e Sauvignon 97 and 98 £8–£9

These two wines are made by an ancient family of winemakers descended from the poet Dante in the Veneto's north-east region. Soave's great white grape, Garganega, is

blended with France's crisp and aromatic Sauvignon Blanc to give a peppery nose, with floral notes, orchard fruits and a hint of hazelnuts on the palate. The 97 is a well-structured serious white with crisp acidity and plenty of stuffing, made to go with a wide variety of food, especially chicken dishes. The 98 is concentrated and interesting with nutty aromas and a hint of petals, ripe pears and nuts on the palate. Try it with mushroom risotto.
Grants

IGT delle Venezie Marchesi de' Frescobaldi/Robert Mondavi Danzante Pinot Grigio 99 £8–£9
A collaboration by giants Frescobaldi and Mondavi, this wine represents an Italian/Californian cross-pollination of the art and science of winemaking. It is pleasing and well made, with a nice balance of ripeness and crispness. Some green apple tartness is counterbalanced by friendly pear notes. Drink it over the next two years.
Allied Drinks

IGT delle Venezie Cesari Mitico Chardonnay 97 £15–£16
As Italian Chardonnays go, this has not broken the rules. It was matured in oak barrel and in bottle before release. The oak influence is expressed in the wine's bouquet by appealing nutty and smoky scents followed on the palate by a combination of tropical and Mediterranean fruit with vanilla oak. The oak is integrated and there is very good fruit with acidity in balance. This is a white wine big enough for main courses, even with red meat. It will drink well up to 2004.
TDL

Portugal

DOC Vinho Verde Casa do Valle 98 £4–£5
Located in Portugal's most northerly vine-growing region, where the weather is cool and damp, Vinho Verde is also its largest DOC region. Vinho Verde ('green wine') indicates that the wine is best when young and is not an indication of its colour. The vines are trained high above the ground to reduce the grapes' sugar and potential alcohol and to ensure high acidity levels. Often a little carbon dioxide is added at bottling to give it a little sparkle. This one is a concentrated, balanced wine with more abundant excellent fruit than is normal for a Vinho Verde. It has plenty of character and good intense fruit on the finish. Take it on a picnic or try it with a summer salad.
WineOnline

Spain

In this section the wines are listed by
- Denominación de Origen (DO) — the Spanish equivalent of the French Appellation Contrôlée
- price

DO Costers del Segre Raïmat Chardonnay 98 £8–£9
Raïmat vineyards date back to 1627, but Chardonnay is a much more recent arrival. Temperature-controlled fermentation in stainless steel tanks makes this Raïmat a thoroughly modern wine. Aromas of white pepper dusted over melon lead on to more melons, peaches and white pepper on the palate. It's a full-bodied oak style and is still a little immature. Fresh, crisp acidity lifts the wine, which will be at its peak in two years. Try it with grilled or roasted vegetables in olive oil.
Grants

DO La Mancha Vega Robledo Airén-Macabeo 99 £4–£5
Wines from La Mancha, Spain's largest DO, have improved beyond measure in the last twenty years. This is a crisp, clean example, made from Airén and Macabeo, with a zingy lime fruit palate. It shows the great value that can come from this area and would be a good partner for fish or white meat.
Bacchus

DO Navarra Chivite Gran Feudo Chardonnay 98 £7–£8
One of the leading firms in Navarra, Chivite hand picks the grapes for this Chardonnay. After brief maceration on the skins, the wine is fermented in stainless steel tanks. It has honey and citrus aromas, with a smooth texture and good balance of honey and lemon flavours, supported by refreshing acidity and a long, impressive finish. This wine could go on for a couple of years.
TDL

> **Penedès**, being a forward-looking and experimental sort of place, grows lots of different white grape varieties. White grapes in this region are grown at high altitudes where temperatures are cooler. The drop in temperature during the night is essential for the retention of acidity, without which the wines would be flabby and dull.

DO Penedès Gran Caus 97 £11–£12
The blend in this wine is 37% Chardonnay, 32% Sauvignon

Blanc and 31% Xarel-lo (one of the Cava grapes). The result is
an intriguing toasty nose of a myriad of fruits. On the palate
there are lemons and some honeyed flavours. Overall, this is a
very well-made wine with a fine balanced finish that will keep
for the next two years.
Approach Trade

DO Penedès Can Ràfols dels Caus Vinya El Rocallís 98 £24–£25

Here is an elegant wine from an award-winning estate, Can
Ràfols dels Caus, which is surrounded by mountains and
woods that create a unique micro-climate. The wine has a
spicy and smoky nose, with ripe citrus and apple. Apples and
pineapples appear on the palate, with spice and butter. The
restrained use of oak gives an elegant structure to the wine,
which has a rich and silky texture. This is one that will mature
for a couple of years, and would go well with roast guinea
fowl or richly sauced crab or lobster.
Approach Trade

DO Penedès Can Ràfols dels Caus Vinya La Calma 98 £24–£25

With its warm apple pie aromas and rich vanilla creaminess,
this is a big wine, but it still retains that vital streak of acidity.
Lovely complex fruit layers with a delicious crisp grapefruit

and lemon peel acidity end with a hint of spice on the finish.
The richness and crispness combine to make a full-bodied,
elegant wine with the potential to age for three years or more.
Richly sauced chicken and fish, full-fat cheese or creamy
mushroom ragoüt would suit it well.
Approach Trade

> **Rías Baixas** wines come from the cool north-west coast
> of Spain. Made from the high-quality Albariño grape,
> which has an aromatic peachy character, it is considered
> one of Spain's best white wines.

DO Rías Baixas Lagar de Cervera Albariño 98 £8–£9
This is a lovely, complex wine with refreshing citrus fruit —
aromatic and classy with an elegant palate of fresh tropical
green fruits. It has a character all of its own and will drink well
over the next year or two.
Molloys

DO Rías Baixas Martín Códax Albariño 99 £9–£10
Albariño's high quality shows to good effect here with citrus
and pineapple aromas and hints of hazelnuts on the palate.
Layered levels of fruit add nice complexity to a long finish.
This has another couple of years to go.
Approach Trade

> **Rueda's** soil and climate suit Sauvignon Blanc. It has
> been grown here only since the 1970s and, with
> Verdejo, was the foundation of the DO Rueda, one of
> Spain's most successful white wines.

DO Rueda Basa 98 £6–£7
Produced by famous Spanish winemaker Telmo Rodriguez,
this wine has striking ripe gooseberry fruit on the nose,
followed by full and fruity flavours. This is good-value,
aromatic, fruit-driven wine — fresh and clean, with a very
pleasant finish.
Approach Trade

DO Rueda Mantel Blanco Verdejo/Sauvignon Blanc 98 £6–£7
This blend of Verdejo and Sauvignon Blanc gives an aromatic
grassy and peachy nose. On the palate there is ripe red apple
fruit and a touch of peach very nicely balanced by a clean
zippy acidity. It has decent length and should go on for a year
or two.
Approach Trade

DO Rueda Herederos del Marqués de Riscal 99 £7–£8
Marqués de Riscal winemakers were determined to produce a
crisp, clean white wine and found just what they wanted in the
Verdejo grape. This 99 has instant appeal, with its lively green
flavours — green grass, gooseberry and lime cordial. It's very
crisp and refreshing.
Findlaters

DO Rueda Mantel Blanco Sauvignon Blanc 98 £7–£8
This wine is an excellent expression of ripe Sauvignon Blanc,
with pure elderflower and gooseberry fruit throughout —
classic. It finishes very well and should retain its vitality for a
year or longer.
Approach Trade

DO Rueda Con Class Sauvignon Blanc 99 £7–£8
Long, hot summers ripen Sauvignon Blanc grapes to perfection in the Rueda area. Sunshine is captured in the elderflower
aromas of this example, followed by ripe green fruit —
gooseberries, citrus and limes — on the palate. Quite substantial, it has good fruit concentration that will last for up to two
years and would suit fish, veal, pork or roast chicken.
Searsons

DO Valdeorras Guitian Godello 96 £15–£16
DO Valdeorras is an up-and-coming wine region in north-west
Spain. Its indigenous variety, Godello, which makes crisp wine
with apple flavours, has the potential to make world-class
wines. Barrel fermented, this example has ripe apples with
some smoke on the nose and a full-flavoured palate of melons
and gooseberries helped by some sharp citrus fruits. Well
rounded, it has a long finish overlaid with creamy wood
elements.
Approach Trade

DO Valdepeñas Viña Luz 99 £4–£5
Airén, Spain's most widely planted grape, was the main
Spanish brandy grape. Now, however, cool fermentation
techniques produce crisp white wines with international
appeal. This one, which is 80% Airén and 20% Chardonnay,
has a distinctive, mild aroma and a palate showing typical
green pepper and waxy elements — the deliberate oxidation
adds style. Ideal as an aperitif, it's very good value and should
keep for a year or more.
Approach Trade

Old World Red

Bulgaria

'**Reserve**' on a Bulgarian wine label indicates that the
wine has been aged in oak for a minimum period, with
the number of years usually stated on the back label.
However, the oak vats are often old wood, which helps
to mellow the wine rather than impart any vanilla
seasoning.

Bulgarian Vintners' Reserve Cabernet Sauvignon 94 £4–£5
This Cabernet Sauvignon is very Bordeaux-like in style.
Restrained blackcurrant fruit and leaf are in harmony with
sappy acidity and moderate alcohol. Fully mature, it doesn't
need food and the tannins are very gentle from cask ageing. A
classy and elegant wine, it would be a perfect match with roast
leg of lamb with garlic or rosemary.
Irish Distillers

France — Bordeaux

The wines in this section are listed by
- Appellation Contrôlée
- price

> **AC Bordeaux** is the generic appellation for white and
> red wines produced anywhere within the Bordeaux
> region. They are generally inexpensive and intended
> for early drinking, two to three years from the vintage.
> The quicker-maturing Merlot is the dominant grape in
> the blend. These wines are matured in vats rather than
> small new oak barrels.

AC Bordeaux Ch. La Croix de Cabut Chevalier Lassalle 97 £6–£7
An easy-drinking claret from the difficult 97 vintage, when
Cabernet Sauvignon ripened better than Merlot, this is
stunning value, offering great quality for the price. With
delicious ripe fruits — blackcurrants and Victoria plums — the
wine is fleshy and accessible with none of the austerity
sometimes associated with variable vintages. It has a long and
fruity finish and is good for another two years or so.
O'Briens

AC Bordeaux Ch. la Freynelle 98 £8–£9
Youthful plummy fruit aromas with a hint of herbs are
followed through on the palate with a spicy note. The tannins
are soft and the wine has good length. This is a text book AC
Bordeaux at a very reasonable price.
Cana

AC Bordeaux Marquis de Chasse 96 £8–£9
The cool summer of 1996 produced some very elegant wines
such as this one, a blend of roughly 50/50 Cabernet
Sauvignon/Merlot. It's a modern style of claret–fruity with
easy tannins and refreshing acidity, making it a great food
wine, especially with rare roast beef. It's a good all-rounder
from a reliable year and will improve for another two to four
years.
Bacchus

AC Bordeaux Sirius 96 £8–£9
Sirius is made by the Sichel family, one of the co-owners of the
famous Ch. Palmer, but this wine is more accessible in style.
The 50% Merlot/46% Cabernet Sauvignon/4% Cabernet Franc

blend was aged in French oak barrels for 14 months and
bottled in 1998. It now has a good concentrated fruity nose,
which is developing complex aromas from the oak ageing,
and a decent weight of blackcurrant fruit on the palate. It's
good value and will improve for two to four years. Lamb with
a herb sauce would be a good match.
Irish Distillers

AC Bordeaux Signatures en Bordeaux 96 £8–£9
With 80% Merlot and 20% Cabernet Sauvignon, this is a quite
typical blend for the AC. The fast-maturing Merlot gives an
easy-drinking style for this still-youthful wine. It's from a
good vintage, with tannins, alcohol and fruit all nicely balanced. Tasty for the price.
O'Briens

AC Bordeaux Michel Lynch 97 £8–£9
Made by award-winning winemaker Michel Cazes, this is
typical generic AC Bordeaux. Blackcurrant and vegetal leafy
aromas are followed by good assertive sappy fruit flavours
with refreshing acidity. Redcurrant fruit persists on the palate
to a long finish. It craves lamb — the perfect partner.
Barry & Fitzwilliam

AC Bordeaux Ch. Bonnet 97 £12–£13
Ch. Bonnet is a huge vineyard owned by the Lurton family of
winemakers in the Entre-Deux-Mers region. Their 97 claret has
blackcurrant leaves and green and black pepper on the nose.
Elegant flavours of crunchy blackcurrant and green pepper
show restraint, initially hiding their fruitiness. Already smooth
and seductive, this wine could still do with another two years'
ageing to allow it to really shine. It would be delicious with
lamb noisettes in pastry.
Febvre

> **Bordeaux Côtes de Francs** is a reliable appellation, east
> of St Émilion, noted for good-value fruity reds. Al-
> though Merlot is the main grape in the blend the style
> is more tannic, and longer lived than generic AC
> Bordeaux.

AC Bordeaux Côtes de Francs Ch. La Prade 97 £9–£10
The slightly jammy red berry fruits in this wine are enriched
with vanilla pod and smokiness. Firm tannins provide support
and balance. The wine will improve for another two years. Try
it with beef medallions with mushroom sauce.
Wines Direct

AC Bordeaux Supérieur contains at least one-half of 1% more alcohol than AC Bordeaux but this should not be taken to indicate superior quality.

AC Bordeaux Supérieur Mitchell and Son Claret 96 £8-£9
The 96 vintage was good, especially for Cabernet Sauvignon. This fairly priced example tempts with a fine aroma of youthful blackcurrant fruit with overtones of red berries. It's in a good Bordeaux style, with creamy blackcurrants and a backbone of gentle tannins, and will age well for another two years. Drink it with red meats, casseroles and cheeses.
Mitchells

☆ ☆

AC Bordeaux Supérieur Ch. Méaume 97 £8-£9
Ch. Méaume is a very reliable domaine north of Merlot country, Pomerol. Its 97 has remarkable concentration and complexity for such a basic AC. Complex aromas of ripe mulberry, tobacco leaf and pencil shavings are followed by intense flavours of black hedgerow fruits infused with cedar wood, tobacco leaf and violets. The flavours are all well integrated and harmonious and the finish is very long. A super wine, this will carry on improving for another two years. A good partner for beef or lamb.
Findlaters

AC Bordeaux Supérieur Ch. Biré 97 £8-£9
Here's a good-value, rich, fruit-driven wine — creamy and richly structured, with flavours of coffee bean and smooth cedar wood. It's a classic wine for classic food — grilled steak, roast lamb and duck — to be drunk before the end of 2001.
TDL

☆ ☆

AC Bordeaux Supérieur Ch. Cadillac Lesgourgues 97 £10-£11
Made from 70% Merlot/30% Cabernet Sauvignon and aged for a year in oak casks, this is a delicious, full-bodied red wine. Soft and velvety, with an excellent weight of ripe blackcurrant fruit, well-balanced tannins and good length, it is drinking beautifully now and will continue at this level for a year or two. For a Bordeaux of this quality it is great value and the perfect partner for red meats such as beef Wellington or roast rack of lamb.
Mitchells

Côtes de Bourg is located on the east of the Gironde estuary opposite the commune of Margaux, and is

similar in style to its neighbour Premières Côtes du
Blaye, producing fresh, fruity and early drinking red
wines. El Niño caused unusual weather conditions in 98
and was blamed for the rain at vintage time. Because of
the very hot August, the early ripening Merlot was the
most successful grape.

AC Côtes de Bourg Ch. Les Forges de Macay 98 £9–£10
This 98 is medium bodied with a mature bouquet of green
peppers and plums. The palate echoes the plum fruit character,
and adds soft tannins and a herbaceous touch. A 'must have'
for Merlot fans who can enjoy it over the next two years. Try
it with beef or lamb burgers.
Cana

AC Côtes de Bourg Ch. Macay 98 £10–£11
Ch. Macay 98 is very well made — round and juicy with good
weight, offering plenty of plum fruit, ripe tannins and a long
finish. Drinking nicely now, it will improve for another two to
three years.
Cana

The best **Côtes de Castillon** wines are similar in style to
good St Émilion — plummy and velvety.

AC Côtes de Castillon Ch. Puy-Landry 97 £7–£8
Merlot is the dominant grape in the vineyards just east of St
Émilion, where this château is located. This offering has plum
and blackcurrant fruit fanning over the tastebuds. Mellow
tannins emphasise the fruit with a sprinkle of spice on the
finish. It will cellar well for another three years.
Wines Direct

Fronsac is in a pretty, hilly area west of St Émilion,
where Cabernet Franc is the dominant grape in the
local Bordeaux blend. The wines are full but a little hard
in youth, requiring a long maturation to soften and
shine.

AC Fronsac Ch. Beauséjour 97 £9–£10
This 97 is a chunky wine with a range of flavours from warm
spicy fruit cake to dark chocolate and dried fruits. Keep it for
two to four years and serve it with pot-roasted guinea-fowl.
Grants

AC Fronsac Ch. de la Rivière 94 £12–£13
A great-value Pomerol lookalike, with terrific depth and
extract, this 94 is mostly Merlot, with Cabernet Sauvignon and
a little Cabernet Franc. It has a rich, leathery, velvety nose and

good weight in the mouth with nice use of wood. Bramble
fruit flavours, firm gripping tannins and a good long finish all
add up to an excellent wine, which will repay ageing for
another three or four years.
Irish Distillers

> **AC Haut Médoc** is a step up from generic AC Bordeaux
> in the hierarchy of ACs. It is a district AC for red wines
> only. The **Cru Bourgeois** category, which is quite
> separate from the AC system, was introduced in 1932
> to indicate wines of quality. The category was updated
> in 1978 and now includes 203 châteaux.

AC Haut-Médoc Ch. Moulin du Cartillon Cru Bourgeois 98 £11–£12

Ch. Moulin du Cartillon is in the heart of the Médoc and is
planted with 30% each of Merlot, Cabernet Sauvignon and
Cabernet Franc and 10% Petit Verdot. The 98 is austere, classic
claret, slowly releasing juicy redcurrant and blackcurrant fruit
through the firm tannins. Keep it for a year or two, as further
ageing will result in greater interest and mature complexity.
Maxxium

AC Haut-Médoc Ch. Tour du Haut-Moulin Cru Bourgeois 96 £14–£15

From a very reliable and conservative producer whose wines
are intense in style, demanding five to ten years to reach
maturity, this 96 will reward keeping for another two to four
years to allow the firm tannins to soften. Its rich fruit flavours
of plums and cassis with liquorice are wrapped in a creamy,
velvety texture.
Wines Direct

AC Haut-Médoc Ch. d'Aurilhac Cru Bourgeois 97 £16–£17

Cabernet Sauvignon, the dominant grape in this blend, fared
well in 1997 when summer rain made ripening difficult. This
Cru Bourgeois is a big, rich, ripe wine with excellent weight of
smoky blackcurrant and damson fruit, and lots of complex
flavours of tar and chocolate. A delicious wine with great
length and finish, it's still very young — give it two to three
years.
Mitchells

AC Haut-Médoc Ch. Beaumont Cru Bourgeois 95 £20–£21

This château has over 81 hectares of ageing vines capable of
yielding wonderful complex wines. The 95 benefited from a
hot, dry summer, which produced grapes with deep concentrated flavours. It's a traditional-style wine with a fruit pie
nose and hints of Christmas cake and figs. Although it's

beginning to show maturity, a little time is still needed for it to soften. At this price you are paying for the scarce vintage, which has a further life of at least four years.
Bacchus

AC Haut-Médoc Ch. Arnauld Cru Bourgeois 94 £19–£20
Although 94 promised to be an outstanding vintage, heavy rain at harvest quenched these hopes. Nonetheless, as in most difficult vintages, good winemakers still managed to make some outstanding wines such as this Cru Bourgeois. It has gentle fruity flavours that slowly evolve to subtle cassis and black pepper. It's a mature claret with soft tannins giving access to the ripe fruitiness. Try it with medallions of venison.
Febvre

AC Haut-Médoc Ch. Coufran Cru Bourgeois 95 £21–£22
Located in the northernmost part of the Haut-Médoc district, this vineyard is mainly planted with Merlot for a more supple and quickly maturing style. The 95 is an elegant and classy claret from a very good and ripe vintage. It has a lovely concentration of summer pudding fruits, very dense and intense, finishing with a grind of black pepper. It could do with another three years' ageing, but waiting for full maturity will be difficult! Partner it with navarin of lamb.
Gilbeys

> The 1855 **Grand Cru** (great growth) classification of the top red wines of the Médoc, Haut Médoc and the dessert wine Sauternes, was based on the market prices of the wines in that year. In the Médoc there are five levels of excellence ranging from the top Premier Cru (First Growth) to Cinquième Cru (Fifth Growth). Apart from the promotion of Ch. Mouton-Rothschild from Second to First Growth in 1973, the system remains unchanged.

AC Haut-Médoc Grand Cru Ch. Camensac 95 £22–£23
Established in the 16th century, this 20 hectare Fifth Growth (5ème Grand Cru Classé) vineyard is now owned by the Forner family corporation. The 95 has a wonderful bouquet of tobacco leaf, tar and cedar wood. The palate has great concentration and depth of flavour with ripe blackcurrant fruit. Very firm tannins will preserve the wine's future for three to four years. A great dinner party wine accompanying magret of duck with wine and cassis sauce.
Grants

Lalande de Pomerol, beside the commune of Pomerol and the port town of Libourne, is a red AC with a rich plummy style like Pomerol and St Émilion. The emphasis on Merlot in the blend makes for a soft and supple style with less tannin than most red Bordeaux.

AC Lalande de Pomerol Ch. Haut-Surget 97 £11–£12

This wine offers a big mouthful of fruits of the forest enriched with vanilla undertones. Softening tannins reveal the fruit, which follows through to a long and lingering finish. The wine will mature for a further two to four years.
Wines Direct

AC Lalande de Pomerol Ch. La Fleur Saint Georges 97 £15–£16

A very enjoyable 97, this offers a big mouthful of plum and blackcurrant fruit with coffee/mocha tones from oak ageing. Will be even better after 2003. Drink it with pork and prunes or côte de boeuf.
Wines Direct

AC Margaux produces wines of exceptional finesse and elegance, rarely heavy. The most famous chateau in the commune is Ch. Margaux, 1er Cru Classé (First Growth).

AC Margaux Private Margaux Réserve 97 £14–£15

The commune tends to use a higher proportion of Merlot in the blend, adding fragrance to the wines. This 97 has a herbaceous nose followed by an elegant, smooth, velvet palate. The fruit and alcohol are well balanced and the wine has a good finish. This is for the person with time and a little money — buy now and allow the elegance of Margaux to come through over the next two to three years.
O'Briens

AC Margaux Ch. La Tour de Mons Cru Bourgeois 95 £24–£25

The Clauzel family has owned this 35 hectare vineyard for three centuries. Their 95 is a wine with the 'wow' factor — it's a beautifully made Bordeaux that shows winemaking as an art rather than a science. Its inviting bouquet delivers its promise of perfumed berries, wood smoke and truffles on the palate with hints of coffee and sandalwood. It's intense without being aggressive — a pleasure, a treat, and an experience to savour

now or keep for four years. Either way, partner it with rib of beef with wine sauce.
Gilbeys

> The **Médoc** was originally named the Bas-Médoc or lower Médoc, but the Bas was dropped many years ago. The land was salt marsh until the mid-17th century, when the Dutch drained the area. The mild and moist maritime climate and the richer soil or sand produces wines less fine than from the gravel soil of the Haut Médoc. The exception is near where the two ACs meet, where pockets of gravel soil yield higher-quality wine.

AC Médoc Ch. Loudenne Cru Bourgeois 96 £13–£14

Purchased by W. & A. Gilbey in 1875, Ch. Loudenne is one of the largest properties in the Médoc. The vineyard lies on a series of gravel outcrops that slope gently down to the Gironde river. The whole crop is matured each year in oak casks and bottled at the château. The 96 has quite concentrated ripe plum and blackcurrant flavours with a blackcurrant leaf and woody finish. Very young still, it will get much better with a couple of years' further ageing and will be delicious with loin of lamb.
Gilbeys

AC Médoc Ch. Laujac Cru Bourgeois 96 £15–£16

The cool summer of 1996 helped to extend the ripening period and allowed the vines time to extract more minerals and trace elements from the soil. The resulting wines have a greater range of aromatics and flavours, as in this full-bodied red with its good weight of ripe plums and damsons and a hint of old wood. It's drinking well now, but still has time to reach maturity in another two years or so.
Mitchells

AC Médoc Ch. Rollan de By Cru Bourgeois 96 £15–£16

This is a family-owned vineyard established in 1983 by the Malcors, with 60% Cabernet Sauvignon, 39% Merlot and 1% Petit Verdot on the garonnaise gravel soil. Their 96 is a smashing wine, beautifully constructed on a deep blackcurrant base with an underlay of new French oak. It's slightly tannic now, but will develop and mellow from 2002 on. Drink it with guinea fowl cooked with mushrooms or leeks.
Wines Direct

> **Pessac-Léognan** covers the northern part of the Graves district and many of the finest vineyards, including Ch. Haut-Brion (one of Bordeaux's top five Premiers Crus

Classés, and the only non-Médoc wine included). The
AC was created as recently as 1987.

AC Pessac-Léognan Ch. Haut-Nouchet 95 £20–£21

Ch. Haut-Nouchet 95 has beautifully integrated flavours of
strawberry, caramel and tobacco, finishing with fabulous
cinnamon spice. This is a treat to drink now or age for two to
three years.
Dalton

Premières Côtes de Blaye is located east of the Gironde
estuary, opposite the Haut-Médoc district. The red
wines are made from Cabernet Sauvignon, Cabernet
Franc, Merlot and Malbec. They are fresh and fruity,
best enjoyed young and often excellent value.

The **97 vintage** was a difficult one in Bordeaux with
uneven flowering in May and rain during the summer,
percolating into the soil, possibly diluting the grapes'
juice. Cabernet Sauvignon did best, as it ripens latest,
allowing time for the soil to dry out and the concentration of fruit to be restored.

AC 1ères Côtes de Blaye Ch. Bertinerie 97 £7–£8

This 97 has earthy aromas of 'cough-drop sweets and hedgerow dark and red fruits. There is a creamy texture on the
palate enveloping bramble berries. Some stalky black fruits
with supporting tannins add a little edge and bite. Roast lamb
is a classic combination with this claret.
Wines Direct

St Émilion is on the right bank of the river Dordogne,
east of the sister port towns of Bordeaux and Libourne.
Merlot is the dominant grape here, as it is quite tolerant
of the compact, moisture-retaining clay soils. The juicy
wines of the St Émilion district tend to mature more
quickly than Cabernet-Sauvignon-based wines of the
west bank. **St Émilion Grand Cru** is a separate AC
established in 1955. Estates are assessed for inclusion in
the classification every ten years, most recently in 1996,
when 68 châteaux qualified.

AC St Émilion Ch. de la Cour 95 £13–£14

This St Émilion 95 is dry and full bodied, with lots of complex
flavours—meaty blackcurrant fruit, spice and tar—all well
integrated, giving a super wine full of character and with good
length. While this wine is drinking well, it's still very young
and hasn't reached maturity—give it another three years or
so. It's very good with roast beef.
Mitchells

AC St Émilion Grand Cru Ch. du Paradis 96 £13–£14
The 1996 vintage had a cool summer which slowed down the
ripening season, giving the vines time to extract more subtle
aromatics and flavours from the soil's minerals and trace
elements. It was a fine year for reds. This 96 is in the classic
traditional style. There are slightly vegetal aromas, green and
sappy, with a hint of rubber. The palate shows fruity blackberries and blackcurrants. A warming sensation at the back of the
throat suggests high alcohol and the tannins are very firm and
assertive, needing a couple of years to soften and mellow. So
cellar until 2003 and then drink it with roast red meat.
Irish Distillers

AC St Émilion Grand Cru Ch. Rozier 97 £13–£14
The Saby family has been making wine at Ch. Rozier since
1796–nine generations. Their 97 has aromas of mature blackberries and plums with a touch of mint and intense flavours of
mature black fruits and soft, mellow tannins. The wonderful
multi-layered complexity peersists on the finish. The wine will
continue to improve for another four years.
Wines Direct

AC St Émilion Grand Cru Ch. de la Cour 97 £15–£16
A delicious well-balanced wine from a challenging vintage,
Ch.de la Cour 97 has a medley of ripe, soft summer fruits, all
well integrated with vanilla and chocolate flavours. It's a
superb wine in perfect condition, with great length–the
flavours linger on and on.
Mitchells

AC St Émilion Grand Cru Ch. La Commanderie 96 £18–£19
Here's a classic Bordeaux with a huge weight of ripe, spicy,
baked fruit; all its elements are in harmony. It's a big wine,
rich, ripe and robust, with excellent length and a wonderful
round finish. Drink it now or let it age for up to four years.
United Beverages

> **St Estèphe** is the largest and most northerly of the four
> great commune ACs in the Haut-Médoc district—the
> other three are Pauillac, St Julien and Margaux. It is the
> most tannic in style, often unapproachable in youth,
> and requires more ageing than the others to tame the
> tannins.

AC St Estèphe Berrys' Own Selection nv £16–£17
This non-vintage wine has been blended from different years. It's full bodied and rich, with a huge concentration of ripe summer berries well integrated with oak, which adds lots of complex flavours. A great wine with long length, this is excellent value and will age for up to four years.
Fields

AC St Estèphe Frank Phélan 96 £17–£18
Yes, there's an Irish connection. Bernard Phelan from Clonmel, who settled in France at the end of the 18th century, was one of the 'wine geese'. Frank Phélan is the second wine of Ch. Phélan-Ségur. The 96 is a dark wine with a big nose, giving hints of cedar and sandalwood with strong blackcurrant notes. Chocolate and fruit compete on the palate and the wine has a medium to long finish. This wine will definitely improve with age–if you've got the time, money and space, keep it for three or more years. If you're drinking it now, decant the wine two to three hours before serving.
Barry & Fitzwilliam

AC St Estèphe Ch. Beau-Site Cru Bourgeois 96 £19–£20
One of several vineyards owned by Borie-Manoux, this is a 22 hectare estate. The 96 is deep in colour, with rich, plummy flavours and tobacco/leather nuances showing some development. It's very smooth and full on the palate with a long finish.
Cassidys

> **St Julien** wines are elegant, with a cedar wood bouquet. The commune is located in the heart of the Haut-Médoc district on the left bank of the Gironde, home to some of Bordeaux's most serious wines. Cabernet Sauvignon is the dominant grape in most of the blends.

AC St Julien Berrys' Own Selection nv £14–£15
This Berrys' Selection is a big wine with well-structured tannins; it's mouthfilling with ripe plummy blackcurrant fruit well integrated with old wood flavours. A delicious wine, with great length and finish, it's worth ageing for a year or two to watch it develop.
Fields

☆

AC St Julien Connétable Talbot 95 £24–£25
This is Ch. Talbot's very good second wine—made from
younger vines or from wine lots considered unsuitable for the
main wine, in this case a Fourth Growth Grand Cru Classé.
This practice was developed commercially in the 1980s, when a
more rigorous selection for the first wine was made at the
blending stage of production. The 95 Connétable is a big wine
with excellent weight of ripe, complex flavours–vanilla, meat,
fruit—all well integrated. Well balanced, this wine still has
three or four years to go, yet it's drinking beautifully now.
United Beverages

France — Burgundy

Except for Beaujolais wines, which are listed by price at the end of the section, the wines in this section are listed by

- Appellation Contrôlée
- price

AC Aloxe-Corton Dom. Latour Louis Latour 96 £20–£21
Latour has a tradition of embracing modern technology — for example, its red wines have been stabilised by pasteurisation (heating to 70°C) throughout the 20th century. This gives the house a style of predictable, early-maturing wines high in alcohol with well-rounded flavours. The subdued bouquet of this wine does not prepare you for the flavours of ripe redcurrant and raspberry fruit, interwoven with an oaky influence. Hints of richly roasted coffee bean emerge on the finish under a cloak of very firm tannins. The tannins do require food to act as a foil. Overall, this is an elegant and refined wine that would suit robustly flavoured red meat dishes.
Gilbeys

AC Beaune 1er Cru Dom. Bouchard Père et Fils 97 £21–£22
Bouchard was founded in 1731 and is the largest owners of top-quality vineyards in the famous Côte d'Or region. This 1er Cru is in classic Beaune style, ripe and full flavoured, without the tightness and focus of its northern neighbours in the Côte de Nuits. The redcurrant fruit finishes in a peppery ending. It will age for another two to three years.
Findlaters

AC Bourgogne Antonin Rodet Pinot Noir de Vieilles Vignes 96 £12–£13
Established in 1875, this company has recently expanded its holdings to some very fine vineyards in the Côte Chalonnaise/Région de Mercurey and Gevrey-Chambertin in the Côte de Nuits near Dijon. Made from Pinot Noir 'vieilles vignes' (old vines), this wine shows the intensity and concen-tration of the promising 96 vintage for both red and white Burgundy. A mature bouquet of wood, smoke and coffee beans with an attractive whiff of the farmyard to add com-plexity heralds a palate of excellent concentration of cherry fruit and spices. However, the tannins are still very assertive and will need a couple of years to soften and mellow before the fruit isrevealed.
Febvre

AC Bourgogne Dom. Denis Mortet Les Charmes au Châtelain 98 £13–£14
This very dark purple/ruby-coloured wine has richly concentrated dark berry aromas and fruit, with good acidity and structure. It is well balanced and has soft, but noticeable, tannins. Drink it over the next two years.
Burgundy Direct

AC Bourgogne Hautes Côtes de Beaune Chanson Père et Fils 97 £9–£10
Here is a friendly wine with ripe, fruity aromas, mirrored and fulfilled on the palate. Delicious, ripe red berry fruits spiked with black peppercorns follow through to a long finish with hints of coffee. It is just starting to evolve into a gamy, savoury character and should develop well over the next year or two. It needs food.
O'Briens

AC Bourgogne Hautes Côtes de Nuits Dom. François Gerbet Cuvée Vieilles Vignes 96 £11–£12
Made from the fruit of old vines, this very good wine has an impressive nose of dark berry fruits. It is medium bodied with fairly soft tannins and decent length. Drink it over the next two years.
Burgundy Direct

AC Givry 1er Cru Pierre Ducret Les Grands Pretans 98 £10–£11
Bursting with summer fruits—raspberry, loganberry—this easy-drinking wine has well-balanced acidity and lots of bodygood weight. It finishes long and is great value for money. It will keep for another two years.
Wines Direct

AC Mâcon Supérieur Chanson Père et Fils 99 £7–£8
A simple and seductive wine that delights the tastebuds with refreshing juicy red fruitiness, this Mâcon is a good introduction to red Burgundy.. It is lively and stimulating, with a good long finish of cherry and redcurrant fruit. It will drink well for up to two years.
O'Briens

> **Maranges**, on the southern boundary of the Côte de Beaune district, is one of the most recently awarded ACs. The 96 vintage enjoyed excellent summer weather, which continued into the autumn harvest. The red wines are rich in ripe fruit with good potential for ageing.

AC Maranges 1er Cru Joseph Drouhin 96 £14–£15

The Joseph Drouhin house, which has been in the wine business for 120 years, has a reputation for producing wines of reliable quality and authenticity. The reds are fermented in open vats with a floating cap of grape skins pumped over the fermenting wine to extract colour, flavour, aromatics and tannin from the skins. This 1er Cru has red berry aromas that emerge on the palate after the assertive tannins subside. There are mocha coffee hints on the finish. Match this one with red game meats.
Gilbeys

AC Mercurey A. et P. de Villaine Les Montots 98 £14–£15

This Mercurey has a lovely mature nose of summer fruit with typical Pinot earthiness, followed by a decent weight of fruit. It has a good, slightly spicy, loganberry finish. It will drink well for two years.
Wines Direct

AC Mercurey 1er Cru Dom. la Marche Les Vasées 96 £20–£21

If you want to taste classic Burgundy, this is it—from its strawberry/lead pencil nose to its gamy, developed, ripe red fruits. With a very long and satisfying length, it's well worth the money.
United Beverages

> The **Beaujolais** district is planted with the Red Gamay grape on granite soil and produces fruity, easy-drinking wines, light in tannin, that mature quickly. A common fermentation method, which suits the Gamay, is **carbonic maceration**, where the grapes are fermented under a layer of carbon dioxide. This process minimises tannins and makes wine with fresh fruit flavours.

AC Beaujolais-Villages Chanson Père et Fils 99 £7–£8

Here's a lively and perky little Beaujolais with crisp red berry fruit bursting forth. In an easy-drinking style with a long, lingering red cherry fruity finish, it does not need food.
O'Briens

AC Moulin-à-Vent Gérard Charvet Dom. des Rosiers 98 £9–£10

Pleasant and flavoursome, this well-made, good-quality wine is ideal for lunch or summer supper. With its light concentration of fruit and acids, it won't weigh you down, yet its decent weight of fruit will help it to drink well for another two years.
Wines Direct

Tartaric acid crystals occasionally form in bottles of wine. They are a sign that the wine has not been heavily filtered and are completely harmless.

AC Fleurie Louis Max 97 £11–£12
From the famous village of Fleurie, this is a very flavoursome and serious mature Beaujolais cru. The tannins have a nice edge and the raspberry and strawberry fruit flavours have an added earthy dimension from the local terroir. Try it with spaghetti Bolognese before the summer of 2001.
United Beverages

AC Fleurie P. Ferraud & Fils Dom. du Clos des Garands 99 £12–£13
Although initially shy on the palate, due to its youth, this wine slowly and subtly opens up, revealing itself to be a fruity but not confected wine of substance. Delicious wild strawberries appear on the finish.
Febvre

France — Rhône

In this section, the wines are listed by
- region
- Appellation Contrôlée
- price

Rhône

Syrah is the only black grape permitted in the Northern Rhône.

AC Côte Rôtie Delas Frères Seigneur de Maugiron 94 £22–£23

Côte Rôtie means 'roasted slope', which describes this hilly, sunny part of the northern Rhône well. One of the great reds of France, this example comes from a single vineyard and is made almost entirely from Syrah. The white grape Viognier is added to give perfume. It's a mature wine with a medley of summer pudding flavours. The fruit is well integrated with a little spice. It has a very long finish, but it's a bit pricey. Drink from now until 2002.
Febvre

> **AC Crozes-Hermitage** surrounds the vineyards of the steep hill of the top-rated AC Hermitage. Crozes-Hermitage wines are in a lighter, more forward style than Hermitage.

AC Crozes-Hermitage Cave de Tain l'Hermitage 98 £7–£8

One of the best-run co-operatives in southern France, Cave de Tain l'Hermitage produces a reliable range of northern Rhône wines. This one has a lovely black pepper and blackberry nose, with black fruit flavours and a typical sprinkling of pepper on the palate. Tannins are juicy and vibrant — this is easy-drinking wine, but not light. Ideal with grilled meats, game or casseroles, it should be drunk within a year — two at most.
Tesco

AC Crozes-Hermitage Louis Max 98 £9–£10

This is an unusual wine. Aromas of black cherries, ripe plums, liquorice and espresso give way to flavours of slightly burnt apple and raisin pie. There's also a hint of walnuts and a whiff of floral perfume at the end. A tart lemony streak makes this a good wine to serve with bacon and cabbage — the acidity will cut through the fat.

United Beverages

AC Crozes-Hermitage Dom. des Remizières Cuvée Particulière 98 £10–£11

Syrah vines over sixty years old and a dependable producer result in a dense, vegetal, mineral nose, hugely pronounced, with a hot gym shoe background. Very spicy baked damson fruit and a big structure with extrovert personality lead to a long, spicy length. On the palate this gives lots of mouth-watering juicy fruit. Acidity is well balanced with firm rounded tannins, making this a very good example of the AC. It should last up to three years — try it with steak and mushrooms.
Wines Direct

AC Crozes-Hermitage Gabriel Meffre Laurus 96 £11–£12

One of the stable of Meffre wines, this well-made example shows typical Syrah characteristics with smoke and spice on the nose, soft, well-rounded tannins, rich and ripe blackberry fruit and a good long finish. On the nose there is moist tobacco leaf, leather and tar. A complex and deep wine with spicy plum pudding fruit and layers of flavour with a big savoury overtone, it's a real winter wine. The finish is long and spicy. Drink it over the next two years with chunky home-made hamburgers.
Dillons

AC Crozes-Hermitage Delas Frères Les Launes 97 £12–£13

Delas is a respected Rhône producer. This Crozes-Hermitage is intensely perfumed and complex with aromas of herbs, lavender, pepper, cherries, blackberries and sandalwood. Red and black berry fruits burst on the tastebuds, tamed with a black pepper lift; the fruit rebounds in the finish and is ampli-fied to the end. This is seriously good Crozes and will drink well for up to two years. Serve it with beef or game casserole in wine sauce.
Febvre

> **Hermitage** is one of France's most full-bodied red wines, with the best examples capable of ageing for fifty years. The vineyards are on an extremely steep hill on granite soils, where the grapes spend all day every day soaking up the sun. Hermitage needs about five years in bottle, to allow the tannins to soften.

AC Hermitage Cave de Tain l'Hermitage Les Nobles Rives 94 £15–£16

With its mature aromas of black cherries and spice with some cedar wood, this Hermitage has good fruit concentration of black cherries and damsons with some added spice and pepper. A powerful and elegant wine from a respectable

vintage, it has a long finish with warmth. It is ready to drink now, but will mature and improve for up to five years. Delicious with rib of beef.
Dunnes Stores

> **St Joseph** is the second-largest AC in the northern Rhône. Up to 10% of the white grape Marsanne may be added to Syrah at the fermentation stage to soften and add perfume to the wine.

AC St Joseph Cave de Tain l'Hermitage Les Nobles Rives 96 £9–£10
Grapes have been grown on this site, on the west bank of the Rhône facing the famous Hermitage hill, since Roman times. This 96 has aromas of ripe dark fruits with hints of spice and white pepper wafting out of the glass — a lovely Syrah bouquet. The wine has a wonderful grip of spice and pepper with an afterburst of ripe summer fruits, blackberries and damsons on the palate, with a lingering attractive finish and lots of flavour layers. Keep it for up to two years; open an hour before serving, perhaps with beef Stroganoff.
Dunnes Stores

AC St Joseph Le Grand Pompée 97 £13–£14
St Joseph wines are fruitier and often more approachable than other northern Rhône wines. This one has a nice mouthfeel, with ripe berry fruits and prevalent but not overbearing tannins. This wine will go well with food. A big, wandering wine, it's very enjoyable, though not classic, and should be drunk within a year or so.
Gilbeys

✓ U·G· **Rhône**

> **Châteauneuf-du-Pape** pioneered the AC concept, driven by Baron Le Roy de Boiseaumarié in the 1920s. Up to thirteen grape varieties are permitted in the blend (some of them white). The style is full bodied and high in alcohol, 12.5% being the minimum volume permitted.

AC Châteauneuf-du-Pape Dom. Roger Perrin 98 £11–£12
Luc Perrin was catapulted into the winemaking business when his father died in a vineyard accident in 1986. He has maintained the estate's excellent reputation, producing wines that lean towards a New World style. The papal arms embossed on the bottle mean that the wine has been estate bottled. This

well-priced Châteauneuf-du-Pape has ripe upfront fruit with hints of cedar wood and spice on the nose. On the palate there is good concentration of rich dark fruits with hints of liquorice and tarry spice and pepper. This is very well-made wine with a long, complex finish. Drink it within two years with game pie or casserole.
Dunnes Stores

AC Châteauneuf-du-Pape Dom. de Nalys 97 £15–£16
Using the carbonic maceration method of fermentation, Domaine de Nalys produces soft, round, fruity, early-drinking wine, using all permitted thirteen grapes. Raspberry aromas are followed by red fruits and some pepper on the palate. Tannins are quite firm and the finish is long and smooth — this is a rich, full-bodied wine. Strawberry jam and caramel are also in evidence. Drink it within two years with game, red meats ot strong cheeses.
TDL

AC Châteauneuf-du-Pape Chapoutier La Bernardine 97 £17–£18
Michel Chapoutier makes La Bernardine with 100% Grenache grapes. He stopped filtering his wines in 1995; unfiltered wines have extra complexity and throw more sediment. This excellent example of Châteauneuf-du-Pape has black fruit and spice, with firm tannins and a soft yet spicy finish. It's drinking well now and is guaranteed to improve for the next three years. Braille information is included on the label.
Grants

AC Châteauneuf-du-Pape Ch. Gigognan Clos du Roi 97 £17–£18
Only five of the thirteen permitted grape varieties appear in this soft, round and fruity wine, which has nicely balanced yet warming alcohol. This is definitely a cold-winter-evening-by-the-fire type of wine. Drink it within the next year.
Taserra

AC Châteauneuf-du-Pape Dom. de Monpertuis 97 £17–£18
The Monpertuis estate is a traditional producer whose wines often need up to five years to mature. Grapes are not destemmed and the wine, which is aged for 18–20 months in oak casks, is unfiltered. These solid foundations show through in the flavours of black cherries, plums and hints of leather and tar. Flavours are rich and gorgeous; drinking beautifully now, this wine will age for at least five years. Try it with game and lentils.
United Beverages

AC Châteauneuf-du-Pape Dom. Duclaux 97 £17–£18

This Châteauneuf-du-Pape is nearly three-quarters Grenache, giving that typical warm, earthy, strawberry jam bouquet. Warming cosseting flavours of baked red berry fruits enlivened with a twist of black pepper comfort the palate. The gentle tannins reveal the jamminess of this powerful wine. It's drinking well now and will improve for up to two years.
Febvre

AC Châteauneuf-du-Pape Gabriel Meffre Laurus 97 £18–£19

Only older vines are used for this wine, which was matured in 275-litre oak barrels for several months. It has a big fresh tar bouquet, with leather, farmyard and hot spice aromas. Hugely complex, with very ripe baked fruit and lots of spice enveloped by oak, this is a big, full-bodied and well-structured wine with ageing potential. It has beautiful balance and lots of body. Tannins are soft and well rounded, allowing the rich blackberry fruit to emerge. The finish is quite long and the wine will age and improve for up to five years.
Dillons

AC Châteauneuf-du-Pape Guigal 96 £19–£20

From one of the best producers in the Rhône, this wine is aged in tank and barrel for two to three years before release. The increased proportion of Syrah and Mourvèdre gives the wine added body and complexity. Liquorice, smoke and black fruit compete for attention on the nose. On the palate, spice and pepper (from the Syrah) with damsons and quite a bit of alcohol (from the Grenache) make for a weighty mouthful with good length. This should drink well over the next two years.
Syrah

AC Châteauneuf-du-Pape Paul Jaboulet Aîné Les Cèdres 97 £19–£20

The négociant house of Jaboulet owns no vineyards in the Rhône and buys its grapes from growers. It has become more difficult to source grapes from old vines, as growers tend more and more to bottle their own wines. Even so, the quality of Jaboulet wines has consistently improved in the 1990s. This is a lovely gentle wine with bags of scented fruit and ripe tannins. Satisfying and classic, it will improve for at least two years. Drink it with venison with apples and blackcurrants.
Gilbeys

AC Châteauneuf-du-Pape Ch. Fortia 97 £20–£21
Fruit of the forest aromas are backed by church incense in this
nicely concentrated wine, which will drink well for another two
to three years. The ample soft red fruit flavours have a refreshing
edge that is a nice counterfoil with food, especially meat dishes.
Taserra

AC Châteauneuf-du-Pape J. Vidal-Fleury 95 £22–£23
The oldest firm in the northern Rhône, dating from 1781,
Vidal-Fleury saw a decline in quality until it was bought by
Guigal in 1984. (Étienne Guigal, who founded the highly
successful Guigal house in 1946, was Vidal-Fleury's ex-head
vigneron.) Gentle aged aromas of blackberries with leather
overtones go on to delicious, complex flavours of black fruit,
Christmas cake and lots of spice, with great depth and concen-
tration and a fabulous finish.
Irish Distillers

**AC Châteauneuf-du-Pape Paul Avril Clos des Papes 98 £23–
£24**
The combination of an excellent vintage for Châteauneuf-du-
Pape and a first-rate winemaker has produced a great wine. A
lower proportion of Grenache and a higher proportion of
Mourvèdre and Syrah result in a very rich yet mellow wine
with great fruit. There is a hint of French oak; this wine has
style and complexity and will continue to improve and mature
for two to ten years. Delicious with Christmas goose.
Syrah

> **Côtes du Rhône** wines account for 80% of the wines
> produced in the southern Rhône and their easy-
> drinking style makes them very popular.

**AC Côtes du Rhône Chanson Père et Fils Les Arpents d'Éole
98 £6–£7**
Produced by a respected Burgundy house that has ventured
south, this reasonably priced Côtes du Rhône has raspberries
on the nose followed by plum and raspberry tart flavours.
Gentle tannins and a spicy, smooth finish make this a good
buy. It will hold for another year.
O'Briens

AC Côtes du Rhône Enclave des Papes Cuvée Spéciale 99 £6–£7
Strawberries and cream all the way, with some pepper thrown
in for good measure, mark this nice, straightforward wine.
With a good tannic structure, it would go well with lamb
stews, grilled kidneys or liver dishes or cheese.
Oddbins

AC Côtes du Rhône Ch. de Ruth 97 £7–£8

With marked mineral and vegetal aromas, this is a farmyardy wine. It has lots of vanilla matched with velvety acidity/tannin balance, spicy plum pudding fruit and medium- to full-bodied warmth. Tannins are soft and well rounded and there is quite a long finish. Drink it within the next year or so with lasagne or moussaka.

Dillons

AC Côtes du Rhone Dom. la Réméjeanne Les Arbousiers 98 £7–£8

Here's a fiery, spicy dragon of a wine – definitely one for those who prefer hearty, strapping wines. Full-bodied and fruit-driven, it should be aged for another year or two to allow the glossy berry fruit to shine.

River

AC Côtes du Rhone Gabriel Meffre La Chasse du Pape 98 £7–£8

Aged in small oak barrels for three months before bottling, this wine has soft tobacco leaf, cigar box and vanilla aromas. Mouth-drying tannins are matched with a complex vegetal palate with Morello cherry and blackcurrant fruit. Dry with medium body and big, spicy length, this would be a great match for roasts or grilled meats and should keep for one to two years.

Dillons

AC Côtes du Rhône J. Vidal-Fleury 96 £8–£9

Vidal-Fleury is a well-known Rhône firm with an excellent reputation. This is good-value fruity Côtes du Rhône with leather and black fruit aromas and concentrated blackberry fruit on the palate. Tannins are gentle and the finish is long and silky, with a savoury touch. It will keep for one to two years.

Irish Distillers

AC Côtes du Rhône Guigal 98 £9–£10

Marcel Guigal ages his wines longer than normal for a Côtes du Rhône and this extra time pays off. Smoky black fruit aromas lead on to lots of spice and black fruit flavours on the palate. Tannins are gentle and length quite decent, giving it wide appeal. Drink it in the next year or so.

Syrah

AC Côtes du Rhône Parallèle 45 98 £9–£10

From a very ripe vintage and made from 50% Syrah/50% Grenache, this is a big wine, full of fruit backed with tannin and lots of acidity, ensuring its potential to evolve. The high proportion of Syrah and the tannic finish mean that it will age for five to six years. A good food match would be rack of lamb or cheese.
Gilbeys

AC Côtes du Rhône Dom. A. Mazurd et Fils Cuvée Mazurka 91 £13–£14

Grenache and Syrah grapes are fermented using the carbonic maceration technique, which makes the wine soft, fruity and very approachable. Damson and black fruit aromas are followed by lovely spicy blackberry and damson flavours, going on to a spicy savoury finish. Drink it within the next year.
Syrah

> **Côtes du Rhône-Villages** wines must contain at least 12.5% alcohol, compared with the minimum 11% for ordinary Côtes du Rhône.

AC Côtes du Rhône-Villages Rasteau Cave de Rasteau Réserve 98 £7–£8

Pliny wrote about the wines of this area, and they're just as good today. The superb, silky flavours of ripe cherry mingle with chocolate truffle and even raspberry ice cream. It's a beautifully structured wine and great value for money. It will keep for up to two years. Serve it with white or grilled meat, roast chicken, or cheese.
Dalton

AC Côtes du Rhône-Villages Rasteau Dom. Martin 95 £8–£9

A tiny village in the Provence foothills, Rasteau is one of the sixteen villages entitled to add its name to AC Côtes du Rhône-Villages. The higher alcohol in Villages wines shows in this crowd-pleaser, which has a distinct whiff of alcohol vapour. It's an all too drinkable style, with ripe strawberry jam fruit. Not designed for ageing, it should be drunk in the next year.
River

AC Côtes du Rhône-Villages Rasteau Cave de Rasteau 97 £9–£10
Made by the local co-operative in Rasteau, this easy-drinking wine would suit café-style food, grilled meats or cheese. It has intense, concentrated flavours of sweet raspberries and blueberries and is fresh, lively and easy to drink—a solid little wine. Drink it over the next year.
Dalton

> **Côtes du Ventoux** wines are made in a soft, easy, uncomplicated style. The blend includes Grenache, Cinsault, Syrah, Mourvèdre and Carignan.

AC Côtes du Ventoux Dom. des Anges 98 £7–£8
This wine is made by Irishman Ciarán Rooney at Domaine des Anges, reckoned by US wine guru Robert Parker as one of the best estates in the region. It's great value, with its raspberry aromas, a solid palate of summer berries with baked spice tones below, gentle tannins and a very smooth silky finish. It will keep for a year or so.
O'Briens

AC Côtes du Ventoux La Vieille Ferme 98 £7–£8
The vines for this wine are grown high on the slopes of Mont Ventoux. Selected and assembled by the Perrin brothers of Ch. de Beaucastel, the wine is lightly fined and isn't cold stabilised, so with time it's normal to find some natural sediment in the bottle. It has plenty of mouthfeel, with dollops of fruit and firm acidity, making it a good food wine for grilled meats, pasta and cheese. It will drink well for up to two years.
Allied Drinks

☆

AC Côtes du Ventoux Dom. des Anges Clos de l'Archange 98 £10–£11
Grapes are selected from the oldest vines on this Irish-owned property to make an 80% Syrah/20% Grenache wine. More care is lavished on the wine by giving it ten months in oak barrels, 25% of which are new. The result is black cherry and tar on the nose with touches of rhubarb and raspberry and quite a spicy, fruity palate with firm tannins and excellent balance. Five years should see this wine at its peak.
O'Briens

Gigondas was one of the first villages in the Côtes du Rhône to be awarded its own AC — in 1971 — reflecting the excellent quality of its wines.

AC Gigondas Dom. Grand Romane 95 £9–£10

Unusually, the white grape variety Counoise is included in the standard blend of Grenache, Syrah and Mourvèdre in this muscular Gigondas. This is for real grown-ups. It has a dark, brooding style with plenty of fruit and spice and is not for the faint-hearted. With a textured palate of peppery black cherry ice cream, leather, tar and a touch of vanilla, it's ready to drink now and will hold for another year.
United Beverages

AC Gigondas Gabriel Meffre Laurus 97 £13–£14

One of the Gigondas pioneers, Gabriel Meffre built his business using surplus World War II US Army earth-moving equipment to carve out huge areas of vineyard. The wine, which comes from old vines and is aged in oak, has a Christmas cake bouquet with lots of musky vanilla and a slight pine background. Very full-bodied, it's big and beefy with baked bitter cherry and damson fruit, some spice and a good finish. Tannins are still quite firm; drink it over the next two years.
Dillons

AC Gigondas Guigal 97 £14–£15

Marcel Guigal has increased the Syrah and Mourvèdre elements in his Gigondas at the expense of Grenache to make a better, richer wine. There's certainly plenty of fruit — sweet ripe black fruits of the forest and strawberry/raspberry compote. It has a big palate with a good backbone of tannin and will mature for at least two more years.
Syrah (SY3)

AC Gigondas J. Vidal-Fleury 95 £14–£15

From a good year and a good producer, this is a super wine. It has an inviting meaty nose followed by liquid velvet — a textured palate of raspberries, almonds, vanilla and spice box notes. The finish is elegant and again velvety with almost caramel flavours. It will drink well over the next year.
Irish Distillers

Formerly a village in AC Côtes du Rhône-Villages, **Vacqueyras** was awarded its own AC in 1990.

AC Vacqueyras J. Vidal-Fleury 97 £10–£11

The quality of the AC shows through in the basketfuls of raspberries in summer sunshine here — powerful fruit flavours and a smooth, creamy vanilla finish. Made with a high propor-

tion of Grenache, this wine should be drunk within the next
year.
Irish Distillers

AC Vacqueyras Montirius 98 £12–£13
Five generations of winemakers are behind this wine. Their
commitment to their terroir includes biodynamic methods and
no use of pesticides or herbicides. The wine has quite a spicy
nose with blackberry fruit. It's very savoury on the palate,
with strong tones of spice and pepper, but it's packed with
blackberries. Very soft tannins and a long finish make for a
good winter warmer wine. It will keep for the next year.
Bubble Brothers

France — South

In this section the wines are listed by
- region
- Appellation Contrôlée/Vin de Pays
- price

Languedoc-Roussillon

Cabardès became an AC in the 1998 vintage, previously being classified as VDQS, hence the classification of the second wine below. The winemakers had worked for years to improve the quality in this region and finally the powers-that-be gave them recognition.

AC Cabardès Dom. Prieuré de Caunettes 98 £7–£8
This Cabardès, from the great 98 vintage, has a wonderfully inviting nose of spicy, ripe red fruits. The same flavours appear on the palate together with hearty tannins.
Mitchells

VDQS Cabardès Ch. Jouclary 97 £8–£9
Plums with hints of pepper appear on the nose of this wine, made the year before Cabardès gained its AC status. Concentrated, mouthfilling fruit flavours with little touches of cedar lead to a long, flavoursome finish.
Bubble Brothers

AC Cabardès Ch. de Brau Cuvee Exquise 99 £10–£11
The organic wines from Ch. de Brau are suitable for vegetarians and this one, which is aged in oak, is also suitable for vegans. It will remind you of Christmas with its aromas of mulled wine spices, Christmas cake and mince pies. The flavours on the palate are full and rich — black fruits, damsons, even a little raisiny note. Fabulous value, it will do nothing but improve over the next four years. Try it with game or red meats.
On the Case

Corbières has an incredible future if it manages to shake off the bad habits of the past and embrace the vineyard and cellar management practices increasingly used by the new pioneers.

AC Corbières Chapelle d'Auriol 98 £6–£7
There's plenty of chew in this fruity wine with its firm tannins, soft, mellow strawberry tart flavours and touch of

cherry. It will drink well for two years — try it with spicy pork ribs or mixed bean casserole.
Searsons

> The **98 vintage** was wonderful in Languedoc-Roussillon, with beautiful weather all through the harvest and a dry wind — perfect for the vines. Red wines benefited most — the best have an impressive tannic structure that is not at all harsh, and are bursting with ripe fruit.

AC Corbières Ch. La Baronne Montagne d'Alaric 98 £6–£7

Made by a family of doctors, this wine receives every care and attention. Lovely raspberry aromas with hints of spice become black fruits on the palate with a peppery kick and hints of spice on the finish.
Wines Direct

AC Corbières Ch. St Marc d'Audéric 96 £7–£8

A smooth, easy-drinking wine, this has bags of red cherries with a spicy kick at the end. It's very soft in the mouth and should probably be drunk by the summer of 2001.
Dalton

AC Corbières Ch. la Bastide 98 £8–£9

One of the pioneers of good management helping to realise the potential of Corbières, Ch. la Bastide produces honest, well-made wines. This one has attractive, rounded plum and blackberry flavours.
Febvre

> **Costières de Nîmes** is fast making a name for itself as one of the areas to watch in the South of France.

AC Costières de Nîmes Ch. Grand Bois 98 £6–£7

The great 98 vintage produced this intense wine, with its aromas of summer fruit and abundant baked black summer fruit flavours.
WineOnline

AC Costières de Nîmes Dauphin de Rozier 98 £7–£8

Raspberries with hints of spice on the nose lead to lush black summer fruit flavours in this wine from the excellent 98 vintage. It has attractive smooth tannins on the palate and a silky finish.
Bubble Brothers

AC Costières de Nîmes Ch. de l'Amarine Cuveé de Bernis 98
£8–£9

This wine should probably be kept for a little while before drinking, but it's so good you may not be able to resist it now. It's packed with ripe mulberries and blueberries with an impressive tannic structure.
River Wines

AC Coteaux du Languedoc Cuvée Antoine de Montpezad 99
£4–£5

An easy-drinking fruity red, this is well made and uncomplicated — what more can you ask for at the price? It has an attractive nose of fruits of the forest, leading to a flavoursome palate of blackberry with a touch of cassis and vanilla undertones.
Dunnes Stores

AC Coteaux du Languedoc Dom. Coste Rouge 96 £5–£6
For this wine the grapes underwent carbonic maceration, which means that the berries were fermented whole to produce a fruity, upfront style. It was matured in oak casks and has intense dark fruits on the nose with hints of spice. Flavours of rich, ripe autumnal fruits fill the mouth with a wonderful, warm, spicy follow through.
Dunnes Stores

AC Coteaux du Languedoc Ch. Ginestière 99 £6–£7
Here's an uncomplicated, well-made wine, full of fruit and sure to please. Its light cherry fruit nose with hints of spice leads to ripe berry fruit flavours.
WineOnline

AC Coteaux du Languedoc Bergerie de L'Hortus Pic Saint Loup Classique 98 £7–£8
Syrah, Mourvèdre and Grenache are the grapes making this lovely soft wine. They were grown in one of the first vineyards to capture the attention of the outside world in the 1980s and demonstrate the quality being produced in Languedoc-Roussillon. This 98 has bramble fruit aromas and intense, concentrated black fruit flavours, with a touch of spice, that just go on and on.
Wines Direct

AC Coteaux du Languedoc Dom. de Terre Mégère Classique 98 £7–£8
Another gem from the super 98 vintage, this wine has a lovely evolved nose with a dark fruit bouquet laced with spice. Ripe, upfront fruit flavours finish with delicious spicy plum with a creamy edge.
Wines Direct

AC Coteaux du Languedoc Gabiam 96 £7–£8

For a wine from this area this 96 is holding its age well. It has ample dark fruit and spicy herbal aromas and is full of damson and blackcurrant flavours with a herbal twist. The finish is great — soft with lots of flavour.
Dunnes Stores

> The vineyard area of **La Méjanelle** is a stone's throw from the city of Montpellier. It is covered with galet stones (round and pudding shaped) more often seen in Châteauneuf-du-Pape, which help to maintain the temperature in the vineyard and limit extremes of heat and cold — creating a wonderful microclimate.

AC Coteaux du Languedoc Dom. Clavel Les Garrigues Terroir de la Mejanelle 98 £7–£8

This wine's rich black fruit aromas are matched by succulent black fruit and cassis on the palate. Warm, spicy flavours, ripe black fruits, soft tannins and impressive length make it very easy to drink. This is just the thing for a cold winter's evening.
Wines Direct

AC Coteaux du Languedoc Ch. de Flaugergues La Méjanelle 96 £11–£12

A lovely, concentrated wine made in La Méjanelle and matured in oak casks this has dark, smoky fruit aromas with spice and pepper. Damsons and plums with plenty of spice and pepper appear on the palate. An impressive finish rounds it all off — the richly concentrated flavours just keep on going.
Dunnes Stores

AC Coteaux du Languedoc Dom. Clavel Copa Santa Terroir de la Méjanelle 98 £12–£13

Another top wine from La Méjanelle, this is absolutely delicious. It has an interesting, complex nose of black fruit with hints of eucalyptus and mint. This complexity carries through to the palate, where there are layers of flavour — dense black fruit, spice and even hints of violet. The tannins carry the fruit well and this leads to an endless spicy fruit finish. This wine will continue to improve for a few years yet.

Wines Direct

AC Côtes du Roussillon Dom. de Bisconte 98 £8–£9
Blended from Syrah, Grenache and Mourvèdre, harvested by
hand and aged in oak barrels, this wine has a wonderfully
complex nose. Cherry jam with hints of ginger and very
seductive cinnamon follow on the palate.
Searsons

**AC Côtes du Roussillon-Villages Dom. des Chênes Les
Grands-mères 98 £7–£8**
This vineyard is set in a breathtaking amphitheatre in the
foothills of the Pyrenees. The 98 has dense black fruits in
abundance on the nose and in the mouth. Soft tannins and
fruit that continues on and on make this an easy-drinking,
value-for-money wine.
Wines Direct

> **Faugères** is a relatively small appellation, one of the
> first to break away from the larger Coteaux du
> Languedoc region. Set in the foothills behind the coast,
> the location is absolutely stunning, with beautiful
> medieval villages nestling in the hills.

AC Faugères Ch. Grézan 98 £8–£9
This good-value wine lives up to its lovely birthplace. Baked
fruit on the nose is followed by mouthfilling flavours of cherry
Bakewell tart and orchard plums.
Bubble Brothers

> **Minervois** has breathtaking scenery, with extraordi-
> nary bridges perched over gorges. It may appear as an
> area time forgot, but behind the doors of the cellars,
> wonderful wines are being made.

AC Minervois Comté de Mérinville 97 £7–£8
From a vineyard surrounded by garrigues stuffed with wild
herbs, it's not a surprise that this wine has intense herbal tones
with mint and lavender on the nose. Delicious fruits follow on
the palate — cranberry, redcurrants and cherries in abundance.
This wonder of a wine has oodles of character with an impressive finish just to round it all off.
Bubble Brothers

**AC Minervois Dom. Borie de Maurel Esprit d'Automne 99
£7–£8**
The name 'Spirit of Autumn' is just right for this wine. It's full
of warm autumn fruits and spice with plums, cherry and

blackberry with some baked spice on the finish.
Oddbins

**AC Minervois La Livinière Ch. de Gourgazeaud Réserve 98
£8–£9**
Set in the craggy foothills, La Livinière is one of the crus of the
Minervois. This attractive red has aromas of dark fruits with
hints of white pepper and liquorice. Very rich and dark in the
glass, the flavour has lots to offer — ripe fruits, warm spice and
a big structure. Maybe not for the faint-hearted — but it will
certainly keep you warm through the winter.
Dunnes Stores

> **St Chinian** has plentiful evidence of Roman viticultural
> practices in the South of France. Gently sloping vine-
> yards leading down to the river make for a peaceful
> setting, though they have to be high enough to avoid
> the flooding!

AC St Chinian Dom. Rimbert 98 £12–£13
A very distinctive aroma of gingerbread wafts from this wine
and turns to stem ginger, black cherries and herbs in the
mouth. All the elements are perfectly combined and finish
very well.
Bubble Brothers

VIN DE PAYS

VdP des Coteaux de Murviel Dom. de Limbardie 99 £6–£7
This promising wine is a little young — try keeping it for a year
and then see how it develops. It has roasted red pepper and
spicy fruit aromas and bramble fruit flavours, with good
length. At the moment the tannins are a bit strong, but age
will soften them.
Findlaters

VdP du Gard Mas des Bressades 98 £10–£11
New World in style, this wine has rich, earthy blackcurrants on
the nose. Attractive mulberry fruit and herbal overtones
dominate in the mouth with a lovely, lingering finish.
Bubble Brothers

VdP d'Hauterive Dom. La Bastide Syrah 98 £7–£8
Made from Syrah, which is known as Shiraz in the New
World, this wine has a spicy blackberry nose. It's smooth and
gently peppery on the palate with sweet, juicy, blackcurrant
and roasted pepper flavours.
Febvre

VdP de l'Hérault Méranée Moulin de Gassac Cabernet Sauvignon 98 £6–£7
Made from Cabernet Sauvignon, the king of Bordeaux, this wine is very peppery on the nose, leading to pure black-currants with pepper on the palate. It could be kept for a year or so.
O'Briens

VdP de l'Hérault Moulin de Gassac Terrasses de Guilhem 98 £6–£7
The second wine from Mas de Daumas Gassac, this is made in conjunction with the local co-operative. Blackcurrants abound on the nose, with hints of chocolate. Beautifully concentrated black cherry flavours give a wonderful lingering finish. This wine will keep for a couple of years.
O'Briens

VdP de l'Hérault Moulin de Gassac Albaran 98 £8–£9
Another good wine from Moulin de Gassac, this one has an earthy, baked fruit nose that leads to a light, fruity, easy-drinking palate, full of sultanas, plums and hazelnuts. This wine should keep on improving for a couple of years.
O'Briens

VdP de l'Hérault Moulin de Gassac Elise 98 £8–£9
An unusual, interesting wine, this would benefit from being decanted at least two hours before drinking. Full of dark fruit aromas with chocolate and mint hints and ripe fruit flavours, it's definitely worth the wait.
O'Briens

VdP de l'Hérault Mas de Daumas Gassac 95 £20–£21
95 was the only rival to the brilliant 98 in terms of vintage quality and this is shown to perfection here. Blackcurrants with earthy hints on the nose lead to a velvet-smooth palate with lots of intense, spicy fruit flavours with notes of tobacco and a cedar finish.
O'Briens

VdP de l'Hérault Mas de Daumas Gassac 97 £20–£21
This wine has a lovely gentle spice box character. An attractive cedar and blackcurrant nose is followed by minty blackcurrant flavours and a smooth, fruity finish. It's a little pricey!
O'Briens

VdP des Monts de la Grage Dom. Gleizes 98 £6–£7
Here's a flavoursome, medium-bodied wine with a touch of

character. Blackberry fruit aromas lead to soft, stewed fruit flavours with spice and pepper. The tannins are firm and altogether the wine is very acceptable and pleasing. It will drink well for two years.
Mitchells

VdP d'Oc Mosaique Grenache/Syrah 99 £5–£6

Light fruit aromas and cherry flavours with a lick of spice mark this perfect party wine. It is wonderfully drinkable without breaking the bank.
Oddbins

VdP d'Oc Tesco Merlot Reserve nv £4–£5

A very subtle and elegant wine, with an enticing bouquet of blackberries and plums mirrored on the palate, this Merlot is quite Bordeaux-like in style. It is a very good example of the diversity of styles and value for money available in the South of France.
Tesco

VdP d'Oc DLC Chevalière Grenache 98 £6–£7

Presented in a bottle whose design dates from the 18th century, this wine has soft fruit flavours with attractive tannins. It's a versatile food wine and great value for money.
Allied Drinks

VdP d'Oc Dom. La Laurie 97 £6–£7

Here's a red wine full of sunshine to lighten up those cold evenings. It has lovely warm, dark, fruits with soft inviting tannins and a lick of spice to sign off. When the days have shortened and the fire is lit, this is the wine to open.
River Wines

VdP d'Oc Jean-Louis Denois Mourvèdre 97 £6–£7

Mourvèdre is a wonderfully flavoursome but fairly gutsy grape that can be quite difficult to manage and needs a skilled winemaker to make the most of it. This pleasing example shows delicious evolution and a remarkable complexity for the price. Its dark fruits meld with leathery, spicy flavours to give a robust wine, typical of the Mourvèdre grape.
River Wines

VdP d'Oc La Cuvée Mythique 97 £10–£11

Here is a perfect expression of the big fruity wines that the South of France is capable of producing. Full of flavour and richness, with a baked fruit nose and an attractive full body, it was aged for a year in small Allier oak barrels and will happily keep for a few years yet.

VdP d'Oc Michel Picard Cabernet Sauvignon 97 £7–£8
Made from 100% Cabernet Sauvignon, this wine is full of
cassis and black fruits. Slightly cedary blackcurrants on the
nose lead to dense black fruit flavours in the mouth. It's is a
well-made wine with ripe tannins and great length.
TDL

VdP d'Oc Michel Picard Merlot 98 £7–£8
Smooth, rich and velvety, this delicious wine is made entirely
from Merlot. Hints of vanilla come from ageing in small oak
barrels, while round and gentle tannins support the soft, dark,
ripe autumn fruits.
TDL

VdP d'Oc Michel Picard Syrah 97 £7–£8
Typical Syrah (famous for the huge dark red it produces in the
northern Rhône Valley), this wine has oodles of black fruit
aromas followed by concentrated dark fruit flavours with a
dash of pepper. The tannins are smooth and soft, making it an
all-round, easy-drinking wine.
TDL

**VdP des Côtes de Thongue Dom. Bassac Cabernet Sauvignon
98 £10–£11**
Dom. Bassac, an organic estate owned and run by three
brothers—Pierre, Henri and Louis Delhon—produced this
super wine suitable for vegetarians. Loads of blackcurrant
fruit aromas and a hint of tar drift up from the glass. The fruit
is certainly present on the palate—black fruits galore, but the
still firm tannins make this a wine to have with food, preferably roast beef and Yorkshire pudding or lasagne with a meat
sauce. It will mature and soften over the next two years.
On the Case

Provence

VdP des Maures Terroirs du Var nv £4–£5
Here's a soft easy-going wine, great for everyday drinking. It
has mint leaf, fruit compote and ripe berry fruit on the nose
and lots of ripe berry fruit flavours.

Taserra

VdP de Vaucluse Dom. des Anges Cabernet Sauvignon Cuvée Speciale 96 £9–£10
With wonderful cassis and blackcurrant aromas, this good-value wine really blossoms between pouring and drinking. It has good body and evolving flavours with juicy plum, raspberry and peppery characters in the mouth and a long, flavoursome finish.
O'Briens

South-West

AC Buzet Dom. du Pech 95 £7–£8
A very agreeable Bordeaux lookalike, this wine has none of the austerity of classic Bordeaux. Ripe redcurrant and blackberry fruits persist on the palate, accompanied by mouth-watering green peppers, and lead to a wonderful, long, lingering finish.
River Wines

AC Buzet Dom. de la Tuque 95 £8–£9
From the excellent 95 vintage, this wine has an intense bouquet, full of vanilla and cigar box aromas. Wonderful plum fruit layers appear on the palate with hints of chocolate, well matched by firm tannins. The wine should continue to develop well over the next two years.
WineOnline

AC Cahors La Tour de l'Impernal 94 £7–£8
Cahors produces very dark, inky wines due to the inclusion of the Tannat grape in the blend. This deep, velvety 94 is almost opaque. It has big cigar box aromas with vanilla hints on the nose followed by stewed blackberry fruit flavours with hints of liquorice.
WineOnline

Greece

In this section the wines are listed by price.

'Achaia' Clauss Belle Hélène Vin de Table Sec £4–£5
This honest charmer offers great value from Greece. It's a non-vintage wine made from a blend of years. However, its mature orange-tinted colour suggests that it contains some older vintages. Fresh and stimulating strawberry fruit flavours and a lingering grip of tannin lead to a long finish. A well-made and well-balanced wine, it's excellent value and would be a good everyday wine to drink with burgers or pizza.
Taserra (TS05)

> **Achaia Clauss** has been making wine since 1861 and is one of Greek's largest producers.

'Achaia' Clauss Pelponnesiakos Topikos Oenos Cabernet Sauvignon/St George 98 £4–£5
The blend of Cabernet Sauvignon with the local variety, St George/Agiorgitiko, lends an international accent to this wine. It's a juicy, fruity red with a refreshing, crunchy, fruit bite — ideal for a party and quite similar in style to a ripe Chinon or Bourgueil from the Loire. It's well balanced with firm tannins and crisp acidity — very tasty and easy drinking but good. Try it with roast lamb.
Taserra

> **Xynomavro** ('acid black') is Greece's most respected grape variety. It lives up to its name, producing deeply coloured, tannic, fresh wines that can age into relatively complex maturity

Tsantalis Dry Red 95 £5–£6
The wine merchant/producer Tsantali, based at Agios Pavlos, uses a native variety, Xynomavro, and a French variety, Cabernet Sauvignon, for this wine which has more international appeal than the traditional styles. Aged in oak for a year, then cellared for two years, the wine has softened and matured. It has a light nose of summer fruits and some vanilla essence and is dry, with a grip of tannin and a mouthfeel of dark, bitter cherries, and a spicy edge. This is a value-for-money, easy-drinking wine, but it needs food. Try it with roasted Mediterranean vegetables drizzled with olive oil and lemon juice. The wine should be drunk over the next two years.
Dunnes Stores

'Achaia' Clauss Ch. Clauss 97 £8–£9

A lovely, inviting, gluggable wine with mouth-watering juicy black fruits and easy tannins, this wine doesn't need food and would go down a treat at a party if you didn't mind paying a bit more than usual. Aged in oak and in bottle to ensure that it's a mellow fellow, it's an ideal partner for pizzas and burgers.

Taserra

Tsantali Merlot 98 £8–£9

This style of winemaking will win many friends. The wine is intense and inky with chunky fruit — ripe blackberries — and may have had some carbonic maceration (the method used in Beaujolais) to bring out the plummy fruitiness and minimise the tannins. The result is approachable and delicious. Serve it with barbecues or spicy foods.

Oddbins

Tsantali Chromitsa Metoxi 96 £9–£10

Cabernet Sauvignon is the dominant grape in this blend with the native Limnio. Aristotle referred to it as the 'Limnia'. Yet, despite its long heritage the local grape is virtually unknown outside Greece. The Cabernet does the main work in this wine. It provides immediately appealing luscious, ripe bramble and berry fruits. The flavours are still at the youthful and fruity stage. Try this with steak tartare or rare meat.

Oddbins

Gaia Estate Nemea Agiorgitiko 98 £12–£13

Founders of the Gaia estate Karatsalos and Yannis Paraskevopoulos cultivate their Agiorgitiko/St George vines according to EU regulations on biological agriculture. Their vineyard is unirrigated, which helps to stress the vines and reduce yields, thus increasing the concentration of fruit. The wine is bottled directly from cask without filtration — to maximise flavour. Judging by the very deep opaque purple colour and the assertive tannins, this wine had lots of grape-skin contact when fermenting. It's a big, Merlot-like wine, made for long ageing. It needs to be kept for another two years to allow it time to develop.

Oddbins

Hungary

The large **Lake Balaton**, from which the region in western Hungary derives its name, acts as an enormous air conditioner by moderating the severe climate in summer and winter.

Chapel Hill South Balaton Cabernet Sauvignon 98 £4–£5
Following the demise of the Soviet Union, the satellite countries are looking for new markets in the West by using international varietals. This Balaton Cabernet Sauvignon is made in a classic claret style. It has a restrained, fruity, blackcurrant nose, followed by sappy semi-ripe blackcurrant fruit flavours, masked in the short term by firm tannins. While it's a little austere, it shows breeding and an understated character. Still needing some time to mature, it's a good food wine. Drink it from 2002.
Barry & Fitzwilliam

Italy

Italian wines are divided into four classes. A small number of wines are classified DOCG (Denominazione di Origine Controllata e Garantita). DOCG rules stipulate a minimum maturation period of three years, including one year in either oak or chestnut casks. Below that is DOC (Denominazione di Origine Controllata) of which there are more than two hundred examples. Below these again are IGT (Indicazione Geografica Tipica) analogous to the French Vin de Pays, and VdT (Vino da Tavola).

In this section the wines are listed by
- region
- quality designation (DOCG/DOC, IGT, VdT)
- price

Abruzzo

The **Montepulciano** grape is one of Italy's finest-quality grapes, not to be confused with Tuscany's Vino Nobile de Montepulciano, which is made from a clone of the Sangiovese grape. Montepulciano performs at its best in the rugged mountainous Abruzzi region on the east central coast. As a grape, Montepulciano can vary in style from low acidity and gentle tannins with ripe fruit to a mid-range of darker and more concentrated fruit with a slight chocolatey edge to full-blown, intensely peppery, velvety and complex examples.

DOC Montepulciano d'Abruzzo Poderi 96 £4–£5
This Montepulciano is crisp with ripe and juicy black fruits. It is really good value for money and a great everyday wine.
WineOnline

DOC Montepulciano d'Abruzzo Colle Secco Rubino 96 £8–£9
The Montepulciano is at its most charming here, with pronounced aromas of dark cherries and an abundance of refreshing acidity and balancing tannins combined with a complexity of fruit and caramel, giving a succulent, lingering finish. A lovely wine for all-round drinking, it will improve over the next three years. Serve it with hearty meat roasts or firm, mellow cheese.
Febvre

**DOC Montepulciano d'Abruzzo Cantina Zaccagnini 98 £9–
£10**
From the Zaccagnini winery, this Montepulciano has an
appealing style. With soft and generous ripe black fruit on the
nose, it's a really hefty wine — full of tannin — but with the fruit
to match. Enjoy it up to 2005.
Searsons

Campania

DOC Piedirosso Taburno Ocone 96 £13–£14
Piedirosso is a native grape variety in Campania and is often
used in a blend with several neighbouring DOCs near Naples.
Taburno received its DOC in 1987 and is still relatively unknown. Its high vineyards enjoy cool breezes and ample
summer rainfall. The soils consist of clay mixed with volcanic
residue and limestone. This interesting example has a fruity
palate of black and red cherries, plum fruits and dark chocolate. Integrated tannins add substance but do not mask the
fruit. The wine finishes long, with the promise of added
complexity. Enjoy it up to 2003.
Dalton

DOCG Taurasi Mastroberardino Radici 96 £24–£25
Arguably the best producer of DOCG Taurasi, Carlo
Mastroberardino uses only the Aglianico grape. The vines are
grown high in the cool Irpinian hills in south-west Campania.
The wines are often unattractively tough and chewy in youth,
but are transformed by ageing. This wine shows the benefits
of ageing, with its intense dark cherry, plum and bitter
chocolate aromas. It is full bodied, with its rich fruit slightly
masked by firm tannins. It will develop into a complex,
balanced, long-lived wine that shouldn't be drunk until 2003.
Select

Friuli

**DOC Friuli Collavini Pucino Refosco dal Pedunculo 98 £9–
£10**
The Refosco vine produced tasty, long-lived wines in Roman
times and has been popular through the centuries. This one is
quite a chewy wine with rich soft fruits, and, like many Italian
reds, it craves food — it would suit a rich beef casserole or
roasted Mediterranean vegetables. It should be drunk over
the next three years.
Ecock

Piedmont

Although the **Barbera** grape is widely planted all over
Italy, it gives of its best in the DOCs of Barbera d'Alba
and Barbera d'Asti — the only two DOCs where Barbera
is unblended with any other variety. Barbera can be
made in any style — light and fruity, rich and savoury,
oaked or unoaked, sweet, dry, sparkling or even white.

DOC Barbera d'Alba Giribaldi 97 £15–£16

This wine has a really intense purple colour with bags of plum
fruit on the nose and the palate and supple tannins. It's
expensive, yes, but worth keeping a few bottles for two to
three years.
Cana

DOC Barbera d'Asti Superiore Alasia 97 £7–£8

This Barbera has plenty of ripe plums and black fruit on the
nose followed by fresh and crunchy fruit flavours with hints of
caramel and vanilla on the palate. This is a fine, full-bodied
wine with lively acidity and a delicious cherry-stone finish. A
good example of well-made Barbera, it will drink well over the
next three years. Match it with full-flavoured meat or game.
Findlaters

> Meaning 'little sweet one', because of its ability to
> achieve high degrees of ripeness on the vine, the
> **Dolcetto** grape produces easy-drinking, deeply col-
> oured purple wines with a perfume of chocolate and
> plums.

DOC Dolcetto d'Alba Madonna di Como Marchesi di Barolo 98 £10–£11

This wine has a myriad of fruits and chocolate on the nose
with spice and pepper. An excellent structure of tannin and
acidity holds the complexity of fruits together to give a wine
of potential for at least another couple of years.
Select

> The **Nebbiolo** grape is one of Italy's finest reds. It is
> named after the autumn mists that swathe the Pied-
> mont vineyards at harvest time in late October
> ('nebbia' — fog). While the wines are tough and tannic in
> youth, they soften with age and are capable of remark-
> able complexity.

DOC Langhe Alasia 96 £9–£10

A lesser-known DOC than its famous neighbours Barolo and
Barbaresco, DOC Langhe is also made solely from the tannic
Nebbiolo grape. This wine shows the need to age Nebbiolo
for at least four to five years. It has pronounced blackberry
and cherry fruit aromas and is a big wine with delicious chewy
black cherry fruit and hints of bitter chocolate. A dark wine for
a cold, dark night, it will continue to improve over the next
three years. Serve it with full-flavoured and gamy foods.
Findlaters

DOC Monferrato Michele Chiarlo Airone 97 £14–£15

Because of the long, cool growing season in the Monferrato
hills, Barbera can produce wines of remarkable quality, as
demonstrated by this wine. It is big, blocky and meaty with
chewy tannins. The quite brooding dark cherry fruit is lifted
by crisp acidity, giving freshness and bite. The wine needs a
year to soften and mellow and will improve over three years
or so.
Taserra

Puglia

Puglia is the heel of Italy's boot, producing mainly table
wines. Its rolling plains were the birthplace of the vine
in Italy. In a vast sea of indifferent Vini da Tavola there
are some exciting and encouraging glimpses of the
potential the region has for full-bodied characterful
quality wines when yields are reduced.

DOC Salice Salentino Riserva Candido 96 £7–£8

This example of a Puglia wine has assertive cherry and bitter
chocolate on the nose. There is a good interesting mix of
flavours here—lots of ripe southern fruits and warm, spicy
notes. Easy to drink with friendly tannins and a pleasant,
warming finish, it will improve further over the next couple of
years. Match this wine with earthy, warming, comforting
foods—casseroles, roast game and mixed grills.
Findlaters

DOC Salice Salentino Riserva Leone de Castris Donna Lisa 96 £23–£24

Salvatore Leone de Castris, apart from being a lawyer and a
professor of economics, is also a winemaker. Produced in his
huge ultra-modern winery on the plains of the Salento
peninsula, the wines are renowned for their consistent quality

and value for money. Big and bold describes this beautiful, warm, spicy and harmonious wine. Aromas of raisiny dried fruits, spice and chocolate lead to complex flavours of wonderful dark fruits, leather and vanilla. A velvety smooth mouthfeel is aided by firm tannins with a long, long finish. It should be kept for two to three years and decanted before serving to open up the wine's flavours. Serve it with hearty casseroles and peppery, earthy dishes.
Select

IGT Salento Barbaglio Santa Barbara 95 £8–£9
This is a shining example of better-quality Salento wine. Warm and comforting, the aromas of smoky leather and jammy spiciness are mirrored on the palate. A rustic earthiness pervades the flavour profile—it's local tradition and culture in a glass. It should be drunk by 2003.
Findlaters

IGT Salento Negroamaro 98 £9–£10
The native grape Negroamaro ('bitter black') grows well in the Salento district of Puglia. This is a big sturdy blockbuster, full of the warmth of the south, with brooding tannins and dark fruit. Cinnamon, bitter cherries, mushrooms and dark, ripe plums tantalise the nose, and there are diverse flavours of damsons, figs and raisins with herbs and a hot star anise kick on the palate. The wine just longs for spicy food—peppery tomato and garlic dishes or steak, roast beef or venison. Drink it over the next three years.
Woodford Bourne

Sicily

IGT Sicilia Il Padrino Rosso 99 £5–£6
Sicily enjoys a growing reputation for its wines. They are mostly non-DOC and use native Italian grape varieties—the blazing Mediterranean sun and the mineral-rich volcanic soils courtesy of Mount Etna ensuring ripe grapes with full flavours. This warm and friendly young wine has an inviting range of red and black berry fruits, perked up with ripe but firm tannin, and a warm finish lingers. This may be cheap, but it's even more cheerful. While lovely now, it will improve for two to three years. It's the ideal match for pizza and tomato-based pasta or tangy cheese.
Oddbins

Trentino/Alto Adige

DOC Teroldego Rotaliano Kettmeir Tridentum 98 £9–£10
This DOC is located on the west bank of DOC Trentino-Alto

Adige's river Adige. These deeply coloured wines, with their
elegant perfume and firm, full fruit, age moderately well. This
Kettmeir example has black cherries and summer fruits on the
nose and strawberries and bitter almonds on the palate. A
balanced wine with a clean, fruity finish, it will be even better
when it has matured for a couple of years. Good with roast
meats, it should be resisted until 2003.
Select

Tuscany

DOC Pomino Tenuta di Pomino Rosso 96 £14–£15
Pomino is a lofty DOC in Chianti's Rufina zone, producing
reds and whites with remarkable finesse. Coming from the
illustrious Frescobaldi family's 75 hectare estate at Tenuta di
Pomino, quality is virtually guaranteed. This red has emerging
aromas of cherries and almonds aided by vanilla. Beautifully
balanced, with intense, ripe red cherry, black fruits and smoky
plums, a massive attack of flavour sensations cascades over
the tastebuds. Assertive, dark, inky bramble fruit fans over
the palate and lingers for ages. Sandy-textured tannins spike
the fruit and add gravitas. It will drink well over the next four
years.
Allied Drinks

> Standards have improved dramatically in **Chianti**. It
> started in the vineyard with plantings of Chianti's
> native Sangioveto clone of Sangiovese, which is more
> sympathetic to the lime-rich and flaky soils than the
> widely planted Sangiovese di Romagna, better suited to
> the warmer climate of its southern home in the Po river
> valley.

DOCG Chianti Classico Riserva Tesco 96 £7–£8
The extra ageing given to Riserva wines pays off in the quality
shown in this wine. Like so many good Italian wines, it needs
to be drunk with food. It has lovely aromas of cigar box, tea
chest and red fruits with some complexity emerging. Rich and
long with lovely red cherries and spice rolled in tobacco leaf,
the wine has great elegance and finesse at a remarkably good
price. Enjoy it with full-flavoured meat and pasta dishes.
Tesco

DOCG Chianti Colli Fiorentini I Mori 97 £8–£9
The Colli Fiorentini area borders the Classico sub-region to
the north and runs along the hills flanking the river Arno,
cradling the Renaissance city of Florence. This zone produces

some easy-drinking Chiantis as well as some of the finest cask-aged Riservas. This example belongs to the former style. Dry, with well-balanced acidity, there is plenty of ripe, almost sweet, juicy fruit and a long finish. Well worth a try for a good-quality Chianti, it should be drunk over the next three years.
Cana

> **Riserva** on a label means that the wine has been aged
> in cask and/or bottle, and has a higher alcoholic
> strength.

☆ ☆

DOCG Chianti Classico Riserva San Giovanni 95 £9–£10
The additional ageing in cask given to Riserva wines has added complexity and a mellow character to this wine. The aromas are of Morello cherries, baked fruits, treacle and dark chocolate. It's dry on the palate with just the right balance of rich fruit tannin and acidity. The flavours are Morello cherries again, liquorice, cinnamon and bitter chocolate, with an elegance leading to a succulent finish. Decant before serving to open up the wine's potential. Enjoy it over the next three years.
Dunnes Stores

DOCG Chianti Conti Serristori 98 £9–£10
This wine is classic Chianti, with a tight structure, elegance, style and breeding. There is a beautifully smooth chocolatey texture on the palate, with the firm promise of added complexity. However, its restrained style requires food — try it with spaghetti carbonara, lasagne or steak and mushrooms. It will benefit from ageing until 2003.
Dillons

DOCG Chianti Fattoria il Palagio 97 £9–£10
Several Vernaccia producers near the Tuscan town of San Gimignano also make Chianti. Fattoria il Palagio's version is a typical, well-made, honest and straightforward Chianti from a very good vintage. Morello cherry aromas abound on the nose and on the palate there are cherries again with a crisp plum-stone character. Serve it with lightly smoked salamis, prosciutto, cheese, game, duck or lamb. This wine should be drunk over the next two years.
MacCormaic

DOCG Chianti Classico Melini Isassi 97 £10–£11
Melini are long-established producers with 126 hectares of vineyards in the Classico zone. The added intensity of a

Classico shows through in this lovely, ripe Chianti from the brilliant 97 vintage, hailed by some producers as the vintage of the century. Still youthful, with firm tannins and fresh acidity muting the soon-to-emerge cherry fruit, its class shines through none the less and it finishes with elegance. Resist it until 2002 and then enjoy it for at least a couple of years.
Gilbeys

DOCG Chianti Classico Castello di Volpaia 97 £11–£12
The splendid estate of Castello di Volpaia sits atop a hill 600 metres high in the heart of the Classico zone. Carlo and Giovannella Stianti Mascheroni have transformed the cellars and vineyards. Wines from the estate are now noted for their perfumed refinement. This wine is no exception, with its lovely, complex Chianti nose of tea leaves, cherries and deep cherry-like flavour balancing the apparent acidity lurking beneath a blanket of tannins. It will be a real classic when the tannins soften. Lay this wine down until after 2003.
Oddbins

DOCG Chianti Classico Riserva Vigneti La Selvanella 95 £12–£13
The 95 vintage was difficult and challenging. Autumn rain diluted the grape juice, but winemakers who waited until the weather was drier in late October made some good wines, as shown by this example. Lots of aromas waft out of the glass — black cherry stones, plums, damsons, cranberries and vanilla pod, with a touch of spice. On the palate bitter cherries pervade. It's a very typical well-made Chianti Classico, beautifully balanced and crying out for grilled or roast red meats — and just the thing with duck. It will continue to improve until 2003.
Gilbeys

> **Rufina** is the smallest of the seven Chianti DOCG zones. Its high reputation for strength, extract and structure can be partly explained by the sandy calcareous lower slopes of the Apennines. The vineyards are in an enclosure that is hot during the day and cool at night. This helps to ripen the grapes fully while extending the ripening period.

DOCG Chianti Rufina Riserva Marchesi de' Frescobaldi Nipozzano 96 £12–£13
Frescobaldi have been in the wine business since 1300. The wine's pedigree is very obvious in this understated and restrained style of Chianti. The extended ageing in cask given to Riservas also adds a dimension to the cherry fruit and gives

the wine an attractive austerity. The dry tannins demand a
food partner and the wine finishes on an earthy note. It will
gain complexity over the next couple of years.
Allied Drinks

DOCG Chianti Classico Lamole di Lamole 98 £13–£14
The year 1998 proved to be a difficult one in the vineyard. A
very hot and dry summer was followed by rain at harvest
time. Good reds were produced, which should mature more
quickly than more serious vintages. Based in Greve, Lamole di
Lamole bottles its Classico from the Salcetino estate at Lucarelli.
This Classico has a good concentration of dark cherries, spices
and blackcurrants well integrated with softening tannins. The ripe
berry fruits linger on the finish. A very good, typical Chianti
Classico, it will improve over the next three years.
Select

DOCG Chianti Classico Lamole di Lamole Barrique 96 £14–£15
The Antiche Fattorie Fiorentine group makes convincing
Chiantis. This wine was aged for nine months in oak
barriques. Happily, 96 was a relatively good vintage for reds,
despite some autumn rain. As a result, the wines should
mature more readily than wines from drier vintages. This is
certainly the case with this Chianti. Nice woody aromas show
that the wine is beginning to mature. The medium-bodied
mouthfeel is of cherries and liquorice and the tannins are well
integrated with the fruit. The wine ends with a long, dry finish
requiring a food accompaniment, perhaps roast lamb with
rosemary or a garlicky bean casserole. This is an elegant wine
to savour with friends. It should be drunk by 2004.
Select

DOCG Chianti Classico Lamole di Lamole 97 £14–£15
The much-acclaimed 97 vintage in
Tuscany yielded near-perfect fruit.
The grapes ripened early in the
summer and the dry autumn
brought a very long ripening season
to give wines of concentration and
extract. This ripe expression of the
vintage shows sweet, almost
blackcurrant, fruit with balanced
acidity at the edges of the palate. The
mellow tannins are quite soft,
perhaps lacking some structure, but
the overall result is a pleasing
mouthful of atypically ripe Chianti.
Select

DOCG Chianti Classico Riserva Tenute Marchesi Antinori 96 £14–£15
Antinori has over six hundred years behind its reputation as one of Italy's most respected modern wine houses. Innovation and clever marketing are at the heart of their success. This Chianti Classico was given 14 months' maturation in small oak barrels and 12 months in bottle. When poured, dark plums and Morello cherries define the aromas. Gorgeous, rich, mature black cherries provide layers of flavour, with a lovely, long, lingering finish. This classic style needs classic food with no fancy sauces — keep it pure. Enjoy this one over the next couple of years.
Grants

DOCG Chianti Classico Castello di Brolio 97 £21–£22
Castello di Brolio's Chianti has been barrique aged for about 18 months and laid down for further ageing in bottle. From the wonderful 97 vintage, this is a huge wine with lovely mature fruit flavours — ripe, inky, blackberry fruit with a good kick of spice. It's a rich, velvety, youthful Chianti, atypical in its fruitiness and opulence and just beginning to mature. Great with venison and smoked bacon, but at a price. It will be at its peak in 2004.
Cassidy

DOCG Chianti Classico Riserva Lamole di Lamole Vigneto di Campolungo 95 £22–£23
Lamole di Lamole makes very convincing Chiantis, especially the Riservas from their 22 hectare estate at Campolungo. The extra cask and bottle age shows in the earthy, ripe cherry and chocolate aromas on the nose. This wine is very rich with lots of concentration. Delicious layers of fruit and spice with warm overtones of coffee and dark chocolate are cut through with acidity and firm tannins. Lovely and long with a slightly bitter finish, it's one to keep and enjoy over the next five years.
Select

> The beautiful Tuscan village of **Montepulciano** (no connection with the grape variety of the same name) is located south of the medieval city of Siena. Its 'noble wine' (Vino Nobile) was one of the first to be elevated from DOC to the DOCG upper tier of quality wine classification in 1981.

DOCG Vino Nobile di Montepulciano Le Pergole 95 £10–£11
This traditionally long-lived wine shows plenty of black cherry

fruit scent with a hint of spice and vanilla. Layers of warm
dark cherry fruit are integrated into a firm tannic structure
and a typical acidic bite leads to a long fruit-cake finish of
quality. It needs two years to mellow further.
Dunnes Stores

DOCG Vino Nobile di Montepulciano Fassati Pasiteo 97 £15–£16

The Prugnolo Gentile grape, a clone of Sangiovese, is used to
make Vino Nobile di Montepulciano. It derives its name from
the plummy colour of the grapes. This Vino Nobile has a
youthful but maturing nose of dark cherries and plums. Black
fruits follow through on the palate, but are slightly masked by
firm tannins. This is a big, structured wine, potentially complex
and intriguing, that will benefit from a few years' cellaring. Try
it with venison or pasta with a spicy sauce.
Select

IGT Toscana Marchesi de' Frescobaldi Rèmole 98 £7–£8

This is a surprising wine, with a burst of flavour on the
tastebuds that the shy aromas do not prepare you for. Delicious juicy red berry fruit dances on the palate and finishes
with a satisfying earthiness — elegance and class in a glass.
Allied Drinks

IGT Toscana Torciano Baldassarre Rosso 97 £12–£13

Chianti meets Bordeaux here, with Cabernet Sauvignon and
Merlot supporting the native Sangiovese grape. The Bordeaux
treatment continues with maturation in French oak barriques
to add an extra dimension to the bouquet and flavour. It
certainly works — the wine has a lovely cigar-box character
followed by a blackcurrant and gamy animal bouquet. The
palate reveals red berry spicy fruit flavours and an appealing
violet tone. It will benefit from further ageing for a couple of
years. Roast game would match it well.
SuperValu-Centra

IGT Toscana Vistarenni Codirosso 96 £18–£19

From the Vistarenni estate of 40 hectares owned by the
Tognanna family, where Director Elizabeth Tognanna and
winemaker Gaspare Buscemi make very respectable Chiantis,
this Supertuscan Codirosso displays a lovely concentration of
chocolate and spice on the nose. There is a big mouthfeel, with
plenty of dark, warm fruits aided by a balance of acidity and
tannin. The wine ends with a long, pleasant, flavoursome finish.
Select

Supertuscan wines evolved in the 1960s, when Chianti winemakers were looking for a sense of new direction. Different methods were experimented with, including planting Bordeaux grape varieties and maturing wine in new oak barrels. The resulting wines, while of superb quality, are not typical of the region and are not classified as DOC.

VdT Falorni Rosso de' Cardinal £6–£7
This is no simple table wine. Aged in oak barriques, it is in a restrained and subtle Chianti style, but without its typical austerity. It is fragrant and fruity on the nose with scents of violets and blackcurrants. The flavours evolve on the palate with red berries and old wood on the mid-palate and a woody, dry finish. Try it with spaghetti bolognese, steak or game.
SuperValu-Centra

Veneto

Amarone wines are rich and almost port-like, with high alcohol and an attractive bitter twist on the finish, hence the name 'amaro' (bitter). Grapes for Amarone are harvested early, while their acidity levels are still high, and dried on straw mats over the winter, a process called 'appassimento'. This shrivelling concentrates the sugar in the grapes, which are then fermented to dryness, resulting in wines with great concentration, high alcohol levels and bittersweet fruit.

DOC Amarone della Valpolicella Villa Cerro 96 £12–£13
The 96 vintage was relatively good in the Veneto. While some rain fell after a fine summer, it did not prevent the grapes from ripening well. However, fully ripe grapes are not of prime importance to Amarone. This is positively cheap for such a good wine. Opening up like a book, the flavours intensify as the wine breathes in the glass. Delicious raisin and dried fruit flavours, sweet and appealing, have a contrasting herbal note to counterbalance the richness. The finish is long and satisfying.
Tesco

DOC Amarone della Valpolicella Classico Masi 96 £16–£17
This Amarone has stunning aromas of black cherry and tobacco notes on the nose, while on the palate there are sharp cherry, lemon peel, cranberry and redcurrant fruits with raisins and spice completing the bittersweet medley of flavours. It can be difficult to find a food match for Amarone because of its richness and powerful concentration, but try

strong game pie, venison, old Pecorino cheese or simply
almonds at the end of a meal. This wine will keep until 2003.
Grants

DOC Amarone della Valpolicella Classico Bolla 95 £16–£17
Although Bolla is a major producer of Valpolicella, the company is perhaps more associated with the white wines of
neighbouring Soave. The Veronese family firm, founded in
1883, own vineyards but also buy grapes from a 'club' of over
400 growers, who receive benefits from the Sergio Bolla
Foundation, aimed at improving local viticulture. Their
Amarone is in a lovely classic style. It is powerful and concentrated, with rich raisiny fruit and a herbal and citrus twist. The
alcohol, though dominant, is well matched by the strength of
flavours. Drink it over the next two years.
Dillons

DOC Amarone della Valpolicella Classico Fabiano Amarone della Valpolicella 95 £18–£19
Although Fabiano's Amarone is crammed with massive
flavours, it is restrained and stylish. Multilayered, with bittersweet fruit and citrus acidity adding balance, it is complex and
still very tight, needing further ageing. The finish is extremely
long and has miles to go. This is a very big, rich, concentrated
wine, offering huge potential. Resist it until 2003 at least — it
will be well worth waiting for.
WineOnline

DOC Amarone della Valpolicella Classico G. Rizzardi 93 £24–£25
Rizzardi has a reputation for some of Verona's most elegant
and charming wines, and this Amarone fulfils that promise.
It's just like a classic port, but without the rich sweetness and
20% alcohol. This is an intense and domineering diva of a full-
bodied Amarone. Attention is focused on the serious mouthful
of contradictory flavours — raisins and herbs, cherries and dry
wood — but the end result is well integrated and harmonious.
It should be drunk over the next three years.
Irish Distillers

DOC Piave Sacchetto Piave Pinot Nero 98 £7–£8
The broad banks of Veneto's Piave river are home to several
French grape varieties. Standards continue to improve, helped
by the research centre at Conegliano. This Piave is a pleasant,

easy-drinking Pinot Noir, with a fruity nose spiked with
oodles of pepper. There's more pepper on the palate with
sweet black cherries—it's very gutsy and has a long finish. A
versatile food wine, it would go well with goulash, venison,
white meats, goats' cheese and roasted Mediterranean
vegetables.
SuperValu-Centra

> **Valpolicella** is made from indigenous Veronese grape
> varieties, principally Corvina, with Molinara and
> Rondinella playing a supporting role.

DOC Valpolicella Classico Santá Sofiá 98 £8–£9
Santa Sofia uses the classic blend of black grapes for
Valpolicella—Corvina, Molinara and Rondinella. Here we have
a light, fruity wine with crisp, juicy cherry fruit and a good
slick of refreshing lemon zest. There is a nice balance of fruit
and acidity with moderate alcohol. Try serving it cool to bring
out the fruity flavour. Drink it within two years.
Select

> **Superiore** denotes that a wine has an extra degree of
> alcohol and a year's additional ageing. The category
> overlaps Riserva.

DOC Valpolicella Classico Superiore Zenato 97 £8–£9
Considered one of the top producers of Valpolicella, Zenato
takes grapes from the Classico area of the DOC, the steeply
terraced hillsides overlooking the city of Verona. This is a
good example of the superior quality and concentration of the
wines from the hilly Classico zone compared to those from
the more fertile river valley, which produce plain DOC
Valpolicella. Generous in fruit with a lot of softness, the wine
isn't heavy or full bodied, but nice and elegant with complex
black cherry flavours and juicy, ripe tannins. It's fun to drink,
but do so within the next two years.
Searsons

> **Ripasso** is one of three types of Valpolicella. Tradition-
> ally it was used to strengthen and preserve the lighter
> styles before the days of stainless steel and bottles. It
> involves pumping the newly fermented Valpolicella
> wine into the vats containing the alcohol-soaked grape
> skins and lees of the just-vacated rich Recioto and
> Amarone wines. This initiates a slight refermentation,
> adding both alcohol and body to the Ripasso, which
> strengthens the wine, enriching it and boosting its
> ageing ability dramatically.

DOC Valpolicella Classico Superiore Cesari Mara Vino di Ripasso 95 £9–£10

Named after Mara, the grandmother of the Cesari family, this wine spent 6–12 months in oak casks and at least six months in bottle before release. Cherries, spice and chocolate are obvious on the nose, with black cherries with delicious hints of spice and chocolate on the palate. A Black Forest gâteau of a Ripasso, it would be good with prosciutto, pizza, lamb, risotto or pasta with tomato and basil. Enjoy it over the next two years.
TDL

DOC Valpolicella Classico Superiore Brunelli Pa' Riondo 97 £11–£12

Giuseppe Brunelli has a reputation for excellent Valpolicella and for his Pa' Riondo in particular. This offering shows a medium-bodied wine with plum and cherry fruit, soft tannins and a respectable finish. This will prove to be a crowd pleaser for the Italian enthusiast. Drink it by 2003.
Cana

DOC Valpolicella Classico Superiore Montegradella Santá Sofiá 97 £11–£12

Superiore is not always an enhancement to a wine that is supposed to typify an easy-drinking, fruity, fresh style, like Valpolicella. However, in this surprisingly long-lived Valpolicella, it works, as demonstrated by cherry and violets on the nose followed by creamy chocolate and cherry flavours with a touch of spice. The excellent fruit is backed up by firm tannins and balanced acidity, giving a long, silky finish. The wine will continue to improve over the next two years. Risotto with mushrooms would be a good food match.
Select

DOC Valpolicella Superiore Villa Rizzardi Poiega 97 £9–£10

The highly respected Guerrieri-Rizzardi family makes Bardolino, Soave, Amarone and this lovely Valpolicella in their family estates. Instantly appealing aromas of ripe cherries are followed by delicious and mouth-watering ripe red cherry fruit with a more serious satisfying edge than most Valpols. Very gentle tannins are followed by a long, fruity finish.
Irish Distillers

IGT del Veronese Masi Campofiorin Ripasso 96 £9–£10

There is a lot going on here in this Ripasso—aromas of freshly cut green pepper and tobacco demand attention. Similarly

demanding is the chewy palate with fruit, spice and warm woody and peppery flavours. It's a complex wine in an assertive style made to suit the food of the region, such as boiled meats. But try silverside of beef, mixed grilled meats or rich risottos and pizzas.
Grants

IGT delle Venezie Cesari Mitico Merlot 97 £15–£16
Merlot is generally made in a soft and round style in Italy's north-eastern region, but occasionally it can produce fuller and richer wines of real class and distinction. This Merlot has been matured in oak and bottle for added complexity. There are richly scented aromas of dark berry fruit and damsons and cherry flavours with white pepper. This is a smoothie with loads of fruit and interesting flavours, many layered. It's got another two years to go, so it may yet become great rather than very good. This rich, fruity style is a wine for all seasons. Try it with beef, lamb, duck, veal, Parma ham or vegetarian moussaka.
TDL

☆ ☆

IGT Provincia di Pavia Fabiano Pinot Nero 98 £6–£7
Here is Burgundy's Pinot Noir, but with an Italian accent. This is a delicious, full-bodied and full-flavoured wine of red cherries and red berries. It has an excellent, though still tight, structure and very elegant and classy style with long, heady length. A great wine at this price, it delivers on all fronts. Enjoy it over the next two years.
WineOnline

IGT Veneto Fabiano Cabernet Sauvignon 97 £7–£8
Bordeaux's blend of black grapes is found here in profusion — Cabernet Sauvignon, Cabernet Franc and Merlot. This Italian version displays a fine balance of ripe black fruits and typical Italian crisp acidity. It's a beautifully made wine with serious class and structure and great integration of flavours that still retain their definition. A very long, gloriously mellow finish rounds it off. A lovable, great-value wine, it should be enjoyed over the next two years.
WineOnline

IGT Veneto Sacchetto Merlot 97 £8–£9
With 85% Merlot and 15% Cabernet Sauvignon, this classic Bordeaux blend has produced a wine reminiscent of generic Bordeaux. Aged in French oak barrels for at least six months,

it makes for very pleasant easy drinking with blackcurrant flavours and hints of violets and cherries. Drink it with roast duck or pheasant.
SuperValu-Centra

Verona

IGT del Veronese Masi Toar 96 £13–£14
Made in a modern style from fresh grapes, two Valpolicella grapes (Corvina and Rondinella) are used in this wine, but the traditional Molinara is replaced by Oseleta. Toar refers to the volcanic soil of the terraced vineyards. Tobacco and black cherry aromas give way to black cherries and Christmas cake spices on the palate. Try red-wine based rich risotto, duck, beef stew or strongly flavoured charred vegetable dishes with this well-structured wine.
Grants

Lebanon

Lebanon has an ancient tradition of winemaking. Vine growing is concentrated in the Bekaa Valley, at an altitude of 1000 metres, and is flanked by high mountain ranges, which provide a cooling influence at night and adequate rainfall.

Ch. Musar Gaston Hochar 93 £14–£15
Amazingly, Ch. Musar missed only one year's production during the wars of the 1980s. Winemaker Gaston Hochar was influenced by Bordeaux winemaking techniques, and the French influence continues. Ch. Musar blends 50–80% Cabernet Sauvignon, with the balance coming from Cinsault. The wines spend two to three years in Nevers oak and up to four years maturing in bottle before release. This extended ageing contributes to the wine's distinctive style. The 93 has warm, earthy, clay-pot-baked Middle Eastern fruit aromas which are mirrored on the palate — dates, figs and damsons with an earthy tone spiked with paprika and finishing with a warm and noticeably alcoholic finish. This is a winning wine with universal appeal because of its approachable fruit and flavoursome maturity. Enjoy this dry and rich port-like wine over the next two years.
Grants

Portugal

Portuguese wines are noticeably different from those of Spain. The Portuguese climate is cooler, with more moisture from the Atlantic Ocean. Its grape varieties are unique and most wines are made from a blend of grapes. Less than 20% of Portuguese wine has the highest quality classification Denominaçao de Origem Controlada .

In this section the wines are ordered by
- quality classification (DOC, IPR, VR, VdM)
- price

Bairrada derives its name from 'bairro' , which is the main soil type, though it's mixed with limestone in pockets. **Baga**, the local grape, must constitute at least 50% of the blend, but it's usually around 80%. The vines are trained low and produce fruity, long-lived wines with medium to high tannins and acidity.

DOC Bairrada Dom Teodósio Vinhas da Faia 96 £5–£6
This is a savoury, dry, gripping wine complemented with lovely sweet fruit. Winter warmth comes from plenty of alcohol and a very long, rustic, spicy finish. It's excellent value for money. Drink it over the next three years. It's made to go with grilled meats.
WineOnline

The rugged region of **Dão** is situated south of Douro (Port country) and is surrounded by mountains. The granite-based soils give an added dimension and concentration to the wines. DOC laws stipulate that at least 20% of Portugal's finest grape, **Touriga Nacional**, must be in the blend and the wine must be matured for a minimum of 18 months in old wooden casks before bottling.

DOC Dão Dom Teodósio Cardeal Reserva 94 £7–£8
This Dão shows a very evolved and attractive cherry fruit bouquet. The tannins are smooth and velvety and reveal smoky cherry and damson fruits that pervade the palate and follow through on the long finish.
WineOnline

Although the Upper **Douro** Valley is port country, up to 60% of the grapes may be used in un-fortified wine. The unfriendly climate has extremes of heat in summer and cold in winter with little rainfall. The soil is made up of granite and schist, which flakes easily once it's broken up (usually with dynamite). The steeply sloped hillsides are terraced and labour intensive to tend.

DOC Douro Duas Quintas 97 £9–£10

One of the few Spanish grapes to cross the border is Tempranillo, known locally as Tinta Roriz. It adds firmness and length to the wine. This wine has a complex and earthy nose of stewed black fruits and a rich and chewy palate with plenty of spicy black fruits and tannin. It needs a couple of years to soften and evolve further and will drink well over three years. Decant it into a carafe before serving and match it with red meat, lightly sauced dishes or hard cheese.
Searsons

The **Ribatejo** is Portugal's second-largest wine-producing area after Vinho Verde. The area spans the broad Tagus Valley upstream from Lisbon. The summers are warm and the winters mild, giving well-balanced wines with ripe fruit and moderate alcohol. Red wines are made predominantly from the **Periquita/Castelão Francês** grape, known locally as the **João de Santarém**.

DOC Ribatejo Serradayres 97 £6–£7

This wine displays attractive strawberry and jammy fruit and has a weighty mouthfeel of baked fruit and dark cherries. While quite firm now, the tannins will soften from 2002 to reveal a decent fruity finish.
WineOnline

IPR (Indicação de Proveniência Regulamentada) is the quality category just below DOC and indicates that

promotion to full DOC quality wine status may not be
far away. VQPRD often appears on the labels of such
wines.

IPR Alenquer Quinta de Abrigada 96 £8–£9

Alenquer is one of the Oeste area's six IPR regions and the
most promising. Made from Periquita, Alicante and Bouschet
grapes, this is a refreshingly different wine with big fruit
flavours of native grape varieties. Luscious baked stewed
prunes and plums fan over the palate. There is a spiciness and
an earthiness to this honest, fruit-driven wine. Enjoy it from
2002 over two years.
River Wines

> **Garrafeira**, a term unique to Portugal, means that a
> wine has been judged by a tasting panel to be of
> outstanding quality and must also have 0.5% higher
> alcohol. In addition, red wines must be aged for at least
> two years in cask and a year in bottle before sale.

IPR Cartaxo Dom Teodósio Quinta d'Almargem Garrafeira 95 £8–£9

Cartaxo is one of the Ribatejo's six IPR regions. This wine has
the distinction of being qualified as Garrafeira and has very
concentrated aromas of damsons and figs with ripe tannins and a
long stewed fruit finish. It will drink well over the next two years.
WineOnline

IPR Palmela Dom Teodósio Almargem 96 £8–£9

Palmela derives its name from the town it surrounds. Castelão
Francês/Periquita is the principal grape. This representation is
a beautifully balanced, smooth, round, fruity wine with plenty
of flavour interest. It's dry and very well made, with the
intense fruit flavour continuing to a great sweet finish. Enjoy it
from 2002 to 2004.
WineOnline

IPR Santarém Dom Teodósio Cabeça de Toiro Reserva 96 £7–£8

This is a classic Portuguese red from one of Ribatejo's six IPR
regions. Very floral aromas of violets lead to a palate with rich
black fruit and cherries enlivened by a juicy acidity. The wine
cleverly balances the weight of fruit and elegance, ending with
a lovely, soft, silky finish. Drink it over two years from 2002.
WineOnline

IPR Tomar Dom Teodósio Quinta de S. João Batista 97 £6–£7

The Periquita/João de Santarém grape, which is dominant in
the blend, produces full and gripping wines that benefit from

ageing in bottle. The palate here displays rustic and chewy
flavours. The dark black cherry fruit has a sweet/sour balancing acidity and is very dry, with a typically Portuguese, dusty
finish. Drink it over two years from 2002.
WineOnline

> **VR (Vinho Regional)** is a classification of table wine
> akin to France's Vin de Pays, where regional character
> is permitted to flex its muscles by experimentation.

VR Estremadura Quinta das Murgas Reserva 96 £6–£7
Estremadura lies along the Atlantic coast north of Lisbon and
the Ribatejo. This wine has a heady aroma full of blackberries and
blackcurrants. It's a big, bone-dry wine with plenty of tannic grip
and power but with sweet, spicy, bramble fruit and violet creams
on the palate. While it's a little chunky and uncomplicated, there is
wonderful fruit combining balance and interest. Leave it until
2002 and then savour it over three years.
WineOnline

VR Ribatejo Casaleiro Puro Sangue 97 £5–£6
This Vinho Regional is well made, warm and typically Portuguese. Quite deep fruity aromas give way on the palate to
great flavours of red cherry with a good balance of acidity and
alcohol and plenty of tannic grip. Enjoy it over the next two
years.
WineOnline

> **Terras do Sado**, in the Setúbal Peninsula south-east of
> Lisbon, has been at the forefront of recent advances in
> Portugal's wine industry, with two firms, JP Vinhos (João
> Pires) and José Maria da Fonseca, leading the way.

VR Terras do Sado José Maria da Fonseca Periquita 97 £6–£7
This wine has lovely ripe damson and date aromas, but the
wine is less fruity than promised by the nose. Still, there are
distinctive flavours of stewed rhubarb and prunes with a tang
of burnt rubber. A good partner for roasts or game casseroles,
the wine will drink well for another two years.
Gilbeys

VR Terras do Sado José Maria da Fonseca Periquita 96 £7–£8
A typical expression of the terroir, this wine has damson, fig
and wood smoke aromas. Very juicy fruit compote flavours
on the palate are earthy but not rustic. This is superb value
and will hold for four years or more. It would be great with
stews.
Gilbeys

VR Terras do Sado José Maria da Fonseca Quinta de Camarate 94 £8–£9

What good value these Vinho Regional wines are! Here we have super aromas of black fruit, plums and blackberries with depth and concentration. Flavours are complex — dark, earthy flavours and some tobacco leaf. Still many years to go — four at least.
Gilbeys

VR Terras do Sado JP Barrel Selection Red Wine 94 £5–£6

One of JP's innovations is oak ageing. This example spent a year maturing in oak casks before being bottled. In this opaque, inky, black wine aromas of wild mountain bush, warm earth and jammy damsons emerge. A delicious smack of gravelly tannins gives way to reveal blueberries, cranberries and loganberries in a fruit compote. This wine is rich and positively rustic. Decant it into a carafe before serving to open up the flavours and partner it with hearty and herby stews.
Tesco

> **VdM** (Vinho de Mesa) is the Portuguese designation for table wines.

VdM Caves Bonifácio £5–£6

With its assertive, earthy flavours this is a very agreeable wine, from a humble table wine classification. It has a good dollop of dried fruit and cake spices bound in macho tannins. This is great value and would make a good partner for rich and savoury winter casseroles. Drink it over the next two years.
Dalton

Romania

> The **Dealul Mare** ('big hill') region is on the sunny, south-facing foothills of the Carpathians, north of Bucharest. It produces very good red wines.

Dealul Viilor Vineyards Special Reserve Cabernet Sauvignon 97 £7–£8

This Cabernet Sauvignon has aromas of ripe bramble berries, blackcurrants and rhubarb. Mouth-watering, juicy fruit pastille flavours are revealed through the firm tannins. Made in a lively and fresh New World style, it would be an ideal party wine and can be enjoyed over the next three years.
Barry & Fitzwilliam (BF28)

Spain

In this section the wines are listed by
- Denominacióne de Origen (DO)
- Denominacióne de Origen Calificado (DOCG) Rioja only
- price

DO Calatayud Marqués de Aragon Garnacha Puro 99 £5–£6
From the largest quality area in Aragón, the same region as Somontano, this 100% Garnacha wine has chewy, spicy flavours and a long and full palate. It's very drinkable now, but will soften further. It's good value and will age for up to two years.
Searsons

DO Calatayud Castillo de Maluenda Garnacha/Syrah 99 £7–£8
Made with 60% Garnacha, 20% Tempranillo and 20% Syrah, this wine has forward, aggressive flavours. It's chewy and inky at the moment, but will improve for up to three years. A big wine, it's good value.
Searsons

DO Costers del Segre Raïmat Abadia 97 £8–£9
The ancient estate of Raïmat was derelict when Manuel Raventós, of Codorníu, began to revive the salt-soaked soil. The first vintage was produced in 1978 and since then the estate has flourished. This blend of Cabernet Sauvignon and Tempranillo was aged for 18 months in American oak. On the nose it's fruity, with chocolate and strawberry. Strawberry and blackberry fruit flavours envelop the palate, making this a pleasant and inviting wine. It will keep for up to three years.
Grants

************** *Best of Wine 2001* **Wine of the Year!** *************
DO Costers del Segre Castell del Remei Gotim Bru 97 £9–£10
A superb wine, at a very friendly price, Castell del Remei Gotim Bru, was unananimously selected as Wine of the Year at the tasting of three-star wines. Founded in 1871, the estate had a fine reputation between 1889 and 1907, but then declined. Since 1982 it has been owned by the Cusine family who are striving to restore it to its former glory. In 1990 the first of the new generation wines was released, including the first vintage of Gotim Bru. The estate has 40 hectares of vines, a stately home, a beautiful chapel and a restaurant—it's well worth a visit. Made from Tempranillo, Merlot and Cabernet Sauvignon, the wine is in the mould of a classic Bordeaux. It's powerful and full-bodied, but not tough, with cedary, complex black fruits. A classy wine, it will improve over the next three to four years. (See also Taster's Choices for another rave review!)
Searsons

DO La Mancha Stowells Tempranillo nv £6–£7
La Mancha is the largest DO in Spain and has made great
strides in quality improvement in the last few years, with
Tempranillo as the main star for reds. Well made in a simple,
easy, undemanding style, this wine is great value.
Allied Drinks

DO La Mancha Vega Robledo Reserva 95 £7–£8
A beneficiary of modern methods of winemaking and a year's
ageing in oak barrels, this wine doesn't reveal its fruit on the
nose, but saves it for a flavour-packed palate with lots of
dense black fruit and great length. Smooth and easy drinking,
it should have wide appeal, especially at the price. It will drink
well for two years.
Bacchus

> **Navarra**, which lies next to Rioja in northern Spain not
> far from the French border, is an area to watch. Most of
> the soil is deep loam over gravel, underpinned by
> limestone — ideal for producing serious wines. The
> region's wine research station (EVENA) is the best in
> Spain. By researching grape growing and winemaking
> and passing their findings on to the local growers and
> winemakers, the scientists have played a huge part in
> catapulting Navarra into the forefront of Spain's wine-
> producing regions.

DO Navarra Cosecha Particular 96 £11–£12
This still youthful wine has deep aromas of blackcurrant laced
with vanilla and pepper, a big mouthful of ripe blackcurrant
fruit, softening tannins and a long finish. A perfectly balanced
wine, it has plenty of alcohol and shows real quality. Well
worth a try, it will last for four years.
Approach Trade

DO Navarra Palacio de Muruzabal 94 £21–£22
Palacio de Muruzabal uses 45% Cabernet Sauvignon, 45%
Merlot and 10% Tempranillo for this deep ruby wine, which
has a meaty, robust nose of weighty dark cherry and fig
aromas. Flavours are classic — it has spice, cherry, cassis and
plums on the palate and a layered chocolate and vanilla
aftertaste that goes on to a terrific finish. A potentially exciting
wine, this is one to keep for at least two years; it will age and
develop for a further three or four.
Approach Trade

DO Navarra Agramont Tempranillo 97 £5–£6
Agramont wines are made by the firm Principe de Viana, a quality-conscious firm with a large export market. The company carries out a lot of research—into new yeast strains and cask fermentation, for example. It is also researching the long history of winemaking in Navarra. This wine has wonderful mature aromas of ripe plums and smooth vanilla with hints of smoke. The palate is well rounded, with a decent fruit intensity of dark summer fruits and a touch of bitter cherries at the end. With fairly soft tannins and a very good finish, it's excellent value and will go on for another two years.
Dunnes Stores

DO Navarra Alma de la Granja Garnacha 99 £6–£7
Garnacha loves the hot climate of Spain; this example has ripe strawberry and cherry aromas with soft bramble and cherry fruit on the palate aided by lively tannins. There are hints of spice and caramel on the decent finish. Drink it over the next two years.
Approach Trade

DO Navarra Palacio de la Vega Cabernet Sauvignon/ Tempranillo 96 £7–£8
Palacio de la Vega is a new, promising bodega ('winery') that makes accessible, fruity wines. The nose here offers blackcurrant and fruit of the forest with spicy vanilla, plenty of blackcurrant fruit on the palate, backed with a touch of spice, and good support from tannins and alcohol. A good-value wine to drink with food, it has a long, warm finish. Grilled rack of lamb or bean and wine-rich stew would be ideal.
Irish Distillers

DO Navarra Quaderna Via 98 £9–£10
Fresh and energetically fruity this young wine has a smooth texture and intense, inky black fruits. Mouthwatering and juicy, with a good grip of tannins, it will benefit from keeping well into 2001. Drink it on a winter's night with peppered steak.
Gleeson

> The word **Crianza** on a label means that the wine has been aged for at least two years before release.

DO Navarra Crianza Agramont Tempranillo/Cabernet Sauvignon 96 £5–£6
Big, juicy reds from international and Spanish grape varieties abound in Navarra. This moderately priced example is a medium-bodied red with blackcurrant fruit and a spicy, earthy character. With its soft tannins and warm finish, it's mature now.
Dunnes Stores

DO Navarra Crianza Las Campañas 96 £5–£6

Wine has been made in Navarra since Roman times, but the
methods have certainly changed — it's all stainless steel and
cool fermentation now. These modern methods have been
used to good effect in this medium-bodied red with lovely ripe
strawberries and plums on the nose. There is nice cherry and
plum fruit on the palate, with a bit of vanilla backing. Tannins
are well under control and it has a good lingering finish — a
value-for-money wine.
Dunnes Stores

DO Navarra Crianza Chivite Gran Feudo 96 £7–£8

This uncomplicated easy-drinking Cabernet Sauvignon is a
drink-in-front-of-TV-Irish-style wine. It has dark berry fruit
flavours and soft, supple, ripe, gentle fruit. It's a good price
and is probably better on its own, without food.
TDL

> **Reserva** on a label means that the wine has been aged
> for at least three years, with at least one year in cask, so
> the wine is quite mature when released for sale.

DO Navarra Reserva Chivite Colección 125 94 £18–£19

Produced to celebrate the 125th anniversary of the Chivite
company, this wine, which first appeared in 1985, is made
from 80% Tempranillo and 20% Merlot. The fruit is succulent,
ripe, sweet and jammy. There is a light dusting of spice — very
pleasing to the palate — and it's easy to drink. Mouthfilling in a
subtle fashion, it has an abundance of fruit. Very well-made
wine, this is the one to choose for that special dinner party. It's
elegant and refined and stands out in the crowd. Keep it for up
to three years.
TDL

DO Navarra Reserva Palacio de Muruzabal 92 £18–£19

Certainly one of Navarra's serious wines, this has abundant
prune aromas, while there is a huge blackcurrant concentration with wonderful vanilla tones on the palate. A long finish
with hints of spice makes this a very good all-rounder with
plenty of fruit and good balance. It's quite pricey, but will age
for two to four years.
Approach Trade

DO Navarra Reserva Chivite Colección 125 92 £20–£21

This wine spent two of the three years of ageing required for
Reserva wines in French oak and the rest in bottle before
release. It's a blockbuster of a wine with rich, ripe, baked fruit,
strawberries dominating, intermingling on the palate with

sweet vanilla essence, spices, welcome drying tannins, and big, big length. Soft and supple, it has a good backbone of tannin and acidity. A serious, complex wine, it has a long life ahead and is an ideal special-occasion purchase. It will develop and mature for up to three years.
TDL

DO Penedès Gran Caus 95 £16–£17
The Can Ràfols dels Caus estate enjoys a unique microclimate, surrounded by mountains and woods. One of the few estates to bottle its own wine, it has won several awards in the last ten years. No Spanish grapes here — the estate uses the French varieties of Merlot, Cabernet Sauvignon and Cabernet Franc. The wine is full of dark-berried fruit with a twist of spice, and has soft tannins and a long finish. Well made, this is international designer wine that should age for at least two years.
Approach Trade

DO Penedès Cristina Colomer 97 £8–£9
Before the 1960s red wine was practically unknown in Penedès, but investment and intelligent use of higher ground and suitable microclimates have brought great success and lots of good wine to the export markets. Many, like this one, are reasonably priced; this is a pleasant, very fruity wine with lashings of oak. It would go well with rich, hearty food and will keep for a year — two at most.
Classic

☆ ☆

DO Priorat Les Terrasses 98 £15–£16
Made by wunderkind Alvaro Palacios on the excellent schist soils of Priorat, this wine is mainly Garnacha and Cariñena. It has a wonderful black cherry nose leading to a spicy, luscious dark fruit palate and a delicious finish. With great structure and elegance, it's a smasher — deeply concentrated and piquant, with soft velvety tannins and subtle oak. It will mature for about four years.
Approach Trade

☆

DO Ribera del Duero Alión 96 £22–£23
Owned by superstar company Vega Sicilia, the Alión estate aims to produce 100% Tinto Fino (Tempranillo) wines to a high quality level. They have succeeded with this lovely wine. The nose is massively layered and intense. It's a whopper, with deep, sweet, ripe fruit, new oak well used, just enough acidity — definitely a keeper. It will go on for at least another two years.
Mitchells

DO Ribera del Duero Reserva Emilio Moro 94 £20–£21
Tinto del Pais (Tempranillo) grapes are grown 500–800 metres
above sea level for this wine. The hot days and cool nights
produce grapes with excellent fruit that retain a shivery
backbone of acidity. A good example of the region, this wine
has a very big structure, but combines it with lovely spice and
damson fruit. There is a long, powerful finish—this would be
great with juicy meats and will go on for a year or two.
Approach Trade

DO Somontano Enate Cabernet Sauvignon/Merlot 97 £7–£8
Cabernet Sauvignon and Merlot grapes were destalked,
pressed and fermented separately in stainless steel for this
wine, after which it was matured for six months in French and
American oak barrels. This modern approach has resulted in
an overtly fruity style with blackcurrants and Victoria plums.
Fairly straightforward, it's well balanced and easy to drink. It
should retain its essential fruitiness for about two years and
will go well with tomato-based sauces and pizza.
Febvre

**DO Somantano Crianza Enate Tempranillo/Cabernet
Sauvignon 96 £8–£9**
The grapes, a blend of Tempranillo and Cabernet Sauvignon,
are destemmed before crushing. The must is then fermented
in stainless steel tanks before being aged for nine months in
oak casks. Blackcurrant fruit pastilles and tar-infused spiciness
promise great things on the palate, but it doesn't quite deliver
the concentration promised on the nose. An easy-drinking
wine, it should hold for two years.
Febvre

**DO Somontano Reserva Enate Cabernet Sauvignon 95 £14–
£15**
The Cabernet Sauvignon grapes for this wine are destemmed
before crushing. The must is fermented and macerated for
two weeks, after which the wine is aged for a year in French
oak casks. Spicy blackcurrant fruit assaults the tastebuds and
opens up even more on the finish. Tannins are gripping, with
polished oak overtones. This is serious quality wine, classy and
excellent value. It will go on maturing for about four years.
Febvre

DO Tarragona De Muller Viña Solimar Tinto 97 £7–£8
Better known in the past for sweet fortified red wines and

communion wines, DO Tarragona now produces lots of light wines — fruity reds, whites and rosés. The lovely example here has a slightly medicinal nose of baked brambles and red berry fruits. Rich and ripe fruits of cherry, bramble and savoury blackcurrant with a touch of spice form a harmonised and warm palate. It has a weighty and balanced finish and will keep for two years.

Approach Trade

DO Terra Alta Dardell Negre 99 £7–£8

Terra Alta isn't a well-known DO area here, but it has the potential to produce terrific wines from its limestone soils and excellent climate. This blend of Syrah, Cabernet Sauvignon and Garnacha has an unusual, earthy, gamy nose. It's a hearty wine that softens quickly. Firm and generous on the palate, with lots of juicy black fruit, it offers value for money and should last for three years.

Oddbins

> **Toro** is in the same region as Ribera del Duero, with a similar climate and soils, but it is less well known. The wines are made from 100% Tinto de Toro (Tempranillo/ Cencibel). It's a region to look out for, as it is offering some excellent and powerful wines at reasonable prices.

DO Toro Dehesa Gago 99 £8–£9

Made by Spanish superstar Telmo Rodriguez from 100% Tinto de Toro (Tempranillo) grapes, this wine has ripe, fruity summer aromas of strawberries and cherries. A touch of vanilla lies behind the deep, rich fruit and spice on the palate. With its well-integrated tannins, this good-value, very pleasant wine has an appealing finish and will hold for two to three years.

Approach Trade

DO Toro Vega Sauco 98 £8–£9

With its meaty, rich blackcurrant nose with spice, brambles and intense fruits on the palate, this is a robust wine with a big structure. Excellent value at the price, it has a long and impressive finish. It will age for up to two years.

Approach Trade

DO Toro Crianza Vega Sauco 96 £9–£10

This Toro has benefited from the extra ageing given to the Crianza version. Intense aromas of dark fruits and chocolate lead to a complex concentration of fruit, chocolate and liquo-

rice flavours. The different layers of wine are well structured and integrated. A powerful offering for the price, it has an interesting finish.
Approach Trade

DO Toro Reserva Vega Sauco 95 £11–£12
The very intense aromas of this Reserva wine lead to huge fruit with great tannins and a long spicy, finish. A bit of a blockbuster, this is for those who like their wines powerful. It will carry on being powerful for around two years.
Approach Trade

> The **Valdepeñas** region, which lies not far south of Madrid, has been making quality wine for centuries. The Valdepeñas vineyards lie high up on the central plateau of Spain, protected from the wind by mountains. This is a hot, dry place, but the underlying limestone subsoil helps to retain enough water to support vines.

DO Valdepeñas Bodegas Real Bonal Tempranillo 98 £5–£6
Bodegas Real is a modern, forward-looking producer and this wine has jammy mature aromas of red berry fruits. On the palate there are strawberries and light oaky vanilla. Well rounded with a nice body of red fruit, the wine is lifted by an oaky vanilla finish.
Approach Trade

DO Valdepeñas Crianza Señorio de los Llanos 96 £5–£6
Cencibel (Tempranillo) is the Valdepeñas grape and this one has the typical aromas of brambles and strawberries. There are mellow autumn fruits on the palate with some spice and the soft tannins go on to a gentle fruity finish. At its best over the next year, it could possibly hold for another year.
Dillons

DO Valdepeñas Crianza Bodegas Real Vega Ibor 98 £6–£7
The vines' struggle for survival in the intense heat of Valdepeñas is justified in the spicy, jammy, strawberry nose and ripe cherry and bramble fruit palate with plenty of tannic vigour. Well-made wine, it's excellent value and has a decent finish.
Approach Trade

DO Valdepeñas Gran Reserva Señorio de los Llanos 90 £8–£9
Made by a highly respected bodega, los Llanos Gran Reserva is one of the top wines of Valdepeñas. One hundred per cent Cencibel (Tempranillo), it has wonderful complex aromas of cherries, black fruit, vanilla and spice. Dark autumn fruit

flavours are matched by supple tannins, making this wine very easy to drink. It will age for a further year and is ludicrously good value.
Dillons

DOC Rioja Bodegas Olarra Añares 96 £11–£12
Established in 1973, making it one of the new kids on the block, Bodegas Olarra strikes a modern note with this wine. A pretty, untypical Rioja, it is quite perfumed and almost floral. It shows a myriad of complex aromas on the nose, from soft, ripe berries to vegetal notes. Liquorice and red berries assert themselves on the palate. Still youthful, it has good tannins and acidity and will improve over the next two years.
Allied Drinks

DOC Rioja Marqués de Murrieta Colección 2100 97 £10–£11
The firm of Marqués de Murrieta is a guardian of tradition in Rioja, but it has recently begun to produce some wines with more upfront fruit in the modern style. There are perfumed roses and juicy raspberries on the nose of this wine. Its deceptively light fruity flavours evolve into an earthier, meaty flavour, which already shows signs of complexity with hints of truffle and a woody earthiness. Duck with cherry sauce would be perfect. It's ready to drink now and will improve for three years.
Gilbeys

DOC Rioja Viña 505 98 £8–£9
Telmo Rodriguez, one of the most influential winemakers in Spain, works with native Spanish varieties in different regions, aiming to produce a classic expression of grapes and terroir. This wine hasn't been matured in oak, which is unusual for a Rioja. Reasonably priced, the wine has pleasant aromas of jammy fruit and boiled sweets. On the palate there are plenty of ripe summer fruits with a caramel overtone balanced by a decent tannin level and a well-rounded finish. It's drinking beautifully now and should continue to do so over the next two years.
Approach Trade

DOC Rioja Crianza Montecillo 97 £8–£9
Owned by the sherry group Osborne, Montecillo was founded in 1874. It has earned a solid reputation as a reliable to excellent producer. This wine is certainly well made, with layers of aromas of black fruit and spice with undertones of forest vegetation. It has a silky and elegant palate of warm summer fruits balanced by a nice touch of vanilla. Those lovely warm Spanish spices, backed by smoothness and rich fruit, make this a fine match for steak.
Dillons

DOC Rioja Crianza Ijalba Múrice 97 £9–£10

Aged for a year in oak casks and a year in bottle, this wine is made from 80% Tempranillo, 5% Mazuelo, 5% Graciano and 10% unknown! It has a velvety, smooth texture. Rich and fruity, yet with a savoury bite, there is a harmonious marriage of mature jammy fruits with the spiciness of oak. This one will age for a further two years.
Greenhills

DOC Rioja Crianza Marqués de Vitoria 96 £9–£10

Matured in new American oak casks and made with 100% Tempranillo, this is a fairly straightforward, easy-drinking, fruit-laden wine with medium body and typical Tempranillo flavours of ripe, warm strawberries. It's elegant, yet with a good concentration of fruit and spice that lingers on the finish. Good value for money, it will keep for the next two years.
Maxxium

DOC Rioja Crianza Viña Hermosa 97 £9–£10

Crianza wines are aged for at least two years before they reach the shelves. This one is at its peak. There are soft summer fruits and caramel on the nose, with darker fruits, Christmas cake and a lingering vanilla undertone on the palate. Well structured with a pleasant finish, this is good-value Rioja.
Approach Trade

DOC Rioja Reserva Bodegas Olarra Añares 95 £8–£9

This Reserva is in its prime. It has a decent depth of flavour and a subtle oakiness at a remarkably good price. On the palate there is a lively patterned weave of fruity flavours, velvety textured and smooth. Although it's ready to drink now, it will keep for up to three years.
Allied Drinks

DOC Rioja Reserva Faustino V 95 £10–£11

From the well-known family firm of Faustino, this Reserva is absolutely delicious. Perfectly mature and ready now, with gorgeous ripe red berry aromas, it has beautifully poised cherry and strawberry fruit suffused with a gentle seasoning of oaky spice on the palate. A harmonious wine with good length, it would go well with roast meats. At its best now, it will be fine for a year or two.
Gilbeys

DOC Rioja Reserva Marqués de Murrieta Ygay 95 £11–£12

The famous firm of Marqués de Murrieta is one of the most traditional Rioja producers, ageing its wines for years before release. Their Reserva is given a minimum of two years' ageing in old 225-litre American oak barrels, followed by two years in bottle. The nose is noticeably woody and spicy. On the palate, it's quite a chewy and chunky wine with blackberry fruit lifted with fresh acidity and toned with woody spiciness. Still evolving, but with a promise to reward patience, it's ready to drink now and will improve for three years.
Gilbeys

DOC Rioja Reserva Campillo 90 £12–£13

A subsidiary of Faustino, this modern estate has been in business since 1990, producing an excellent range of wines. Mature, jammy blackberries and cassis on the nose lead to soft fruity flavours of black cherries with spice, vanilla and undertones of chocolate. Ripe, creamy tannins and a soft, spicy finish make this a wine that will stand up to quite rich food with a good sauce—lamb and redcurrant jelly, roast turkey or guinea fowl. It would also suit a good strong hard cheese, such as mature Cheddar. It's in perfect condition now.
Barry & Fitzwilliam

DOC Rioja Reserva Ijalba 95 £13–£14

Aged for a year above the minimum requirement, this Reserva is made from 90% Tempranillo and 10% Graciano. It has a palate of blackberry fruits and black cherries infused with oaky spiciness, amplified by black pepper on the finish. Gripping tannins don't interfere with the ripe fruit flavours and will ensure that the wine will last for another three years.
Greenhills

DOC Rioja Reserva Marqués de Vitoria 94 £13–£14

The practice of ageing wine in new French oak casks indicates that this is a non-traditional producer. Using 100% Tempranillo, with its juicy berry flavours, results in an excellent concentration of fruit and spice that's very well integrated. This is a big wine, big on everything. It attacks the palate, filling it with fruit of the forest flavours, washing it with pleasant yet firm and integrated tannins, and, best of all, the flavours are never-ending. Rich, ripe and supple, this would be great on its own or with strongly flavoured food. It has a long life ahead of it—at least four years—and is very good value.
Maxxium

DOC Rioja Reserva Viña Salceda 95 £14–£15

Viña Salceda, which makes red wine only, is on the boundary of the Rioja Alavesa and Rioja Alta districts. The Tempranillo grapes for this wine were hand picked. Wood smoke, raspberry, strawberry and blackberry aromas abound and the fruit on the palate is very intense and concentrated. Flavours ripple over the tongue, carrying tons of red berries and blackberries with a fresh and lingering finish. An ideal match for roast meats, this wine is perfect now, but will improve for three years.
TDL

DOC Rioja Reserva Conde de Valdemar 95 £15–£16

Produced by the highly successful firm of Martinez-Bujanda in their state-of-the-art winery from 80% Tempranillo and 20% Mazuelo, this mature and elegant wine has juicy black fruits with an intense richness spiked with firm tannins. It will continue to mature for at least three years.
Febvre

> **Gran Reservas**, which are made in only the best vintages, are aged for a minimum of five years, at least two of which must be in cask.

DOC Rioja Gran Reserva Montecillo Viña Monty 89 £13–£14

Matured in French oak casks, this Gran Reserva has mature, complex aromas of strawberries and cherries with hints of dark chocolate following through on the palate. With its lovely complexity, perfect balance and long, lingering finish, this is a super wine that will keep for another two years at least.
Dillons

DOC Rioja Gran Reserva Faustino I 94 £16–£17

This Gran Reserva comes from the superb 94 vintage. With sweet fruit, oak and big, rich, broad flavours in abundance, it has massive concentration of fruit and spices, fruit cake flavours and a fabulous finish that lingers long after the wine has been swallowed. Just at the beginning of its maturity cycle, it has a long life ahead — at least four years.
Gilbeys

DOC Rioja Gran Reserva La Granja Remelluri 94 £23–£24

The Remelluri estate is known for its organic production and pure expression of fruit. This Gran Reserva has also benefited from the wonderful 94 vintage and explodes with damson fruit. There are hints of vanilla, impressive tannins and a long finish — this is excellent, classic Rioja Gran Reserva, though it's expensive. It will go on maturing for around four years.
Approach Trade

New World White

The wines in this section are listed by
- *grape variety*
- *country*
- *price*

Chardonnay

Argentina

Grapes are grown in Argentina in desert-like conditions. Only the irrigation supplied by the melting snow of the Andes makes it possible to grow vines at all. Argentina's Chardonnay wines tend to be full-bodied and ripely fruity with a dash of pepper from the use of oak. They are made in an easy-drinking style to mature quickly and should be drunk within five years of the vintage.

Finca Flichman Mendoza Chardonnay 98 £7–£8
A full bodied dry wine with lovely oily fat buttery flavours, this is quite mouthfilling with a delicious creamy finish. It's very good value and would go well with a number of foods including poultry and pasta.
TDL

Trapiche Oak Cask Chardonnay 98 £7–£8
Trapiche is one of Argentina's leading wine companies. As the name suggests, this wine was fermented in new French casks. Its lovely aromas of melon fruit turn to green apple and tropical fruit flavours with a hint of vanilla. It has a long crisp clean finish and would be good with Christmas turkey.
United Beverages

Trapiche Chardonnay 99 £8–£9
Trapiche's 99 Chardonnay is fresh and crisp with wonderfully combined lime and tropical fruits, pineapple, some vanilla and a hint of warm buttered toast. It's appealing and inviting wine with a long pleasant finish — perfect with guacamole and tortilla chips.
United Beverages

Finca Flichman Chardonnay Reserva 99 £9–£10
Although young, this Reserva is still attractive and supple. It has a good intensity of fruit showing tropical and citrus flavours of pineapples and limes. The vanilla finish from the use of oak is a touch heavy, but give it a little time for it shows promise. It's a versatile food wine.
TDL

Australia

Chardonnay from Australia tends to be full-bodied with upfront, super-ripe exotic fruits, moderate acidity, high alcohol and a vanilla, butterscotch character from oak cask fermentation. It is sometimes blended with Semillon, a grape which does not dominate its partner.

Hardys Stamp of Australia Chardonnay/Semillon 99 £6–£7
Beautifully integrated fruit salad flavours characterise this well-balanced wine, with ripe peaches and citrus-marmalade to the fore. It is exceptionally smooth with a super finish. Try it with seafood mayonnaise, a rich salad or spicy fish casserole.
Allied Drinks

Stowells of Chelsea Chardonnay nv £6–£7
With its inviting butterscotch aromas, pleasant savoury apple flavours and restrained use of oak this is a decent wine. It is a typical, well-priced Aussie Chardonnay.
Allied Drinks

Stowells of Chelsea Chardonnay/Colombard nv £6–£7
Colombard was California's most widely planted grape variety until Chardonnay ousted it from prime position a few years ago. Well rounded, super-peachy and warm, this appealing blend has a palate of pure peaches and cream, with a hint of green fruit giving a fresh touch. There are some floral notes on the finish.
Allied Drinks

Tyrrell's Hunter Valley Long Flat Chardonnay 98 £6–£7
Long Flat refers to the vineyard and not the wine! This interesting Chardonnay is dry and fruity but with a powerful kick of oak. The flavours are of ripe Galia melon with a cocktail of peaches, pears, and kiwi, seasoned liberally with white pepper. The spiciness dominates and follows through to the finish.
Maxxium

Hardys McLaren Vale Nottage Hill Chardonnay 99 £7–£8
Hardy's original cellars at McLaren Vale were sited at Nottage Hill. It was named in honour of Thomas Nottage, who managed Hardy's vineyards and cellars for over 60 years. This namesake has inviting toast and honey aromas and a classic smooth buttery texture. It's full of tropical fruit, soft peaches and mango with a touch of rhubarb and cashew nuts.
Allied Drinks

Jindalee Murray Darling Chardonnay 99 £7–£8
Vanilla/oak aromas waft from this wine, followed by ripe
juicy melon and mango. It's dry and wonderfully round with
no hard edges.
Koala

Fiddlers Creek Chardonnay 97 £8–£9
This is an unusual, crisp, pleasing wine. Full of sweet apples,
pineapple, icecream sundaes and some tart rhubarb and
gooseberry, it has a lingering finish.
Bacchus

Miranda King Valley High Country Chardonnay 97 £8–£9
This Chardonnay has a ripe tropical fruit nose with some
toast. It is full-bodied and robust with buttery vanilla flavours,
red apples and some spice.This is due to part barrel and part
malolactic fermentation, with some ageing on the lees. The
finish is very warm and pleasant. Good with chicken or pasta
dishes.
Taserra

Penfolds Koonunga Hill Chardonnay 99 £8–£9
Penfolds likes to use wood and this Chardonnay is no exception, being matured in oak as well as bottle. It has tropical
fruits and vanilla on the nose, buttered toast and melons on
the palate. With a lovely creamy texture, it is dry and has a
mouth-watering, medium-long finish. Match it with stuffed
turkey.
Findlater

Serentos Chardonnay Soft Press 98 £8–£9
'Soft Press', explained on the back label of this wine, means
that the grapes are gently pressed without bruising the skins
so as to prevent bitterness and oils entering the wine. The
wine is for those who like oak. Its tropical fruit and vanilla
aromas lead to baked apples flavours and an elegant finish.
Gleeson

Wakefield Clare Valley Unwooded Chardonnay 98 £8–£9
Fermented at low temperature, this delicious wine, as the label
makes clear, is completely unoaked. However, it can develop
nutty nuances which in blind tastings can be put down to oak
influence — unoaked Chablis often develops similar nuances.
This wine is made from grapes grown in the terra rossa soils
of the Promised Land vineyard. It has apple, pear and subtle
butterscotch aromas and ripe apple and pear flavours well
balanced by acidity. Try it with Thai chicken curry.
Koala

New World Wine Specialists

With over 35 stores open Next-Door is bringing an exciting mix of New World wines to every corner of Ireland.
Currently you will find us in:

· Next-Door Arklow	0402-23963
· Next-Door Athy	0507-33600
· Next-Door Ballybofey	074-30568
· Next-Door Ballyheigue	066-7133154
· Next-Door Ballytrain	042-9745162
· Next-Door Ballyshannon	072-51481
· Next-Door Castleisland	066-7142471
· Next-Door Clonakilty	023-33250
· Next-Door Clonmel	052-21069
· Next-Door Enfield	0405-49261
· Next-Door Enniscorthy	054-38000
· Next-Door Kildare Town	045-521214
· Next-Door Kilkee	065-9056771
· Next-Door Kilrane	053-33661
· Next-Door Kiltimagh	094-81795
· Next-Door Longford	043-45154
· Next-Door Navan	046-76051
· Next-Door Old Castle	049-8541217
· Next-Door Rhode	0405-37011
· Next-Door Roscommon Town	0903-25404
· Next-Door Sallins	045-879294
· Next-Door Sligo Town	071-61431
· Next-Door Tipperary Town	062-51474
· Next-Door Tralee	066-7129194
· Next-Door Tramore	051-393730
· Next-Door Wicklow Town	0404-68441
· Next-Door Wexford Town	053-21273
· Next-Door Ashbourne	**Opening Christmas 2000**
· Next-Door Buncrana	**Opening Christmas 2000**
· Next-Door Edenderry	**Opening Christmas 2000**
· Next-Door Ennis	**Opening Christmas 2000**
· Next-Door Kilmuckridge	Opening Christmas 2000
· Next-Door Letterkenny	Opening Christmas 2000
· Next-Door Monaghan Town	Opening Christmas 2000
· Next-Door Waterford City	Opening Christmas 2000

nextDoor

GET IT ALL - NEXT DOOR!

H.Q. VFI House, Castleside Drive, Rathfarnham, Dublin 14
Tel: 01 4923400 Fax: 01 4923577
Email: nextdoor@vintners.ie

MAKING A GRE
IMPRESSI

HARD

Wakefield Clare Valley Chardonnay 97 £8–£9
Here's another Wakefield Chardonnay from Clare Valley but
this time it's matured in French oak. Made from low-yielding
vines, it has vanilla, cream and ripe apples on the nose and an
elegant balance of tropical and citrus fruit flavours held
together by subtle oak. With a long finish, this is a very good
wine.
Koala

John James McWilliams Chardonnay 98 £9–£10
What a beautiful use of oak! McWilliams have produced a
smooth, complex wine with many layers of peach and apple
flavours integrated with buttery and creamy vanilla. It's full
and robust yet elegant, with a great finish. A gorgeous wine,
just the partner for smoked chicken salad, grilled fish or
creamy scallops.
TDL

**Evans & Tate Two Vineyards Margaret River Chardonnay 98
£9–£10**
Notwithstanding the name, this wine comes entirely from one
vineyard at Jindong in the more northerly part of Margaret
River where the soil is richer and the climate is warmer. It has
lots of ripe tropical fruit flavours with a layer of warm vanilla
and toast giving quite a long finish, all balanced with crisp
acidity. Good with Far Eastern spicy dishes and rich Mediterranean cuisine, it should be drunk by the end of 2001.
United Beverages

McGuigan Hunter Valley Bin 7000 Chardonnay 98 £9–£10
Deep golden in colour, with subtle aromas of vanilla and ripe
tropical fruit this is an assertive, full-bodied wine. It is made in
a fruit-driven style with ripe apple and peach flavours and a
long, luscious finish.
Barry & Fitzwilliam

**Milbrovale Hunter Valley Owens Family Chardonnay 99 £9–
£10**
This wine has a pronounced and aromatic nose with citrus,
pine, lanolin and butterscotch. Bursting with juicy opal fruits in
the mouth, the wine is beautifully structured and dry with a
touch of oak. Drink it with seafood or white meat.
Koala

Schinus Chardonnay 98 £9–£10
Made by Garry Crittenden, at his Dromana Estate in the
Mornington Peninsula, Victoria, this is a flavoursome, pleas-
ant, balanced wine. It has sweet peach and melon fruit,
underlaid with light oak.
Wines Direct

**Brokenwood Harlequin Unwooded Chardonnay/Verdelho 99
£10–£11**
Brokenwood are known for their eclectic blends and this one
is a good example. Verdelho is a grape of real character. It's a
Portuguese variety, perfectly suited to hot climates and in a
dry style gives rich lime-flavoured wines with a lively acidity.
Here it has been blended with Chardonnay, which was first
oaked. It is possible to detect the two grapes both on the nose
and on the palate. It's lively and spritzy in the mouth with an
uplifting middle palate of juicy fruit, predominately limes and
watermelon. Drink it with seafood, white meats, pasta, risotto.
Oddbins

Jim Barry Clare Valley Chardonnay 96 £11–£12
This Chardonnay has lovely ripe fruit, with buttery caramel
from maturation in a mixture of new and one-year-old French
oak barrels. It is medium-bodied with nice complexity and
weight.
Cassidy

**Sandalford Mount Barker/Margaret River Chardonnay 97
£11–£12**
Delicate vanilla and toast aromas appear on the nose of this
appealing wine. Soft, ripe tropical fruit flavours, with hints of
nuts and spice linger on the finish. Try it with poussin with an
apricot and almond stuffing.
Irish Distillers

Scarborough Hunter Valley Chardonnay 98 £11–£12
Made by Ian Scarborough who, after spending many years as
a wine consultant took the plunge and started producing his
own wine, this is an elegant Chardonnay, with a subtle use of
oak. It has toasty almonds and ripe apple aromas, and well
integrated fruit and oak. It is well made in a typical Aussie
style.
Wines Direct

Rosemount Estate Hunter Valley Show Reserve Chardonnay 98 £13–£14
A wonderful example of restraint and elegance from Australia, this is a beautifully balanced, complex Chardonnay with a range of flavours of mineral, fruit and spice. Fermented in French and American oak barrels and matured for ten months on its yeast lees in barrel, it will reward keeping for another two years or so. Just right with Christmas turkey.
Grants

Lindemans Padthaway Chardonnay 98 £14–£15
Barrel fermented and matured on lees in new and one-year-old French oak barrels, this is a rich wine. Nutty and creamy aromas are confirmed on the palate which is rich and soft with subtle flavours of nuts, baked apples and a hint of butter-scotch. With excellent long length, this wine will continue to improve in bottle for another two years. Scallops with pineapple salsa would be a good match.
Gilbeys

Brookland Valley Margaret River Chardonnay 97 £18–£19
Here is an excellent example of Margaret River Chardonnay displaying great elegance and concentration. Its ripe tropical fruit and acidity are finely balanced in a rich yet tangy style.
Fields

Tyrrell's Hunter Valley Vat 47 Pinot Chardonnay 96 £19–£20
This is a big wine in every sense. The nose is full of butter and vanilla, and is even a little oily. Big rich fruity flavours with honey and nut explode on the palate with a spritzy tingle. Bone dry, with the lovely subtle new oak adding creaminess, it ends with a crisp dry finish.
Maxxium

Chile

With an attractive Old World meets New World style Chardonnay wines from Chile often have a mineral influence, as an expression of the vineyards. The wines are well-balanced with complementary exotic and citrus fruits — pineapples and lemons. They range from formulaic to rich and exciting with spicy oak, hints of caramel and butter, cut with zesty grapefruit. In general, the wines are made in a fresh style, for drinking young, especially if unoaked.

Concha y Toro Sunrise Chardonnay 99 £6–£7
The brand name Sunrise refers to wines from 100% of one
grape variety with minimal or no oak aging. This good value
Chardonnay has a hint of sweetness and tastes of apples, ripe
melons and tropical fruit. Drink it over the next year. Chicken
curry with coconut would be a good match..
Findlater

Concha y Toro Casillero del Diablo Chardonnay 98 £7–£8
One of Concha y Toro's oldest labels (the Devil's Cellar) the
Chardonnay for this wine is selected from the Casablanca
district. It is light, yet generous, subtly oaked, with mango,
apple and citrus flavours. It will drink well for another two
years and would be good with spicy baked chicken.
Findlater

Las Casas del Toqui Chardonnay Grand Réserve 97 £7–£8
After significant investment in 1994 Las Casas del Toqui is
now a very modern winery producing big, mouthfilling styles.
Their Grand Réserve 97 is a big broad oaky style of
Chardonnay, matured in oak barrels for eight months. Try it
with monkfish in a rich sauce.
Dunnes Stores

Millaman Reserve Chardonnay 98 £7–£8
Here is a supple and easy wine with spicy melon and tropical
fruit flavours. It offers good value and quality and goes well
with chicken salad, light pasta, fish or chicken gratin.
Barry & Fitzwilliam

San Pedro Chardonnay Reserva 99 £7–£8
San Pedro is a sister winery to Santa Helena, whose wines are
also listed here. The wines are made by the same winemaker
from the same source of grapes. This barrel-fermented
Chardonnay has lively acidity and apple fruit flavours. It is a
good quality, well made wine with concentrated fruit, to be
drunk over the next two years. Pair it with Thai style chicken
or noodles with coriander.
Dunnes Stores

Santa Helena Selección del Directorio Chardonnay 98 £7–£8
Full of flavours, this wine has an inviting perfume of vanilla
and tropical fruit. Apples, well-integrated oak and some spice
appear on the palate. It has a lovely long finish and will
develop for up to two years. Try it with fish pie.
Greenhills

Viña Porta Chardonnay 98 £7–£8
Smooth and appealing, with kiwi, melon and mango flavours and a dusting of vanilla, this wine should be enjoyed over the coming year.
Taserra

Concha y Toro Trio Chardonnay 98 £8–£9
Behind the Trio series lies the vinous trinity of soil, climate and winemaker. The grapes come from Casablanca — one of the coolest areas in Chile with predominately alluvial soils. Fermented in stainless steel for ten months, this unoaked Chardonnay is floral in character with lively citrus and tropical fruit flavours and a hint of white pepper. It has a firm structure and a lingering finish.
Findlater

Santa Carolina Chardonnay Reservado 98 £8–£9
This is a crisp dry refreshing wine with its oak aromas of butter and cream in balance with the fruit. The style was produced by the winemaking technique — stainless steel cool fermentation, and some ageing in small French oak barrels. Try it with fried chicken and bananas.
TDL

Santa Rita Chardonnay Reserva 99 £8–£9
Part barrel fermentation and cask ageing produced this wine's fine but not exaggerated toasty element. A honeyed and vanilla nose gives way to flavours of ripe apples and kiwi. The restricted vine yields show in the weight and intensity of the fruit. Ready to drink now it will last for two years. Try it with baked chicken in a bacon and tomato sauce.
Gilbeys

Undurraga Estate Bottled Chardonnay Reserva 97 £8–£9
This is a characteristic Chardonnay with its balance of fresh-ness and lively green apples, tropical fruit and creamy vanilla texture. It's good value and to be enjoyed over the next year. Drink it with chicken or pork kebabs.
United Beverages

Carmen Maipo Valley Chardonnay Reserve 97 £9–£10
A classic oaked Chardonnay, this Reserve boasts lots of vanilla and toast flavours and ripe tropical fruit. Any overexuberance is tempered by balancing acidity. It's a fine and full-bodied wine representing the best of New World Chardonnay, with the potential to age for up to three years. Try it with creamy chicken or fish pie.
Dillon

Errazuriz Casablanca Valley La Escultura Estate Chardonnay Reserva 97 £11–£12
Errazuriz produces three levels of Chardonnay from this estate in Casablanca, of which this is the second level. The wine is fermented in oak barrels and is aged on its lees for nine months. This results in a buttery, generous wine with flavours of golden syrup and apples, with well-integrated, subtle toasty oak. The wine will drink well for two years.
Allied Drinks

Errazuriz Casablanca Valley Wild Ferment Chardonnay 98 £11–£12
The Chadonnay Wild Ferment began as an experiment in 1995 and is now the top Chardonnay from Errazuriz. 100% fermented in casks with natural yeasts, 80% undergoes malolactic fermentation which gives a smooth velvety texture. Notes of butterscotch and white chocolate are balanced with fresh melon and apple fruit.
Allied Drinks

Santa Rita Medalla Real Special Reserve Chardonnay 97 £11–£12
The Medalla Real series is one of Santa Rita's higher quality ranges. The Chardonnay is fermented in oak barrels and the wine has a creaminess due to complete malolactic fermentation (which softens the acidity of the wine). The oak gives the apple fruit flavours a honeyed, generous rich finish. Drink this delicious wine with roast chicken or turkey.
Gilbeys

New Zealand

The cool maritime climate of New Zealand's narrow North and South islands produces Chardonnays with elegant fruit with very crisp acidity. North Island is a little closer to the Equator and riper fruits — pineapple and mango — are more common around Hawkes Bay. By contrast, the Chardonnays from the cooler South Island's Marlborough region suggest melons and grapefruit with lemon and lime aromas. Oak, when used, is subtle, giving a nutty character to the wines.

Villa Maria East Coast Private Bin Chardonnay 99 £9–£10
Villa Maria produces some terrific wines and this Chardonnay is one of them. Aromas are of toffee apples, the palate has concentrated apple flavours with well-integrated gentle oak. The long savoury finish tapers slowly, delivering more fruit and herbal characteristics. Try it with white meats or seafood.
Allied Drinks

South Africa

South Africa's 500-year-old winemaking tradition is reflected in
the European style of the wines. The Chardonnays are restrained,
subtle and elegant with ripe fruits well matched by very crisp
acidity. A French influence can often be seen in the taste of the
terroir — the environment where the grapes were grown. South
African Chardonnays make excellent partners for food.

Long Mountain Western Cape Chardonnay 98 £4–£5
Apple, pear and greengage on the nose lead to clean citrus fruit
flavours with a touch of vanilla. This is a versatile wine with a
clean crisp finish and would be a good match for creamy pastas.
Irish Distillers

Bon Courage Chardonnay Prestige Cuvée 99 £8–£9
Fermented and matured for six months in French oak, this
Chardonnay has tropical and ripe apple fruit on the nose. The
oak comes through in pleasant creamy wood tastes with
accompanying apple fruit flavours. Finishing pleasantly dry, it
would go well with white meat or fish.
Gleeson

Fairview Chardonnay 98 £8–£9
Such complexity and maturity in a wine so young! A lovely
mature bouquet of field mushrooms and butter follows
through on the palate, accompanied by a ripe melon fruitiness.
With a very long finish and great elegance this a wine to
accompany Christmas dinner roast turkey or pheasant.
Oddbins

Dieu Donné Chardonnay 97 £8–£9
New French oak barrels were used to ferment this wine which
was then aged for ten months. The oak, though dominant, is
very well-integrated. The big rich wine is toasty, with upfront
vanilla and caramel together with apple fruit flavours. Very
well made and impressive, it has a long finish. Try it with
chicken and spicy noodles.
Gleeson

L'Avenir Chardonnay 97 £9–£10
Here'a a big, broad, barrel-fermented Chardonnay with ripe
melon and apples, pineapples and banana intermingling with
oak and toasty almonds. It would work well with brill or
turbot in a creamy sauce.
Dunnes Stores

Bergkelder Estate Stellenryck Chardonnay 98 £10–£11
Bergkelder, which means 'mountain cellar' is part of the
Distillers Corporation. They produce a number of ranges of
prestige wines of which the Stellenryck collection is one. The
Chardonnay has a restrained nose of apricots and light oak
and subtle, but complex, tropical fruit flavours with vanilla
notes. The finish is long and delicate. Try it with chicken in a
seafood sauce.
Febvre

Koopmanskloof Chardonnay 98 £10–£11
The Koopmanskloof Estate is just outside Stellenbosch. Their
100% barrel fermented Chardonnay has aromas of vanilla and
tropical fruit with a waxy note. Harmonious tropical fruit and
toasted oak flavours are balanced by a good bite of acidity.
This wine has potential.
Findlaters

Klein Constantia Chardonnay 96 £11–£12
Constantia wines have been appreciated and enjoyed for a
long time: their legendary dessert wines consoled Napoleon in
his exile on St Helena and were praised by Charles Dickens
and Jane Austen. This Chardonnay was fermented in French
oak and matured for six months in the same barrels. It has an
attractive smoky vanilla nose and concentrated citrus and
tropical fruit flavours. The finish is warm and lingering. It
would go well with baked chicken in a herb crust.
Gilbeys

USA – California

Berrys' Own Selection California Chardonnay 98 £10–£11
A wine to convert ABC members! This is a really classy
Burgundian-style Californian Chardonnay made by Paul
Moser and Tony Cartlidge at Ehlers Grove winery in the Napa
Valley. Barrel fermented in French oak, it has a gorgeous
mature Burgundian bouquet with suggestions of compost,
ripe melon, apples and nuts. Flavours of red apples, ripe
melon and nuts in a buttery texture offer richness to savour,
with a long peppery finish. This is a wine to sip rather than
drink, but if you want to serve it with food try guinea fowl or
pheasant.
Fields

Stratford Chardonnay 98 £10–£11

If you like the upfront New World style, this youthful wine is for you — an oaky, hazel nuttiness overlays subdued green apple fruit aromas. Quite assertive buttery fruit and nutty fudge flavours linger into a long, very creamy finish.
Barry & Fitzwilliam

J. Lohr Riverstone Monterey Chardonnay 97 £14–£15

The Arroyo Vista vineyard in Monterey, on the north central coast of California, grows the grapes for this premium Chardonnay. It's utterly butterly all over the place! A satiny smooth, complex palate marries apple, honey, double-cream toffee and lime leaves in a match made in heaven. The super-duper finish lasts even longer than an unwanted house guest. And it'll go on improving for another three or four years.
TDL

Geyser Peak Sonoma County Chardonnay 97 £15–£16

Grapes were selected from different parts of Sonoma County for this wine. Fermentation was 50% barrel and 50% tank, with the wine being matured on the lees (yeast sediment) to give it depth and flavour. With a nice combination of power and restraint, the ripe melony fruit is balanced by spicy oak. Ready to drink now, it will continue to mature for two years.
Maxxium

Clos La Chance Santa Cruz Mountains Chardonnay 97 £20–£21

New-style Californian Chardonnay, this is a lovely elegant wine. Barrel-fermented and aged on the lees in white French oak, it underwent malolactic fermentation, producing an enticing nose of citrus and vanilla spice, creamy mouthfeel and tastes akin to buttered marietta. The flavours are rich and concentrated, with a long buttery finish. It will keep for at least three years.
Oddbins

Kendall-Jackson Grand Reserve Chardonnay 95 £21–£22

A special occasion wine, with a restrained, mineral, Burgundian-style nose, this Chardonnay was fermented in Monterey barrels and aged on its lees in small French oak barrels. It's full-bodied, smooth and silky in the mouth, with nutty ripe apple flavours spiked with nutmeg. It's expensive, but would be lovely served with pheasant or guinea fowl.
Cassidy

Chenin Blanc

South Africa

Long Mountain Western Cape Chenin Blanc 98 £4–£5
A fresh and easy wine for everyday drinking, this has lemons,
limes on the nose, and citrus and spice on the palate. Try it
with spring rolls.
Irish Distillers

KWV Chenin Blanc 99 £6–£7
A crowd pleaser, made to drink young, this wine is good value
for money. It's dry and fruity with refreshing acidity and lots
of fruit. Try it with chicken dishes, within two years of the
vintage.
TDL

Robert's Rock Chenin Blanc/Chardonnay 99 £6–£7
Light-bodied, with a crisp dry finish, this is an easy drinking,
fruity wine. It is fresh and floral with flavours of melons,
nectarines and stewed apples. Try it with barbequed fish or an
omelette.
TDL

Stowells of Chelsea Chenin Blanc nv £6–£7
This wine's subtle aromas of spring blossom give way to a
savoury palate with crisp acidity and a touch of citrus. It's an
uncomplicated, fresh and pleasant wine with notable length of
flavour.
Allied Drinks

Blue White Irina von Holdt Chenin Blanc 97 £7–£8
The grapes from which this wine is made are from old vines
and are often affected by noble rot, although not in this case.
Honey and lemon aromas are followed by slightly honeyed
apple and citrus fruits on the palate, balanced with crisp acidity
and a very pleasant long finish. This is a good match for lightly
spiced Chinese food.
Barry & Fitzwilliam

Berrys' Own Selection Chenin Blanc 99 £8–£9
Produced by the Simonsig Estate for Berry Bros & Rudd, this
delicious Chenin Blanc delivers liquid sunshine. It has deeply
concentrated ripe, fleshy fruits with a touch of honey. With
well balanced alcohol and a very long finish, this is a charmer.
Fields

Drostdy-Hof Steen/Chenin Blanc 99 £8–£9
In South Africa, Chenin Blanc is known as Steen. This example
has flavours of very ripe pears and peaches which are counterbalanced by crisp citrus fruit. Slightly yeasty, the finish is more
savoury than fruity. It's a good match for curry.
Febvre

Pinot Gris

New Zealand

Babich Marlborough Pinot Gris 98 £8–£9
A remarkable range of flavours appear in this delicious wine —
ripe exotic fruits, rose water, pineapple and pears — with
ginger spice on the very long finish. A slightly oily texture
unifies the diverse flavours. This lovely wine is drinking well
now and would be good with vegetarian quiche.
Gleeson

Shingle Peak Marlborough Pinot Gris 99 £10–£11
Citrus and melons on the nose are followed by a weighty
mouthfeel of ripe melons and some lemon curd, with a long
finish. This is a balanced and well-made wine with potential to
improve over the next two years or so. Try it with vegetable
flans.
Mitchell

Shingle Peak Marlborough Pinot Gris 97 £10–£11
An aromatic wine, with lively citrus and vanilla aromas, this
Pinot Gris has aged sufficiently to develop an oily character,
together with ripe tropical fruits. It is light-bodied with a dry,
nutty finish.
Molloys

USA – Oregon

King Estate Pinot Gris 96 £17–£18
The cool climate of Oregon suits white grape varieties well.
Pinot Gris, more usually found in Alsace or Italy, provides a
grab-bag of surprises in this wine. A light but complex nose
rewards a sincere sniff. The palate goes everywhere — green
apples, soft honey notes, rhubarb. A really unusual wine to
relax with, rather than a food wine, it has good length.
TDL

Riesling

Australia

Riesling is originally from Germany. In the warm climate of Australia Riesling ripens more quickly than in Europe and the wines mature more quickly in bottle, developing the unique petrolly bouquet. They maintain the characteristic racy and refreshing acidity.

d'Arenberg White Ochre Riesling 99 £6–£7
This Riesling has rounded and balanced ripe apple fruit flavours with a touch of oranges and a very fresh finish. It will drink well for up to two years.
Taserra

Hardys Stamp of Australia Riesling/Gewürztraminer 99 £6–£7
Unusual aromas of lime cordial, cloves and spice waft from this blend of two aromatic grapes. The palate is just as unusual, with limes and lychee fruit, crisp acidity and reasonable length. This is definitely something different and would go well with spicy Asian cuisine.
Allied Drinks

Wakefield Clare Valley Promised Land Riesling 96 £8–£9
With a classic Riesling kerosene or petrol nose, this wine is packed with limes and lemon flavours, very crisp and fresh. There is also a mineral backbone. This wine should keep for up to two years.
Koala

Mitchelton Blackwood Park Riesling 98 £8–£9
Named after the vineyard on which Mitchelton was established this is a good-value, classic Australian Riesling. Very nicely concentrated for the price it has lovely tangy lime flavours complemented by a smooth waxy oiliness. It would work well with smoked fish.
Cassidy

Peter Lehmann The Barossa Eden Valley Reserve Riesling 94 £12–£13
A fine example of New World Riesling this is lemon gold in colour with lovely aromas of limes and lemons. The same citrus fruit emerges on the palate with a hint of honey, and the finish is long and pleasant.
United Beverages

New Zealand

Rieslings from New Zealand are typically dry, delicately perfumed and elegant. Quite full-bodied, the wines have rich honey and peachy fruit flavours with a degree of complexity.

Villa Maria Private Bin Marlborough Riesling 98 £8–£9

A wonderful example of New Zealand Riesling, this has a very attractive nose of limes and flowers with a creamy note. the palate is silky smooth, and superbly concentrated with zesty acidity. There are a wealth of flavous—lush apricots, honey, citrus peel, limes and vanillia ice cream and a really long finish. Try it with tempura or spicy fish cakes.

Allied Drinks

Framingham Marlborough Dry Riesling 98 £9–£10

The Framingham Winery produces three styles of Riesling of which this delicious example is one. With apple blossom and lime cordial aromas and a hint of petrol, it has long and intense flavours of lime, with mineral slatiness and a ginger note. With its crisp acidity, this wine would work really well with spicy food. It has the potential to develop further over the next two years.

Gleeson

Shingle Peak Marlborough Riesling 98 £10–£11

The slight touch of petrol on the nose, with citrus fruits and some grapefruit, shows that this wine is developing. Fresh green apple and lemon flavours appear on the palate. Beautifully balanced, it would made a good partner to fish cakes with lemongrass and coriander.

Mitchell

Sauvignon Blanc

Australia

Sauvignon Blanc is not well suited to hot climates which tend to blur its varietal character. Australian Sauvignons are usually fruitier, fuller and richer than examples from cooler climate and would suit those who don't like lean styles. Typically the flavours are not so much green and herbaceous as ripe gooseberry with subdued acidity. The wines mature very quickly and should be drunk within two years of the vintage. The oaked examples are even more full-bodied, and may last a year longer, while gaining a little spiciness.

Fiddlers Creek Sauvignon Blanc 98 £8–£9
A distinctly floral Sauvignon, with blossoms and wild flowers, this wine has a beautifully concentrated fruity palate of apricots, apples and gooseberries. Crisp acidity is perfectly balanced by the concentration of fruit and floral flavours and the finish is long and lingering.
Bacchus

Rymill Coonawarra Sauvignon Blanc 96 £11–£12
This is a rich, full and elegant wine with flavours of ripe melon, kiwi, mango and ripe red gooseberries. No wood was used and the richness may be a hallmark of its age as well as super-ripe fruit. Try it with prawns and peppers.
Gleeson

Vasse Felix Sauvignon Blanc/Semillon 98 £12–£13
Inspired by white Bordeaux Pessac-Léognan, which is also a blend of Sauvignon Blanc and Sémillon, this is a delicious, full-bodied wine in a classic style. Gorgeous aromas of honeysuckle, honey and white fleshy fruits lead to an intense but reserved mélange of flavours from grass to lanolin, peaches to green apples, all beautifully married, with a long and satisfying finish.
Cassidy

Chile

Chile presents Sauvignon in its natural state — crisp, grassy and green, in a style quite similar to the grape's native Loire. The wines have a pungent and herbaceous character of thirst-quenching crunchy, green apples, gooseberries and sometimes asparagus. Mouthwatering acidity makes it a good food wine. Sauvignon matures quickly and should be drunk young, at most within two years of the vintage.

Antu Mapu Sauvignon Blanc Reserva 98 £6–£7
A very crisp and lively Sauvignon, this wine has green fla-vours of gooseberries, cut grass and nettles. Match it with a goats' or feta cheese salad or very lightly cooked salmon.
Barry & Fitzwilliam

Casa Lapostolle Sauvignon Blanc 98 £6–£7
Here is a rich and complex wine with a wealth of fruit and flavours — gooseberries, citrus, melon and asparagus. It has a long and satisfying finish.
United Beverages

Undurraga Sauvignon Blanc 99 £6–£7
Clean and refreshing, this wine has classic Sauvignon Blanc grassy and gooseberry aromas. The palate is full and heavy with melons, spicy mango and a hint of honey. Not intended for long keeping it should be drunk young, say with a fish salad.
United Beverages

Carmen Central Valley Sauvignon Blanc 98 £7–£8
Fresh and crisp, with a subtle nose of green apples, peapod, elderflower and asparagus,.this wine has a lot of fruit on the palate, notably gooseberries and grapefruit. It has a long finish and would be a fine match for pasta with a tomato and courgette or bagna cauda sauce.
Dillon

Concha y Toro Casillero del Diablo Sauvignon Blanc 98 £7–£8
Juicy gooseberries on this wine's nose give way to more savoury and tangy citrus flavours on the palate. It has a long finish. Wood will not be used in making this wine from the 1999 vintage which should give an even crisper and fresher style.
Findlater

Cousiño-Macul Sauvignon Blanc 99 £7–£8
Here's a mouthfilling delicious wine with lemons, gooseber-ries and stewed apple flavours. A little steely with a crisp dry finish, it is well made and good value.
Ecock

Errazuriz La Escultura Estate Casablanca Valley Sauvignon Blanc 99 £7–£8
The nose of this estate wine gives very little away with its muted asparagus and green pea aromas. This doesn't prepare you for a surprisingly concentrated and savoury palate with fresh, green apple acidity. Try it with tomato salad or a simple fish dish with a tomato or pepper sauce.
Allied Drinks

Viu Manent Sauvignon Blanc 98 £7–£8
With fresh nettle aromas, this is a refreshing zippy wine with an abundance of gooseberries and Granny Smith apples. There are further elements of slate and flint probably from stainless steel fermentation. This would be very good with a starter salad of advocado, tomatoes and cheese.
Ecock

Santa Rita 120 Sauvignon Blanc 98 £8–£9
'120' is a range of Santa Rita wines, named after 120 patriots, led by General Bernardo O'Higgins, who found refuge in the wine cellars which now stand on the Santa Rita winery. This Sauvignon Blanc crackles with freshness and has intense gooseberry, citrus and apple fruit. Match it with a salad of mozzarella cheese, peppers and aubergines.
Gilbeys

Carmen Casablanca Valley Sauvignon Blanc Reserve 97 £9–£10
Aromatic and luscious, with grassy, pink grapefruit and crisp green fruit flavours this wine will get your gastric juices going. It has good length and would go well with stir-fried prawns with green vegetables.
Dillon

Viu Manent Reserve Fumé Blanc 99 £9–£10
Fresh and lively with a faint spritz, this is a crisp wine with predominately gooseberry fruits. There is an excellent weight as a result of leaving the wine in contact with the skins after pressing and the two months aging in oak casks. Try it with chicken with strong flavours such as feta and sundried tomatoes.
Ecock

New Zealand

New Zealand produces wonderful Sauvignon Blancs — some would maintain the best in the world. While the grapes ripen well in the heat-retaining volcanic soil, they never lose their aromatic, vegetal, nettley character. Flavours of green pea pod, asparagus and gooseberries are typical, but with an uncommon intensity and focus, and alway with crisp, zesty acidity. The more serious wines have a chalky minerally quality to add interest. The wines are at their best within two years of the vintage.

Stoneleigh Vineyard Marlborough Sauvignon Blanc 99 £8–£9
Assertive and attention grabbing, this wine gives instant pleasure on the palate. It has bracing and invigorating lime juice flavours fleshed out with gooseberries, finishing long in the memory. Partner it with shellfish and drink it over the next two years.
Irish Distillers

Babich Marlborough Sauvignon Blanc 98 £9–£10
This 98 has a refined nose of gooseberries and nettles with a good weight of citrus fruit and asparagus on tasting. It's quite intense, with a reasonable finish and would be a match for seafood with mayonnaise.
Gleeson

Babich Winemakers' Reserve Sauvignon Blanc 99 £9–£10
The grapes for this wine were grown on the Wakefield Downs Vineyard in the Awatere Valley in Marlborough. Fermentation was predominately in stainless steel with a lesser proportion in French oak barriques which softens the wine and adds a delicate touch of spice. The aromas are of freshly cut grass, the flavours are of tart green apples, limes and lemons.
Gleeson

Villa Maria Private Bin Marlborough Sauvignon Blanc 99 £9–£10
A stunning wine, this will stop you dead in your tracks. The nose is pure asparagus while the palate is complex with a mixture of asparagus, gooseberries and limes. The finish is superb. This outstanding wine is ridiculously good value for money. Try it with baked stuffed red peppers.
Allied Drinks

Saint Clair Marlborough Sauvignon Blanc 98 £9–£10
Bone dry with lively acidity, this wine has mineral flavours side by side with contrasting ripe, intense, kiwi fruit. It has a long finish and would go well with a zesty seafood salad.
Greenhills

Berrys' Own Selection New Zealand Sauvignon Blanc 99 £10–£11
From the Stoneleigh vineyards in Marlborough, this is classic New Zealand Sauvignon Blanc – pungent and aromatic, with gooseberry fruit wrestling with blackcurrant leaves for attention. Crisp and refreshing it should be drunk young.
Fields

Nautilus Marlborough Sauvignon Blanc 99 £10–£11
Here's a super-ripe example of Marlborough Sauvignon with tropical fruit on the nose but on the palate displaying a classic nettle and herbaceous character with sweet gooseberries. It's a lovely tangy style which would work with Thai seafood noodles.
Cassidy

Hunter's Sauvignon Blanc 99 £12–£13
This still youthful wine has a pronounced nose of gooseberries and nettles and a touch of blackcurrant leaves. It has a weighty mouthful of citrus and apple fruits with a zippy acidity. The finish is delicious.
Gilbeys

Lawson's Dry Hills Marlborough Sauvignon Blanc 99 £12–£13
Beautifully assertive, yet classy and elegant, this is a fantastic wine. Gooseberries, grapefruit, nettles and salt on the nose prepare the way for flavours of intense, ripe red gooseberries with sappy orchard fruits, such as pears and apples. The long, clean finish has a salty tang. Try this wonderful wine with poached salmon.
Febvre

USA – California

Californian Sauvignon Blancs are assertive and full bodied, with none of the green character of examples from cooler climates. Floral and honeyed aromas lead to intense tropical fruit flavours of pineapples and apricots with softened acidity. Oak maturation is not uncommon and adds an extra layer of spicy character to the wine.

Beringer Napa Valley Appellation Collection Fumé Blanc 98 £11–£12
In California, Fumé Blanc is Sauvignon Blanc – usually matured in oak. The cool climate and well-drained soils of the

Napa Valley give this wine a concentrated fruit palate. Fresh and crisp, there is a herbal quality mingling with citrus. It has a long finish and will retain its freshness for a year or so.
Allied Drinks

Semillon

Australia

In Australia Semillon discovers a personality never imagined in its native Bordeaux. Styles vary depending on the region, from tropical fruit-laden with a non-oak nutty and oily character to grassy wtih citric flavours, to more vegetal and lemony characteristics. The wines often have great depth of flavour with only moderate alcohol. Semillon is a good grape to use in blends as it does not dominate. When partnered with Chardonnay the wines have a pronounced peach and melon character. Oak is often used in vinification and/or maturation.

Jacob's Creek Semillon/Chardonnay 99 £4–£5
Here's a great value blend with lots of citrus fruits on the nose, and soft green plums and Granny Smith apple flavours on the palate with an appealing dash of lemon. With a clean, crisp finish this wine goes well with food — try it with a creamy pork casserole.
Irish Distillers

Miranda Opal Ridge Semillon/Chardonnay 99 £6–£7
This lovely wine has butterscotch and tropical aromas followed on the palate by flavours of light vanilla, peaches and lemons. Fruity and well rounded, it is aided by a balancing acidity and has a decent, lengthy finish.
Taserra

Penfolds Rawson's Retreat Bin 21 Semillon/Chardonnay/Colombard 99 £6–£7
This is an ideal house wine, immediately appealing and versatile with food. It has a ripe pineapple and melon nose and green apple and lime flavours which linger on to the finish. It would be particularly good with stirfried chicken or pork
Findlaters

Peter Lehmann The Barossa Semillon 99 £6–£7
A classic Barossa Semillon style, this has toast, lanolin, citrus and green pepper aromas on the nose. The palate has a good concentration of lemons and ripe pineapples, with more toast and a slightly waxy finish which is very pleasant. With crisp

acidity and a long, smooth finish this is a value for money
Semillon which should continue to develop over the next few
years. Drink it with pork in a creamy sauce.
United Beverages

Penfolds Barossa Valley Semillon/Chardonnay 98 £8–£9
Another enjoyable Semillon/Chardonnay blend this example
has lots of ripe tropical fruit, with a very pleasant nutty
aftertaste, balanced by lively acidity, giving a very clean finish.
Try it with Chinese style chicken with cashew nuts.
Findlaters

Ironstone Semillon/Chardonnay 98 £10–£11
Partial barrel fermentation gives extra weight and structure to
this classic Australian blend. The wine has tangy, savoury
flavours of apples, pears and vanilla and great length. It's just
that little bit different from straight Chardonnay.
Findlaters

**Milbrovale Hunter Valley Seven Stones Reserve Semillon 98
£11–£12**
An early released Hunter Valley Semillon, this is a big and
dense wine with whiffs of hot Formula One tyres. It has fine
concentration of fresh limes and lemons.
Koala

Mount Pleasant Elizabeth Hunter Valley Semillon 94 £11–£12
This 94 had over four years bottle maturation before it was
released for sale and it has potential for further cellaring. A
fresh, lively nose leads to a more restrained palate with
flavours of Granny Smith apples, lemons and limes. The long
finish gets more and more citrussy. Relatively inexpensive, this
is an excellent introduction to the taste of aged Hunter Valley
Semillon. Try it with brill in a creamy sauce.
TDL

Torrontés

Argentina

Etchart Rio de Plata Torrontés 98 £6–£7
This Torrontés has very ripe tropical fruit on the nose, followed by concentrated pineapple flavours with a slightly
smoky tone. Try it with grilled fish such as red snapper in a
ginger sauce.
Irish Distillers

Norton Mendoza Torrontès 99 £6–£7
Aromas of spring flowers waft from this dry, light, lively wine.
Slightly spritzy, it has honeyed tropical fruit on the palate.
Oddbins

Santa Julia Mendoza Torrontés 97 £6–£7
This wine has a floral perfumed nose.Limes and pineapples
appear on the palate, with gentle acidity. A light delicate finish
round it all off.
Taserra

Correas Torrontés/Chardonnay 98 £6–£7
Here's an unusual blend with a light, refreshing character — a
bowlful of limes with a hint of fennel, a touch of honey and
just enough acidity. The finish is very pleasant finish. Asparagus rolls would be a good match.
Gilbeys

Verdelho

Australia

Milbrovale Ownes Family Hunter Valley Verdelho 99 £8–£9
An unusual but not unpleasant nose of lanolin, butter, petrol
and floral notes marks this Verdelho. It's rich and rounded in
the mouth with greengage, citrus and lemon fruits. It's dry
and is a good wine for spicy oriental dishes.
Koala

**Bleasdale Langhorne Creek Sandhill Vineyard Verdelho 99
£9–£10**
Refreshingly unusual and distinctive, this wine's crisp citrus
fruit slowly emerges from under a blanket of riper fruity
flavours of melon, mango and gooseberries. Keep it for a year
or two to see how it develops.
Oddbins

Viognier

Argentina

Santa Julia Mendoza Viognier 98 £6–£7
Here's a well-made, value for money wine. Apricots and
peaches appear on the nose, while on the palate the fruit is
quite rounded and almost fat and gives a nice oily and lengthy
finish.
Taserra

Australia

Heggies Viognier 99 £13–£14
Rich is an understatement for this wine! Think candied citrus,
currants, sultanas and a lovely round mellow, intensely rich
finish. Try it with duck with orange sauce.
Cassidy

Yalumba Barossa Valley Viognier (Limited release) 97 £10–£11
Here is a blockbuster Viognier made from grapes grown in
the Vaughan Brothers vineyard at Angaston. It has a wonderful aromatic nose of perfume and marmalade, followed by a
rich palate with layers of flavours from candied orange peel to
apricots to lovely fresh flowers, none of which are overpowering. Very tasty, with a long finish, it would be good with rich
creamy dishes.
Cassidy

USA – California

Fetzer North Coast Viognier 98 £10–£11
The aristocratic Rhône variety Viognier has brought its
wonderful aromas and finesse to the cool north Californian
coast. With a very aromatic nose of almond blossom, rose
petals, ripe apricot and light nutty tones, the palate doesn't
disappoint – it has lots of warm, ripe, peachy fruit flavours
with a good spicy kick leading to a lovely lime juice finish. Age
this one for a year or two and preferably drink with Asian
food or meaty shellfish such as crab or lobster.
Dillons

Other white

Australia

Brown Brothers Victoria Dry Muscat 99 £7–£8
The Muscat of Alexandria, which is used here, is an aromatic
grape with pronounced fruit character. True to form the nose
is honeyed and very aromatic. It's in an off-dry style that is
emphasised by ripe melons, tropical fruit and honey on the
palate, and is very refreshing with a soft, fruity finish. Try it
with grilled asparagus or similar vegetable salad.
Woodford Bourne

McWilliam's Inheritance Colombard/Chardonnay 98 £7–£8
Here's a refreshing white wine with lots of stewed apple fruits
and hints of spice. Ideal for summer drinking, with a good
whack of alcohol it's good with food — try it with fish, chicken
dishes or smoked salmon.
TDL

Ch. Tahbilk Marsanne 98 £8–£9
A fine and elegant wine, this unwooded Marsaanne is charac-
terised by lemons, some honey and ripe pineapple fruit with a
slightly oily texture which gives a very pleasant, long lasting
finish. It's very well balanced with crisp acidity. Match it with
pork or chicken in coconut milk.
United Beverages

Pitchfork Margaret River White 99 £8–£9
Made by the energetic and innovative winery, Hay Shed Hill,
in Margaret River, this is a wine full of ripe tropical fruit
flavours with a good balance of acidity and alcohol giving it
structure. It would be great on its own on a hot summer day
and is good value for money.
Wines Direct

New Zealand

**Lawson's Dry Hills Marlborough Gewürztraminer 98 £12–
£13**
Exceptionally luscious, opulent, exotic fruit suggests an off-dry
or sweeter style, yet this is a dry wine. Apricots and ginger
persist in a long finish. Drink with oriental dishes especially
Chinese, crab cakes or Thai green curry.
Febvre

South Africa

Malan Family Vintners Stellenbosch Adelblanc 99 £4–£5
Tropical and citrus fruit show on the nose of this light, easy-
drinking wine. It has flavours of soft apple with some lime and
lemon fruit, crisp acidity and a short clean finish.
United Beverages

USA — California

Francis Coppola Presents Bianco 97 £9–£10
Yes, it's the movie director of Godfather fame — his interests
run to vineyards and winemaking. His Bianco has plenty of
ripe peach fruit aromas and flavours with a lovely cut of green
apple acidity, giving a clean and pleasant finish.
Molloys

New World Red

In this section, the wines are listed by
- *grape variety*
- *country*
- *price.*

Cabernet Sauvignon

Argentina

In Argentina, Cabernet Sauvignon is less fleshy than in other New World countries. It has a firm, tannic structure with spice, leather, coffee beans and complex dark fruit. These full-bodied wines are often oak-aged, giving a liquorice and vanilla bouquet, and require two to three years bottle ageing to tame the tannin.

Santa Julia Mendoza Cabernet Sauvignon 97 £6–£7
This reasonably priced wine is a typical example of Cabernet Sauvignon from Argentina. It has a good weight of fruit on the palate with hints of vanilla and oak, firm tannins, crisp acidity and a long, clean finish. Try with barbecued beef.
Taserra

Finca Flichman Mendoza Cabernet Sauvignon 97 £7–£8
A big wine, with a huge weight of baked rich blackcurrant fruits with hints of vanilla, this mouthfilling wine is great value. It has good length and would go well with meatloaf or grilled meats.
TDL

Trapiche Oak Cask Cabernet Sauvignon 97 £7–£8
With a classic, still tight structure, this Cabernet has full red berry fruit flavours, and an elegant texture with spicy and smoky layers underneath, with a herby smoky twist on the finish. It's a lovely wine at a great price and is perfect with steak.
United Beverages

Weinert Cabernet Sauvignon 91 £13–£14
Here is a big, complex wine, still drinking really well after nearly ten years in bottle. It has an attractive nose of blackberries, some fruit cake and cigar box, and lots of concentrated ripe berry fruit on the palate with hints of spice and cedar wood, cigar box and dark chocolate. Well balanced with firm tannins and crisp acidity, it has a lovely long, flavoursome

finish. It's a great wine with red meat — try it with steak.
Molloys

Famiglia Bianchi Cabernet Sauvignon 96 £20–£21
This 96 has developed a mature smoky character. It has a big
bouquet of Ribena blackcurrant fruit and flavours of bramble
berries, spice, mushroom overtones with cigar box and tar.
With a hot and spicy length, it is a definite winter warmer. It is
drinking well now and should continue to do so over the next
three or more years.
Oddbins

Australia

Cabernet Sauvignon in Australia has aromas of blackcurrant
and mint.

McWilliam's Hanwood Cabernet Sauvignon 97 £7–£8
A mouthfilling wine, this has good concentration of baked
blackcurrant fruits, with some chocolate and black cherry
notes, and good length. It is fairly high in alcohol and is likely
to improve over the next one to two years.
TDL

Ch. Tahbilk Cabernet Sauvignon 97 £8–£9
Chateau Tahbilk is Victoria's oldest family-owned winery and
vineyard. Founded in 1860 it lies in the Goulburn Valley, in
Central Victoria. Made from 90% Cabernet Sauvignon and
10% Cabernet Franc this 97 has ripe blackberry fruit with a
touch of violets and a slightly smoky finish. The structure is
excellent as firm tannins are balanced with crisp acidity and the
finish is long and warm. Try it with duck with apples.
United Beverages

Kingston Estate Murray Valley Cabernet Sauvignon 96 £8–£9
Maturation in French oak has given this Cabernet subtle oak
nuances. It has ripe, pleasant, soft berry flavours with firm
tannins and good length.
Gleeson

**Miranda High Country King Valley Cabernet Sauvignon 95
£8–£9**
Aged in new American oak, this Cabernet has a hot, almost
jammy, nose. It's got lots of very concentrated fruit flavours,
well balanced by acidity and a medium to full-bodied palate
with a long, clean finish.
Taserra

Wakefield Clare Valley Cabernet Sauvignon 98 £8–£9
A very pronounced fruity nose does not disappoint on the
palate of this 98. It has an abundance of blackberries and the
finish is long, warm and spicy. It will keep for up to two more
years. Try it with lamb marinated in thyme and whiskey.
Koala

Tesco Coonawarra Cabernet Sauvignon 98 £9–£10
'Typical' is the word for this restrained and elegant Coonawarra
Cabernet matured in French oak barrels. It has super, concentrated, blackcurrant fruit surrounded by well-integrated oak and
offers a decent weight of fruit and richness for the price. It's a
good match for lamb noisettes and ratatouille.
Tesco

Wyndham Estate Bin 444 Cabernet Sauvignon 96 £9–£10
This lovely elegant wine shows some restraint, more typical of
the Old World than the New. With vanilla and mushrooms on
the nose it has a good weight of minty fruit and spice, balanced by softening tannins which give the wine a nice silky
texture. The finish is long and lingering.
Irish Distillers

**Bleasdale Langhorne Creek Mulberry Tree Vineyard
Cabernet Sauvignon 98 £10–£11**
Here's a very dark and dense wine with complex, vegetal
complex aromas. It's hugely structured with concentrated
baked fruit with lashings of tar, leather and tobacco, and hot,
spicy length. It has ageing potential.
Oddbins

Brown Brothers Victoria Cabernet Sauvignon 98 £10–£11
An excellent, great-value wine, this Cabernet has a deep and
dense cigar box nose, with a mineral core. In the mouth it is very
savoury with deliciously ripe bramble and baked fruits and some
tar and eucalyptus. Although velvety, the tannins are very firm
and the wine has a wonderful structure and a long spicy finish.
This wine would work well with a beef casserole.
Woodford Bourne

**D'Arenberg McLaren Vale The High Trellis Cabernet
Sauvignon 98 £10–£11**
Mintiness evolves into eucalyptus on the nose of this very
well-made wine. On the palate there is a great weight and

Wake Up To Wakefield

Australia's most awarded wine-maker

International Wine Challenge, London
Medals Awarded
1999   Seven out of seven
2000   Ten out of ten

WAKEFIELD

1998

SHIRAZ
CABERNET

CLARE VALLEY

AUSTRALIA

Year after year, medal after medal

ripeness from firm blackcurrant fruit and a great grip of
supporting firm tannins. With a long finish, this is a perfect
wine for a leg of lamb. It will continue to improve and drink
well for many years yet.
Taserra

Angove's Sarnia Farm Padthaway Cabernet Sauvignon 96 £11–£12

Elegant vanilla, spice, mint and ripe red berry fruit aromas
appear on the nose of this enjoyable wine. Smooth and
mouthfilling with vanilla, spices and ripe blackcurrant flavours, well-balanced tannins it has a long mellow, warm
length that gives a glorious 'glow'.
O'Briens

Sandalford Mount Barker/Margaret River Cabernet Sauvignon 97 £12–£13

Lovely aromas of ripe blackberry fruits, spice and vanilla
intoduce a wine with flavours of black fruits, spices and black
pepper. This is a beautifully crafted wine of great style and
class. It should keep for another few years though it is drinking well now.
Irish Distillers

Wolf Blass President's Selection South Australia Cabernet Sauvignon 96 £12–£13
Well-made, in a beautifully structured classic style, this 96 has plenty of firm autumn fruits of figs, dates and damsons with lovely spice. It's beginning to develop much more complexity, so resist the temptation to drink immediately and you'll be well rewarded. Try it with fillets of beef.
Dillons

Maglieri McLaren Vale Cabernet Sauvignon 97 £13–£14
The aromas of ripe blackcurrants on the nose of this 97 are a pure expression of the Cabernet grape. The wine was oak-aged for 18 months and has an abundance of blackcurrants and touches of vanilla, from the oak, on the palate. Chewable and complex, with an elegant finish, this is a worthy match for roast fillet of beef.
Gleeson

Geoff Merrill Cabernet Sauvignon Reserve 95 £15–£16
Made from a limited production of premium Cabernet Sauvignon grapes selected from three areas in South Australia—Coonawarra, McLaren Vale and Goulburn Valley, this wine was barrel fermented and matured in new French and American oak for 31 months prior to bottling. The result is a delicious fruit-driven wine with a wonderful mix of cassis, baked red fruits and dark chocolate with pleasing notes of tar and tobacco from its time in wood. It has a long, lingering finish and still some time to go.
United Beverages

Ebenezer Estate Barossa Valley Cabernet Sauvignon 96 £18–£19
A very serious wine at a serious price, this Ebenezer deserves superlatives—stunning, seductive, memorable and worth every penny! The nose is complex and multi-flavoured and so is the palate, with intensely concentrated classic ripe fruit flavours of plums and spice and soft supple tannins, all perfectly integrated. It will continue to drink really well for some time. Well-flavoured dishes would go well with this delicious wine, but it can also be enjoyed on its own.
Allied Drinks

Orlando St Hugo Coonawarra Cabernet Sauvignon 93 £20–£21
When first released in 1980, Orlando St Hugo became a benchmark Cabernet Sauvignon. In a competitive field it is still a very high standard bearer for Cabernets from Down Under. While it has characteristic Australian abundant ripe blackberry fruit, this is tamed by a classy earthiness and spiciness that flatter rather than amplify the fruit flavours. It's the perfect drink with grilled meats and vegetables.
Irish Distillers

D'Arenberg The Coppermine Road McLaren Vale Cabernet Sauvignon 97 £22–£23
The name comes from a road adjoining the vineyard, which in fact has four different names along parts of its not very great length, which is somehow appropriate. It spends 18 months in new and used French and American oak and has a very complex palate with a great weight of fruit, layered with oak and mint. The wine is still very young with firm tannins. It is definitely one to keep in the cellar and enjoy over the next decade.
Taserra

Chile

Cabernet from Chile is very French in style. The wines have a classic claret profile but with riper fruit. The intense and luscious cassis fruit and smoky character from ageing in toasted barrels have herbaceous and herbal overtones and robust but ripe tannins.

Luis Felipe Edwards Pupilla Cabernet Sauvignon 99 £6–£7
Made from the fruit of relatively young vines, without any contact with wood, this is a very pleasant wine with the emphasis on freshness. It has upfront ripe brambles and blackcurrants with a steely mineral background. Drinking well now it has another two years to go.
Oddbins

Carmen Central Valley Cabernet Sauvignon 98 £7–£8
Here are style and elegance at a very good price. The wine has a silky, smooth texture with lots of ripe blackcurrant fruit, and some mint and vanilla. Try it with hearty casseroles or grilled vegetables.
Dillons

'The Cork Wine Merchants'

- Over 500 quality wines
- Quality staff on hand for advice
- 8 shops to choose from
- Full party/function service
- Wine consultancy service available
- Corporate and private tastings arranged
- Direct wine deliveries nationwide arranged
- Wholesale price-list for on-trade available on request
- Wine list available on request
- Wi\ne Club—Douglas and Bishopstown Wine Club

Main Office
Unit 27, St Patrick's Mill Douglas, Cork
Phone: (021) 489 5227/746
Fax: (021) 489 3391
Wine consultant—Gary O'Donovan 087 263 2211

Branches
Douglas (021) 436 3650 Bishopstown (021) 434 3416 Blackpool (021) 439 8177 Summerhill (021) 450 5444 Oliver Plunkett St (021) 427 7626 Shandon St (021) 439 9121 Midleton (021) 461 3001 Riversdale Shopping Centre (021) 461 3792

'We have all the wine in the world'

MOËT & CHANDON
Fondé en 1743

Nederburg

Barton & Guestier
La passion du vin depuis 1725

LUPÉ-CHOLET

I.L. RUFFINO

BLUE NUN®

CONTI SERRISTORI

FOUNDED IN 1850

CARMEN

SANDEMAN
EST 1790

BOLLA

MATEUS®
PRODUCED AND BOTTLED IN PORTUGAL

Señorío de los Llanos®

FETZER.

SANTA ROSA
ESTATE
Mendoza   Argentina

FONTANA CANDIDA   MONTECILLO

Fine wines from Edward Dillon & Co. Ltd.

Carta Vieja Cabernet Sauvignon Reserva 96 £7–£8
Grapes from the oldest vines are used for this Reserva from
Carta Vieja. It has full ripe fruit with a judicious amount of
toast and vanilla from careful oak maturation and a lovely
finish. Drink it before the the summer of 2001. It would be
perfect with veal or steak and kidney pie.
Barry & Fitzwilliam

**Concha y Toro Casillero del Diablo Cabernet Sauvignon 98
£7–£8**
A peppery wine with soft raspberries and blackcurrant
flavours, complemented by a good dose of oak, this will
reward decanting. It will drink well for two years.
Findlaters

**Errazuriz El Ceibo Estate Aconcagua Valley Cabernet
Sauvignon 98 £7–£8**
A classic and elegant wine, though still a little young, this is
great value for money. 20% was aged in oak barrels for about
eight months, resulting in a restrained and not overoaked
style with blackcurrant and red cherry fruit. Match it with
beef, game or strong cheeses.
Allied Drinks

San Pedro Cabernet Sauvignon Reserva 98 £7–£8
An inviting wine, in a ripe and supple, fruit-driven style, this
has abundant blackcurrants on the nose and palate and
softening tannins. Good value and quality, it will drink well for
two years and would be perfect with barbecued meats and
sausages.
Dunnes Stores

Viña Porta Cabernet Sauvignon 98 £7–£8
This Cabernet, sourced from the Maipo Valley, is rich in extract
with a good deal of very ripe blackberries with a hint of mint
and cedar wood. Classic and harmonious, with a long finish it
will be good for two years.
Taserra

Casa Lapostolle Cabernet Sauvignon 97 £8–£9
A value-for-money wine, this is rich and complex with brambles and black fruits, chocolate and toffee and also some mint
and spice. It has good supporting tannins and acidity and a
fruit-driven, long finish. Drink it from now to three years.
United Beverages

Miguel Torres Santa Digna Cabernet Sauvignon 99 £8–£9
Here'a a big wine, with an excellent weight of ripe, baked
plummy fruit, and some tar and chocolate flavours. Beautifully
balanced and structured, it's a bit young yet, but will improve
and soften out with time. It would be great with game and
barbecued or grilled meats.
Woodford Bourne

Santa Carolina Cabernet Sauvignon Reserva 98 £8–£9
A mouth-filling, juicy wine full of blackcurrant fruits, this
Reserva has a lovely supple finish. It should keep for up to
three years. Grilled lamb is a classic match.
TDL

Santa Rita 120 Cabernet Sauvignon 98 £8–£9
Offering complexity at a good-value price this is a supple
concentrated wine with lots of flavours — blackcurrant and
blackberry fruit, vanilla and spice plus a hint of chocolate. It
will drink well for another two years. Try it with kebabs and
pitta bread.
Gilbeys

Viña Tarapacá Cabernet Sauvignon Reserva 96 £8–£9
Fermented and macerated in stainless steel, and aged in
French and American oak barrels, this wine has luscious,
mouth-watering blackcurrant jammy fruit infused with spice.
A long, lingering finish rounds it off. It's a good partner for
roast rack of lamb.
Gleeson

Undurraga Cabernet Sauvignon Reserva 97 £8–£9
Classic and elegant, this Reserva has lovely ripe autumn fruits,
smoky tobacco box warmth and a long, mellow finish. It has
the potential to keep for two or more years and would be
perfect with pheasant and lentils.
United Beverages

**Carmen Maipo Valley Cabernet Sauvignon Reserve 97 £9–
£10**
A good, complex wine, this has concentrated flavours of
brambles, cherry and toffee plus spice, mint and pepper.
Softening tannins suggest that it will improve even more over
the next few years. Pair it with strong flavours such as roast

guinea fowl with bacon and rosemary, duck or very rich pasta
sauces.
Dillons

Alto de Terra Andina Valle de Cachapoal Cabernet Sauvignon Reserva 97 £10–£11

Made in a big, powerful style, this good value wine's fruit is
very ripe and almost sweet. With smooth tannins and a long
length, it packs a punch on the palate. It will continue to drink
well over the next two years. Partner it with highly flavoured
meat dishes such as lamb with ginger, cumin and coriander
salsa.
Irish Distillers

Canepa Private Reserve Cabernet Sauvignon 96 £10–£11

Classy and elegant, this is an upmarket intriguing wine. It has
wood smoke, sappy black fruits, bramble berries and pepperiness and will continue to develop over the next two years.
Partner it with Irish stew.
MacCormaic

Cousiño Macul Antiguas Reservas Cabernet Sauvignon 97 £10–£11

Excellent structure is the hallmark of wines from this winery,
one of the oldest in Chile—firm tannins, a good weight of
blackcurrant fruits and a long finish. With wild strawberries,
blackberries and mineral nuances, the fruit is enveloped in
oaky smoke. Still young, it will soften out with time. Drink it
with food, such as rack of lamb with herbs.
Ecock

Carmen Maipo Valley Grande Vidure Cabernet Reserve 94 £11–£12

This is an exciting blend of Cabernet Sauvignon and
Carmenère. It's medium-bodied and rounded with very sweet
blackcurrants on the nose and palate. There are also nuances
of toast and herbs. Try it with magret of duck and glazed
shallots for an impressive dinner party.
Dillons

Errazuriz Don Maximiano Estate Aconcagua Valley Cabernet Sauvignon Reserva 97 £12–£13

Made in a classic style, and offered at a great price, this wine
oozes elegance and finesse. Though the wine is aged in cask
for 14 months the oak does not overshadow the rich concen-

tration of mellow, black fruit flavours. Continue to drink this
delicious wine for three years plus.
Allied Drinks

☆ ☆ ☆

Montes Alpha Cabernet Sauvignon 97 £12–£13
One of Chile's great red wine, Montes Alpha is harmonious
and classic. It's a highly perfumed wine with bramble fruit,
subtle pepperiness and firm tannins. It should keep for four
years plus and is a testimony to Chile's potential. Try it with
roast duck with a spicy stuffing.
Grants

South Africa

Cabernet Sauvignon wines from the Cape are usually oaked
and full-bodied. The ripe blackcurrant fruit can be matched by
very firm tannins and sometime with vegetal and complex
flavours.

Long Mountain Western Cape Cabernet Sauvignon 99 £5–6
With summer and autumn fruits on the nose, and flavours of
bramble fruits, violets and cherry this is a great-value barbecue. It has good body and a very fruity finish.
Irish Distillers

Nederburg Paarl Cabernet Sauvignon 97 £7–£8
A splash of Merlot is added to this good value Cabernet for
extra fruit and drinkability. It is 60% matured in wood and has
delightful creamy aromas of vanilla and toffee. Full-bodied
and fruit-driven, with flavours of crushed strawberry and
blackberry fruit, it has great body and structure, good length
and a creamy, fruity finish. Be adventurous and try it with
grilled ostrich steaks or red meat.
Dillons

L'Avenir Cabernet Sauvignon 97 £10–£11
From a brilliant vintage, this is a good-quality, well-made wine,
with another two years to go. Some Merlot has been added to fill
out the mid-palate. Sweet cassis and rich blackcurrant fruit
mingle with spice, soft chocolate and a hint of mint, with a
long, velvety finish. It will keep for another two years or so.
Dunnes Stores

Plaisir de Merle Paarl Cabernet Sauvignon 96 £13–£14
Made by Stellenbosch Wine Farms in a soft, easy style, this
single-estate wine has ripe autumnal fruit aromas with a minty
character. Ripe blackcurrant fruit bursts through on the palate

with some spicy complexity. Well-rounded and balanced, with integrated fruit and spice, it has a nice long finish. Serve it with lamb casseroles (including rosemary), or braised mushrooms dishes,
Dillons

Saxenburg Private Collection Cabernet Sauvignon 95 £22–£23
A copybook example of high-quality South African Cabernet this wine could easily be taken for a fine Bordeaux. Its lovely, tangy blackcurrant fruit is complemented by rich oak. There is also a slightly stewed tea influence normally associated with Pinotage.
Fields

USA – California

California produces Cabernet Sauvignon wines with rich and intense aromas and bold flavours of spicy blackcurrant fruit and dark chocolate, with a firm tannic structure. The wines can be powerful, with warming alcohol, yet maintain a reserved austerity. The more serious and tannic wines can age for five to ten years.

Vendange California Cabernet Sauvignon 97 £6–£7
If you're accustomed to thinking that good Californian Cabernets are expensive, think again! This reasonably priced example has intriguing, complex aromas and flavours — cigar box, blackcurrant and smoke, with a ripe palate balanced with softening tannins. This is a refined and elegant wine that will keep everyone happy. It's a good party wine and should go on being a crowd pleaser for up to two years. For a simple meal try it with hamburgers or pasta with meatballs.
Barry & Fitzwilliam

Ernest & Julio Gallo Sonoma County Cabernet Sauvignon 94 £9–£10
The Gallo company grows the Cabernet Sauvignon grapes for this wine in the Cabernet-friendly Alexander Valley, which results in plenty of ripe blackcurrant and medicinal aromas. With firm tannins and loads of ripe fruit, spice, herbs and smoky bacon flavours, it has a really nice character and finish.
Irish Distillers

**Fetzer Valley Oaks Grande Vidura Cabernet Sauvignon 97
£9–£10**
Fetzer sources the grapes for this wine from three different
parts of California—the north coast, Lodi and San Luis Obispo.
Very fruity and full bodied at present, the wine has well-knit
delicious blackberry fruit and some nice toasty oak. It should
develop well over the next two years or longer and is great
with steaks.
Dillons

**Ironstone Vineyards Sierra Foothills Cabernet Sauvignon 97
£10–£11**
The Sierra Foothills, where the 1848 gold rush started, are
intensely hot during the day but cooled by breezes at night—
ideal conditions for ripening Cabernet Sauvignon. The quality
of the grapes comes through in the ripe blackcurrant aromas
with a touch of vanilla and mint in this made-for-food wine. It
has a weighty mouthfeel of ripe blackcurrant fruit with hints
of spice and pepper and a touch of vanilla. Tannins balance the
fruit and the finish is very satisfying. It should improve for
about three years.
Gilbeys

Stratford California Cabernet Sauvignon 98 £10–£11
Here's a flavoursome and intense wine of blackcurrants, with
hints of black pepper and mint, made in an elegant, fruit-
driven style. It will drink well now and over the next year.
Barry & Fitzwilliam

Sebastiani Sonoma County Cabernet Sauvignon 96 £11–£12
Sonoma has the ideal conditions for growing Cabernet—
warm days, cool nights and the gravelly soil that Cabernet
loves. This one has wonderful sweet blackcurrant richness on
the nose. It's rich on the palate, too, with a lovely concoction
of juicy blackberries and a hint of smoky bacon. With nice
mouthfeel and great length, it's a dinner party wine that will
age well for about two years.Try it with roasted lamb or
grilled meats
Barry & Fitzwilliam

**Wente Vineyards Charles Wetmore Reserve Cabernet
Sauvignon 96 £11–£12**
This is a good-quality, mid-price Californian Cabernet from
the Wente estate which was founded in 1883 and is reputed to

be tbe oldest winery in the USA. Big, broad and spicy, it has a
rich blackcurrant nose and intense, good sweet fruit — very
flavoursome. A good example of new, more subtle, Californian Cabernet, it will mature for four years. Match it with
duck with a fruit sauce.
Dunnes Stores

**Beringer Vineyards California Cabernet Sauvignon 96 £12–
£13**
Beringer produces 1.3 million cases of wine a year, but being
on the large side doesn't mean that they stint on quality. Aged
in small French and American oak barrels, this wonderful
Cabernet has a classic style — a coolness and restraint on the
palate — yet delivers excellence in everything, everywhere! A
super wine for the most discerning palates, it has so much
character. It will mature for three years.
Allied Drinks

**Bonterra North Coast Organic Cabernet Sauvignon 95 £12–
£13**
Organic pioneering company Fetzer aims to extend their
range of wines made from organic grapes. It's a worthy cause,
but does the wine live up to the aspiration? The answer has to
be 'Yes' — it has a lovely concentration of ripe strawberry fruit
on the nose and classic Cabernet Sauvignon flavours of
blackcurrant on the palate. This is an elegant wine, but still a
little immature and in need of some time to soften. Keep it for
two or three years.
Dillons

**J. Lohr Seven Oaks Estates Paso Robles Cabernet Sauvignon
97 £16–£17**
Jerry Lohr takes the grapes for this excellent wine from his
Seven Oaks vineyard in Paso Robles, where he also grows
Merlot and Cabernet Franc. The nose smacks of loads of ripe
blackcurrant fruit and a subtle touch of liquorice with whiffs of
spice. Restrained yet typical Cabernet Sauvignon, with soft
integrated tannins and subtle use of wood, it has a smooth
finish. It's a classic wine and should mature for three more
years.
TDL

Ernest & Julio Gallo Sonoma Frei Ranch Vineyard Cabernet Sauvignon 93 £17–£18
Sonoma Cabernets are wonderfully fruity in their youth, but have the ability to mature and evolve. This one is a magnificent, highly concentrated classic Cabernet. While there are oodles of blackcurrants and a nice touch of oak, restraint is the keyword. The fruit is not overdone, but is really well knit into the structure. It has great tannins and fabulous length—a real treat. Buy up lots of it and enjoy it maturing over the next three years.
Irish Distillers

Cabernet blends

Australia

Angove's Stonegate The Arch Cabernet/Shiraz 98 £7–£8
Barrel-aged for a year, this blend is well made and great value. It has baked summer berries on the nose with a smoky spicy aroma. Mouthfilling and weighty, with ripe bramble fruits and some creamy vanilla, the flavours linger on. Char-grilled lamb steaks would be a good accompaniment.
O'Briens

Fiddlers Creek Cabernet/Shiraz 98 £8–£9
Fiddler's Creek is in a gold-mining area in the Pyrenees, Western Victoria. After two miners struck gold, their jubilant fiddle-playing attracted others to the creek, hence the name. Winemakers were also attracted to the area, because of its cool climate. This blend of Cabernet and Shiraz has a very appealing initial 'sweetness' of fruit on the palate that is unusual. It's classic Aussie, beefy but attractive, finishing warm and smooth.
Bacchus

Hardys Nottage Hill Cabernet Sauvignon/Shiraz 99 £8–£9
A fabulous wine of finesse and elegance, this classic Aussie blend reflects great attention to detail in winemaking. It has a texture which is fleshy and meaty yet smooth. With an abundance of attractive rich berry fruit flavours, it lingers on and on to a mellow finish.
Allied Drinks

Yaldara Reserve Cabernet/Merlot 98 £8–£9

This classic blend has fruits of the forest in abundance, with touches of leather and spice, and soft, gentle tannins. It has a smooth finish. Partner it with marinated, grilled lamb steaks and a herb relish.
Barry & Fitzwilliam

Evans & Tate Margaret River Barrique 61 Cabernet/Merlot 98 £9–£10

A blend of 70% Cabernet and 30% Merlot, this is a beautifully structured wine which is rich and complex. It has a gamy and savoury edge, yet it is a fruit-driven style with an abundance of plums, damsons and blackcurrant fruits, and some spice and vanilla, ending in a long, flavoursome finish. It will reward keeping over the next year or so. Drink it with gourmet sausages or pork.
United Beverages

Dromana Estate Mornington Peninsula Cabernet/Merlot 98 £12–£13

From a very fine vintage, this wine was made from low-yielding older vines and aged for 18 months in French barriques. It has layers of flavours with a huge weight of ripe baked blackcurrant and black cherry fruits, smoky with some cigar box and leather and a spicy finish. Delicious and warm, elegant and seductive, it has the potential to improve further in bottle as it ages.
Wines Direct

Bethany Schrapel Family Vineyards Barossa Valley Cabernet/Merlot 98 £13–£14

A Bordeaux blend, which also includes 10% Cabernet Franc, this is a big, mouth-filling, delicious wine with treacle and Christmas cake on the nose. Full-bodied with an excellent weight of ripe blackcurrant fruits, tar and chocolate, it has great structure, good length and a fruity finish.
O'Briens

Ch. Reynella Basket-Pressed Cabernet/Merlot 96 £15–£16

Ch. Reynella is one of the few Australian wineries still to use a basket press for rich, soft pressings. This super wine was

matured in French and American oak for 14 months. With an
elegant texture, intensely creamy and smooth, it is packed full
of classic flavours of blackcurrant, cassis, chocolate and cedar
wood. Long and mellow with a spicy finish, it is drinking well
now and will continue for a few years yet. Venison and
redcurrant casserole would match it well.
Allied Drinks

Jamieson's Run Coonawarra Cabernet/Shiraz/Merlot 97 £10–£11

Jamieson's Run is named after the original property where
Mildara was established in 1888. This blend has been matured
in small French and American oak casks, typically for about
twelve months. A complex and full-bodied wine, its strong
eucalyptus, mint and ripe red berry fruits, lots of spice and
well-integrated oak make for a long lingering finish that will
get better in time. Enjoy it with fresh tomato and aubergine
pasta.
Gilbeys

Peter Lehmann The Barossa Mentor 93 £21–£22

The blend for Mentor changes from year to year. This 93,
made from Cabernet Sauvignon, Malbec, Shiraz and Merlot, is
a deep and concentrated wine with intense baked fruits —
damsons and plums — also mint, spice, cinnamon and chocolate
plus a slightly earthy or smoky character. The finish is long.
This big wine has complexity and was built to last for another
two to three years. Drink it with spicy beef.
United Beverages

Peter Lehmann The Barossa Mentor 94 £21–£22

Made from 67% Cabernet and 33% Malbec, the 94 Mentor is a
beautifully crafted wine of style and class, full-bodied and
weighty with pure (as opposed to jammy) fruit with lovely
flavours of vanilla from a judicious use of new and used oak.
Very well balanced it's still very young — it will become
something very special over the next four to five years.
United Beverages

Yalumba The Signature Cabernet/Shiraz 95 £21–£22

The Signature is Yalumba's finest red wine of the vintage,
hand selected and matured for 28 months in American oak.
Each release bears a different signature of members of the
Hill-Smith and the Yalumba corporate family. A blend of
Cabernet and Shiraz, in varying proportions, it is now sourced
from Coonawarra and Barossa. The 95 Signature, released in

1999, are very fresh, ripe blackberry fruit flavours, with classic mint and chocolate nuances, supported by a good grip of tannins.
Cassidy

Chile

Mont Gras Ninquén Barrel Select Premium Red 97 £13–£14
Big, rich and intense, this classic Bordeaux blend of Cabernet and Merlot has exotic and opulent black fruits and eucalyptus, with firm tannins to hold the fruit in check and a peppery finish. It will keep and improve for some time yet — up to four years.
Maxxium

South Africa

Nederburg Cabernet Sauvignon/Shiraz 97 £6–£7
Lovely, ripe, juicy berry fruits, with a smattering of green peppers, are well balanced in this pleasant blend. The wine is very smooth and has a quite remarkable length of flavour. Drinking well now, it's a good match for pork or poultry.
Dillons

Bon Courage Cabernet Sauvignon/Shiraz 98 £8–£9
The spiciness from the Shiraz blends well with the fruitiness of the Cabernet in this youthful wine. It's very fruity, with red berries and summer pudding fruits, and can only improve over the next year.
Gleeson

Malbec

Argentina

Malbec is probably Argentina's finest red grape variety and in its hot climate and irriagated vineyards it arguably does much better than in its homeland of South-West France. The fruits can appear hard at first and the style can be a little austere with black tarry fruit and spice on the palate but ageing in American oak helps to mellow the tannins.

Etchart Rio de Plata Malbec 96 £4–£5
A very distinctive wine, which has matured and developed nicely for the price, this has oodles of ripe bramble and juicy plum fruit with a streak of herbal flavours running through. Try it with lamb kebabs.
Irish Distillers

Santa Julia Mendoza Malbec 99 £6–£7
More earth than fruit appears on the nose of this good value
wine. It is well balanced, with firm tannins giving good grip,
and has a long finish.
Taserra

Stowells Malbec/Tempranillo nv £6–£7
With plums on the nose and soft, ripe fruit on the palate this
good-value wine is for everyday, easy drinking with simple
food.
Allied Drinks

TriVento Malbec 98 £6–£7
An abundance of juicy ripe black fruit is balanced nicely by a
fresh crisp finish in this well-priced wine. Drinking well now it
is still youthful and should develop over the next two years.
Findlaters

Trapiche Oak Cask Malbec 97 £7–£8
Deep damson in colour, this wine has nice, complex, earthy
aromas. Black summer fruit flavours, with a hint of chocolate
and spice, are backed by firm tannins giving good grip, and
the wine has a nice balance of wood and spice. It has a long,
lingering finish.
United Beverages

Valentin Bianchi Malbec 97 £7–£8
This Malbec has a fresh fennel nose. Lots of squashed sweet
blackcurrant fruit and morello cherry flavours end in a long
finish.
Oddbins

Viña de Santa Isabel Malbec 97 £6–£7
An ideal quaffer for parties and receptions this Malbec is made
in an easy-drinking style with some complexity and lots of
spicy fruity flavours.
Dunnes Stores

Weinert Pedro del Castillo Malbec 98 £8–£9
A delicious, unusual wine with great structure, this wine has a
big blackcurrant liqueur nose, with mint and eucalyptus. Its
excellent weight of ripe blackberry fruits, with a hint of mint
and eucalyptus, ends in a dry fruity finish.
Woodford Bourne

Finca Flichman Malbec Reserva 98 £9–£10
Flying winemaker Hugh Ryman has been working with Finca
Flichman since 1997 as part of a growing trend in Argentina to
make smoother, export-driven wines. This Malbec is laden
with ripe, dark berry fruits and eucalyptus. It would go well
with Mexican food.
TDL

Alamos Ridge Malbec 97 £10–£11
A deep and dense wine, with a serious character, this full-
bodied Malbec is quite beefy with lots of gravy and
eucalyptus. The creamy mouthfeel exudes spicy plum pudding
flavours.
Searson

Luigi Bosca Malbec 93 £13–£14
Long ageing in wood and bottle has benefited this wine by
taming the firm tannins and amplifying the black fruit and
medicinal qualities. This medicine is good for you. It's
remarkably seductive and at its best — drink it before the end
of 2001.
Maxxium

Weinert Malbec 95 £13–£14
This wine is perfect for drinking now. It has huge juicy
flavours of sweet wild strawberries, blackberries and cedar
which taper into a superb, smooth, perfectly balanced finish.
It's really good stuff from one of the best Argentinian
producers.
Woodford Bourne

Merlot

Argentina

Santa Julia Mendoza Merlot 98 £6–£7
With an array of ripe bramble fruit, a hint of cedar and oak
this wine has a typical elegant Merlot nose. It is packed with
fruit flavours, and is smooth and supple with a long and
pleasant finish.
Taserra

Australia

**Miranda High Country King Valley Owens Valley Merlot 98
£8–£9**
Aromas of ripe blackcurrant fruit with a hint of chocolate and
mint lead to a smooth fruity palate, and a long, clean finish.
The tannins are firm, and the alcohol is very evident. This wine
may benefit from decanting, as it may throw a sediment. It
will drink nicely for two years.
Taserra

Schinus Merlot 99 £9–£10
Made by Garry Crittenden in an upfront style, this Merlot has
appealing, ripe, soft plummy fruit, with a touch of earthiness
and eucalyptus. It's a light, easy-drinking wine and should be
drunk young.
Wines Direct

Wolf Blass South Australian Merlot 97 £10–£11
A delicious, full-bodied, big wine, this Merlot is beautifully
structured. It has strawberries and creamy vanilla aromas. The
tastes are more complex with a mixture of plummy fruits,
spice and creamy vanilla flavours with a touch of meatiness, all
ending with great length.
Dillons

Tatchilla Clarendon Vale Vineyard Merlot 98 £14–£15
A typical full-bodied, voluptuous Aussie wine this Merlot has
complex flavours of violets and blackberries bursting with
luscious ripeness. Ripe, firm tannins support the opulent fruit.
The finish is very long. Try this delicious wine with barbecued
ribs or stir-fry beef and peppers.
O'Briens

Chile

In Chile for many years Merlot was used as the name for a
different grape, Carmenère. Nowadays, true Merlot from
Chile produces chunky concentrated ripe wines full of black
cherries, bitter chocolate and Victoria plums with firm but

friendly tannins. It matures more quickly than Cabernet
Sauvignon.

Concha y Toro Sunrise Merlot 99 £6–£7
This is a very agreeable fruity Merlot with ripe plum and
roasted red pepper flavours, and a long finish. It will drink
well for another two years.
Findlaters

Viña La Risa La Palmeria Merlot 99 £6–£7
Definitely a winter wine, this Merlot is gutsy, full bodied and
meaty. Appealing and intense, it has lots of baked black fruits
and some tar. It will age for up to two years.
Oddbins

Carmen Central Valley Merlot 98 £7–£8
This is a delicious, lively Merlot with super-ripe blackberry
fruit in good concentration. It's minty, with a touch of leather,
and an underlying toastiness. Try it with lighter meats or
baked tunafish.
Dillons

Concha y Toro Casillero del Diablo Merlot 98 £7–£8
This good-value wine has cherry sundae ice-cream flavour
with gentle hints of roasted nutmeg and vanilla.
Findlaters

Errazuriz El Descanso Estate Curicó Merlot 99 £7–£8
An excellent example of well made Merlot, this wine is
concentrated with delicious lingering flavours of black fruit
and mellow notes of coffee and chocolate. It's a forward and
fruit driven style. Try it with a plate of mixed salami antipasti.
Allied Drinks

Viña Tarapacá Merlot 98 £7–£8
Soft nutmeg and cinnamon notes spice up this fruity, gutsy
wine. Great value at the price, it is drinking well now. Try it
with pizza.
Gleeson

Santa Carolina Merlot Reservado 98 £8–£9
A charming fruity Merlot this has a good weight of crushed
strawberry and blackberry fruit. It's mouthfilling, with good
length and will drink well for another two years. Match it with
calf's liver with a red onion confit.
TDL

Santa Rita Merlot Reserva 99 £8–£9
Self-confident and assured, this is a perfumed and fruity wine
of violets, ripe plums, cherries and blackberries. Young and
juicy, it will improve over this year and would be great with
homemade lasagne.
Oddbins

Mont Gras Merlot Reserva 98 £9–£10
Intense and velvety textured, this is a very seductive wine. A
small percentage of Cabernet Sauvignon was blended to add
complexity to the Merlot. The wine has purple plum flavours
with a touch of pepper and will age well for up to three years.
It would be a good match for grilled tuna steak.
Maxxium

Casa Lapostolle Cuvée Alexandre Merlot 97 £13–£14
Made from low-yielding 50-year-old vines, and aged in small
French oak barrels, this is a mouthfilling Merlot, fruity and
rich with pronounced plum, damson and Christmas pudding
elements. It is soft with a long, pleasant finish. It will keep and
improve for three years or so.
United Beverages

New Zealand

The Merlot vines are maturing in New Zealand, and are now
producing grapes that are ripe in fruit with rich fruit perfume,
rather than semi-ripe and vegetal. Refreshing acidity and
plummy flavours are well balanced by firm but accessible
tannins.

Saint Clair Marlborough Merlot 99 £8–£9
This Merlot has full ripe flavours of blackberries, damsons, figs
and assertive green peppers. Elegant, quite full-bodied and
satisfying, it has a very persistent finish which goes on and on.
Try it with pasta in a spicy sausage sauce.
Greenhills

Saint Clair Rapaura Reserve Merlot 99 £12–£13
A superb Merlot from New Zealand, this 99 has an excellent
weight of ripe strawberries and blackberries well integrated
with the wood, which gives a lovely creaminess. Elegant and
delicious, it has great length and finish. It is drinking well now
but will improve over the next few years. Divine!
Greenhills

South Africa

Jordan Merlot 94 £15–£16
This is a complex broody wine which needs careful decanting.
It is intense but reserved — classy and elegant in its restraint.
The flavours are of red and blackberry fruits with a sappy bite,
and long ageing has softened the tannins. Try it with grilled
red meat.
Maxxium

Meerlust Merlot 95 £16–£17
A sturdy wine, with still gripping tannins, this is is a classy
Merlot, with fresh tangy plums which soften to fleshier fruit.
It's a good match for beef stroganoff or Irish farmhouse
cheeses.
Febvre

USA – California

Ernest & Julio Gallo Turning Leaf Merlot 97 £8–£9
The giant producer Gallo turned quality up a notch in their
Turning Leaf series. The Merlot has complex aromas and
flavours — spicy plums on the nose and concentrated ripe
summer red fruit flavours with a touch of fruit cake. Well-
integrated oak and soft tannins produce an elegant wine that
should suit most occasions when a fruity, well-structured,
delicious wine is called for.
Irish Distillers

Wente Vineyards Crane Ridge Reserve Merlot 97 £11–£12
Fourth-generation Californian wine producers Wente
produced the first Californian Chardonnay in 1936. Better
known for their white wines, this lovely Merlot enhances the
family reputation. A dry wine, well structured and laden with
warm, spicy, soft-berried fruit, it is velvety and mellow, with a
delicious fruit finish and excellent length. Keep it for around
two years.
Dunnes Stores

Clos du Bois Sonoma County Merlot 97 £13–£14
Clos du Bois is well known for its Merlot — at one time the
company owned more Merlot vineyards in California than
any other producer. Such long experience bears fruit in this
initially shy wine. The fruit slowly emerges and evolves, with
peppery spices on the palate asserting themselves. An elegant
and restrained style, more classy Bordeaux than California, it's
in peak condition and would be wonderful with fillet of beef
or grilled lamb cutlets with rosemary.
Grants

Pinotage

Pinotage, a grape unique to South Africa, is a crossing of
Cinsault with Pinot Noir developed by Professor Perold in
1925 at Stellenbosch University. The wine styles vary from
flamboyantly ripe with a paint-like pungency to rich, deeply
coloured with a wild fruitiness but always with an underlying

smouldering volcanic smokiness. The wines have a curious tendency to mature into a toffee and marshmallow softness.

South Africa

Cape Indaba Pinotage 98 £6–£7
A percentage of the proceeds of the Cape Indaba range go to fund wine apprentice scholarships for South Africans. Their 97 Pinotage is very fruity. Mixed berry fruits bounce out of the glass — it has a very fruity palate with a delicious touch of mint and is best enjoyed young. Try it with barbecues or grilled meats.
Barry & Fitzwilliam

Beyers Truter Pinotage nv £7–£8
From Stellenbosch this is classic stuff so typical of its variety and origin — rubber, stewed tea, leather, pink elastic bandage — the works! It's not the richest wine but for the Pinotage lover it's great value. Try it with hamburgers
Tesco

Cape Mountain Pinotage 98 £7–£8
Summer pudding with vanilla custard? Actually, yes — a mélange of berry fruits combines with gentle vanilla notes in this very pleasant wine.
Gleeson

Clos Malverne Basket Pressed Pinotage 98 £8–£9
For a Pinotage, this wine is big and broad. It's spicy with a good weight of cassis, brambles and fruits of the forest plus some earthiness. Nicely balanced, it is very good value. Try it with chunky grilled sausages.
Dunnes Stores

Groot Constantia Pinotage 95 £11–£12
Herbal, vegetal aromas reflect the maturity and development of this wine. There is more fruit on the palate than on the nose — raspberries and redcurrants with vegetal nuances of truffles and olives and lots of spice. It has style, elegance and character while retaining a subtlety. A match for beef in Guinness.
Irish Distillers

Pinot Noir

Australia

The first inkling that Australia could produce a serious Pinot Noir came when Tyrrells 76 Pinot Noir won the wine Olympics in Paris in 1981 beating off competition from Burgundy. The wines are perfumed with raspberry jam aromas. Flavours of melted milk chocolate and soft strawberries with a creamy, silky texture are sometimes accompanied by smoky oak. On the cooler island of Tasmania the wines have a mintier and herbaceous style with crisp acidity and refreshing raspberry fruit.

Pipers Brook Tasmania Pellion Pinot Noir 98 £15–£16
Fantasic value for such a quality, Burgundian-style Pinot this 98 has an elegant nose of crushed strawberry fruit with a hint of cinnamon. It's a delicious wine with a good weight of ripe soft berried fruits, well integrated with the vanilla flavours from the wood and balancing tannins. This lovely, elegant wine's soft velvety flavours linger on. It's quite young yet but will develop further.
Irish Distillers

New Zealand

The cool climate in New Zealand has produced some exciting Pinot Noir wines. They have a herbal, strawberry and spearmint quality. Chewy, cherry fruit and coffee and chocolate sometimes appear.

Babich Winemakers' Reserve Pinot Noir 98 £11–£12
A premium quality, limited edition from Malborough, this Pinot shows how far New Zealand has come in terms of red wine production. It has all the subtlety and complexity expected from a well made Pinot, with a slightly floral, raspberry nose, and very ripe redcurrant and raspberry flavours. It is rich and balanced, with well-integrated oak, a silky soft texture and excellent. length. Try it with duck or roast lamb.
Gleeson

USA – California

Buena Vista Carneros Pinot Noir 96 £9–£10
Founded in 1857, Buena Vista was California's first premium winery. The Pinot Noir grapes for this wine are grown in Carneros, one of the best Californian sites for Pinot. An

inviting nose promises a taste of things to come — spicy sausage/bratwurst, smoky salami flavours and a hint of fungal undergrowth. There is also some ripe redcurrant fruit with a savoury bite, a good balance of fruit and acidity, and a decent finish. Age this one for up to two years.
Greenhills

Kendall-Jackson Vintner's Reserve Pinot Noir 97 £13–£14
Pinot Noir plantings in California have been overtaken by Merlot and Zinfandel. Pinot is a difficult grape to grow and vinify and has to be planted in the right spot, so a lot of winemakers give it a wide berth. Kendall-Jackson's Pinot is impressive, however, with ripe red berry fruits and some added complexity, with maturing compost heap aromas. The flavours evolve on the palate and finish meaty and savoury. It's a little bit pricey, but worth it. Try it with roast salmon.
Cassidy

USA – Oregon

King Estate Oregon Pinot Noir 96 £20–£21
Oregon's reputation for wine rests on its Pinot Noirs. Its climate is cooler and damper than California (and much more like Pinot's native Burgundy), and the Pinot vines struggle to ripen. It pays off. This wine's nose is very farmyardy, with wet saddle, tar and liquorice to boot. A dry wine, with attractive strawberry, baked fruit and spice flavours, it's soft and elegant, yet complex, with a steely mineral background. It has a dry, fruity finish.
TDL

Shiraz/Syrah

Argentina

Shiraz is called by its original French name, Syrah, in South America's largest wine-producing country. The wines show ripe bramble berry fruit flavours with an oak-influenced tobacco leaf or cigar box bouquet.

Finca Flichman Syrah 96 £7–£8
Flichman is one of the leading exporters of wine from Argentina. Their 96 Syrah is a big, very concentrated, wine with lots of rich ripe spicy blackberry fruits and a flavoursome fruity finish. Serve it with roasts or cheese.
TDL

Marañon Syrah 98 £7–£8
Made for Marañon by Australian winemaker Linley Schultz, the 1998 Syrah has full rich flavours of pepper and liquorice

with blackberry and plum fruit. Try it with winter stew or a
spicy buffet casserole.
Barry & Fitzwilliam

> **Navarro Correas** is one of the leading wine producers
> in Argentina. Master of Wine Martin Moran (then with
> Gilbeys, now an independent consultant) helped them
> to develop a range for export, under the 'Correas'
> label, two of which are featured below..

Correas Syrah/Sangiovese 96 £6–£7
Argentina uses the Old World name 'Syrah' rather than New
World 'Shiraz' for this classic grape variety. Here it is blended
with Sangiovese to give attractive cherry aromas and flavours,
along with soft blackberries and a touch of typical Shiraz spice.
It's most enjoyable and has a nice lengthy finish. Try it with
barbecued meats.
Gilbeys

Correas Estate-bottled Syrah 97 £7–£8
Made by Alfredo Despons, this is a delicious Syrah with its
aromas of vanilla and strawberries, sprinkled with pepper.
Ripe summer red fruits are nicely balanced by the tannins. It
has a very pleasing, lingering finish.
Gilbeys

Australia

Australian Shiraz wines typically have ripe tannins, super-ripe
opulent fruit and concentrated flavours.

☆ ☆

Jindalee Shiraz 99 £7–£8
Black Forest gateau in a glass! Delightful aromas of black
cherries and dark chocolate suggest great flavours and the
wine lives up to the promise. Delicious, seductive and full of
character it has a delicate balance of mouthwatering fresh ripe
blackberry flavours and tannins.
Koala

Lindemans Bin 50 Shiraz 98 £7–£8
Lindemans have had great success with their Bin range. Their
Bin 50 Shiraz has plum and spice aromas with soft summer
fruit flavours, and a touch of liquorice, nicely balanced by
tannins and acidity. Pleasantly full in the mouth, it has a soft
appealing finish. It's a good match for roast meats, particularly
pork or try it with spicy beef and chilli beans.
Gilbeys

McWilliam's Hanwood Shiraz 98 £7–£8
A rich, ripe and robust Shiraz, with vibrant spicy blackcurrant
flavours and a touch of oak, this is good value wine and is
drinking well now. Try it with rack of lamb or veal.
TDL

Baileys Shiraz 97 £8–£9
For sipping by the fire on a dark winter evening, this Shiraz is
better than central heating! It has lots of peppery spice on the
nose with cigar box in the background. Moist savoury tobacco
leaf flavours and big tannins give plenty to chew on.
Koala

Kingston Estate Murray Valley Shiraz 97 £8–£9
Kingston is a small estate in New South Wales producing true-
to-Aussie-style varietals with consistent good quality across
the range. Their Shiraz has spice, leather and blackberry
flavours, with nice oak nuances and a long, peppery finish. It
would be great with red meat and pasta.
Gleeson

McGuigan Millennium Shiraz 99 £8–£9
Brian McGuigan is one of Australia's best-known winemakers,
consistently winning awards. His Millennium Shiraz is dense,
dark and concentrated with blackberry, plum and vanilla
flavours, a spicy finish and good length. Try it with mildly
spiced Indian dishes.
Barry & Fitzwilliam

**Miranda King Valley Kieur River Valley High Country
Shiraz 97 £8–£9**
The High Country of King Valley is in Victoria. Miranda have
a small estate here and the wine is supplemented with grapes
from Kiewa. Aged in new American oak barrels this 97 has a
huge Shiraz varietal nose of chocolate, hot peppers, spice,
cedar wood and brambles. Strong, fruity flavours of plums
and damsons are layered with spice and a hint of chocolate
with a long and complex finish. This is a very impressive wine
for the price. It's a good partner for spicy dishes or traditional
beef or lamb.
Taserra

**Tyrrell's Old Winery McLaren Vale/Hunter Valley Shiraz 97
£8–£9**
The Tyrrell family is one of Australia's oldest wine-producers
dating back to 1870. Many of their great Shirazes are blends

from different regions in Australia and this one is a real crowd-pleaser. Aged in American and French oak, it is bursting with ripe blackberry fruit, well balanced by soft tannins. It would be ideal for a small party and does not need food.
Maxxium

Baileys 1920's Block Shiraz 95 £12–£14
When Rothburys bought this estate a question mark hovered over the 1920s vines that grow this wine. But they survived to produce this 1995 vintage. It's a super, old-style wine with a big sweaty and eucalyptus nose dashed with tar. Complex, spicy, Christmas cake flavours fill the mouth.
Koala

Cranswick Estate Nine Pines Vineyard Shiraz 98 £9–£10
A most intriguing wine, this has so much plum and damson fruit it could be confused with Merlot, and the pepper usually expected from Shiraz takes a back seat. It's got a very long finish and would be a good match for richly flavoured lamb dishes.
MacCormaic

Wakefield Clare Valley Shiraz 99 £9–£10
This typical Australian Shiraz is made from grapes grown in terra rossa soils (red earth over limestone). Oak barrel matured, it is warm and rich with plenty of mouthfilling, chewy, classic black fruit and pepper, and is long and lingering. Try it with steak in a peppercorn sauce.
Koala

Wyndham Estate Bin 555 Shiraz 97 £9–£10
A very typical up-front Australian Shiraz, laden with ripe blackberry fruits and spice, with a long finish this is just right for those who like a big wine with a huge whack of alcohol. It's especially good for winter nights when you need some extra warmth.
Irish Distillers

Milbrovale Owens Family Hunter Valley Shiraz 98 £9–£10
Definitely a winter warmer, this Shiraz was made from handpicked low-yielding vines, and matured in one and two-year-old French oak. It has enticing, lively flavours with lots of spice and baked fruit flavours.
Koala

Brown Brothers Shiraz 98 £10–£11

John Brown made his first wines in the King Valley Victoria in 1889. Today the fourth and fifth generations continue to operate the winery. Partial fermentation and maturation in oak barrels bring out the varietal and regional flavours of this fruity, succulent spicy Shiraz. It's an ideal partner for a solid, classic roast beef — allow at least an hour for it to open up after uncorking — that way the flavours will emerge as soon as you serve the wine.

Woodford Bourne

d'Arenberg McLaren Vale The Footbolt Old Vine Shiraz 98 £10–£11

The oldest Shiraz blocks at d'Arenberg were already planted by the turn of the last century, and still contribute to this wine. D'Arenberg like to give their wines a name with a story and this one is named after a racehorse. It has very concentrated black summer fruit aromas followed by complex flavours of damson fruit with layers of spice and vanilla, balanced by firm tannins, with a long finish.

Taserra

McGuigan Shareholders' Shiraz 97 £10–£11

With super, dense black fruits, spice, leather and a peppery finish this wine offers good complexity at a reasonable price. It's a very traditional Australian Shiraz, and it will drink well over the next few years. Try it with a robust beef casserole.

Barry & Fitzwilliam

Wolf Blass Shiraz 97 £10–£11

The producer, Wolf Blass, made a huge contribution to the revolution in Australian winemaking which introduced fruit-driven friendly wines for early drinking. With warm, mellow, spicy, earthy flavours this wine has a velvety, chocolate mouthfeel, well rounded tannins and a long, lingering finish. Try it with barbecued lamb.

Dillons

Wolf Blass President's Selection Shiraz 96 £12–£13

Here's a very typical characterful and stylish Australian Shiraz. It has pronounced chocolate and spice on the nose and very ripe cocentrated fruit flavours with spice and pepper. It's an excellent wine, but still very young so try to hold it for a year or two before enjoying it. Try it with beef fillet in soy and garlic.

Dillons

Bethany Schrapel Family Vineyards Barossa Shiraz 97 £13–£14

Here is another example of a well-crafted delicious Australian Shiraz true to the style of the Barossa region. Powerful aromas of jammy, black summer fruit, spice, and pepper emerge from this still developing wine. Its lovely ripe fruit flavours are shot through with spice and mint, finishing with warmth and elegance. It would be good with beef or what about cheddar cheese?

O'Briens

Maglieri McLaren Vale Shiraz 97 £13–£14

After aromas of blackberries and spice, black fruits explode on the palate — don't drink this warm sturdy wine too quickly — savour the dense fruit on the palate and the spicy finish. It will drink well for another two years and could stand up to mildly spicy dishes.

Gleeson

Penfolds Kalimna Bin 28 96 £13–£14

According to Penfolds' chief winemaker, John Duval, 96 was an exceptional vintage with the fruit slowly reaching full ripeness over a long, cool growing season. Warm weather towards the end of the season gave the fruit 'an extra dimension of complexity and maturity'. This 100% Shiraz from Penfolds' premier vineyard, Kalimna, in the Northern Barossa Valley, was matured for 12 months in American oak. Black fruit, chocolate and spice plus vanilla, smooth tannins and a long, lovely, finish combine to make it a stunner. Try it with osso bucco.

Findlaters

Penny's Hill McLaren Vale Shiraz 98 £14–£15

A muscular wine with big chunky appeal, dark and dense and a lovely long finish, this Shiraz was made by Susi and Tony Parkinson on the small Penny's Hill Estate. It has flavours of smoky ripe morello cherry with developing nuances of tobacco, cigar box and lots of tar and leather. It will improve further if kept for three years or more.

Oddbins

Chatsfield Mount Barker Shiraz 97 £15–£16
Matured for nineteen months in French barriques, this Shiraz
has a very deep bouquet of cigar box and smoke. Layers of
black fruit and spice flavours are underlaid by black chocolate
and mint. It's a big wine with a balanced structured finish. Try
it with duck with an apple sauce.
Mitchell

Elderton Barossa Shiraz 96 £16–£17
A lovely mature Australian Shiraz, this 96 ia assertive without
being brash. Menthol and mint aromas lead to a fully packed
palate of black plums, damsons, leather and spice from
maturation in oak and a long peppery finish.
Fields

Jim Barry McCrae Wood Shiraz 96 £16–£17
In a rich and robust, fruit-driven, style with excellent ripe
blackcurrant fruits and peppery notes, this Shiraz spent 12
months in new French and one-year-old American oak. It has
developed beautifully into a very elegant wine of great length.
Try it with venison.
Dunnes Stores

De Bortoli Yarra Valley Shiraz 97 £17–£18
This is perfect Australian Shiraz with its dense black fruit,
spice, chocolate and pepper, smooth, round tannins and a
finish that goes all the way to Australia. Try it with steak au
poivre.
Febvre

St Hallett Old Block Barossa Shiraz 96 £17–£18
A delicious wine from the excellent 96 vintage, this is made by
Stuart Blackwell, and is named after the 80-year-old vines. Big
and mouthfilling, it is a benchmark Shiraz laden with ripe and
baked blackcurrant fruit with hints of cinnamon and nutmeg.
It strikes a luscious balance between ripe and baked fruit,
smoke and spice, tannins and acidity. Although drinking well
now it has lots of time to go — ten years at least. This is Shiraz
at its very best.
Dunnes Stores

Craiglee Sunbury Victoria Shiraz 98 £19–£20
Craiglee's winemaker, Patrick Carmody, has roots in Co
Clare — he and his wife are avid readers of *The Clare Champion*
which is sent to them every month. Here he has produced a
lovely elegant style of Shiraz, warm, rich and mouthfilling,
with a weight of subtle spicy fruit. All the elements are
beautifully integrated, leading to a delicious finish and long
length. A treat.
Wines Direct

d'Arenberg The Dead Arm McLaren Vale Shiraz 97 £22–£23
Oddly named after a vine disease, which reduces an arm of the
vine to dead wood, this is a super wine. It is made from grapes
grown on very old vines affected by Dead Arm which produce
small bunches and low yields of highly flavoured grapes. The
wine is matured in American and French oak barrels for 22
months. The result is a very complex wine with hints of tar
and spice and flavours of rich damson fruit, firm tannins and a
long finish.
Taserra

Shiraz blends

Australia

Angove's Butterfly Ridge Shiraz/Cabernet 99 £6–£7
The two classic grape varieties, Shiraz and Cabernet
Sauvignon, are blended here to produce a good value easy-
drinking, quaffing wine. It's got pronounced blackcurrant fruit
flavours with hints of pepper and spice. Good for a quick
supper with pepperoni pizza.
O'Briens

Drayton's Oakey Creek Shiraz/Cabernet 99 £6–£7
Draytons, a Hunter Valley producer with a long history, make
honest, full-flavoured wines at good value prices. The 99
Shiraz/ Cabernet has strong complex Shiraz aromas of spice.
With short fermentation and short maturation in wood it is
not a heavy hitter but is fresh and lively with ripe blueberry
and blackberry fruit flavours. It will drink well for up to two
years.
Wines Direct

**Hardys Stamp of Australia Shiraz/Cabernet Sauvignon 99
£6–£7**
BRL Hardy is one of Australias biggest wine producers. This is
a well made medium bodied wine with the typical fresh fruit
character of Shiraz and Cabernet — blackcurrant, plum and

cherries. It is soft, smooth and easy drinking. Drink this one young, it's not for cellaring.
Allied Drinks

Jacob's Creek Shiraz/Cabernet 97 £6–£7
Complex, meaty aromas are matched by strong spicy robust flavours in this blend from Jacob's Creek, one of the most popular brands in Ireland. It's a lovely elegant wine with a herbal quality, and a touch of liquorice, with the ripe plums and initial spice. Great value, it offers lots of character for the price.
Irish Distillers

Miranda Opal Ridge Shiraz/Cabernet 99 £6–£7
A lovely velvety wine, with ripe spicy fruit aromas and flavours, this classic blend finishes smooth and long with a pepper twist. It is good value and would go well with lots of dishes: meat, poultry, cheese, creamy pasta.
Taserra

Penfolds Rawson's Retreat Bin 35 Shiraz/Cabernet Sauvignon/Ruby Cabernet 99 £6–£7
Penfolds, one of four giant Australian companies which dominate the wine scene, make great red wines: they are the producers of Australia's premier red wine, Grange, developed by the legendary Max Schubert. At the lower end of the price spectrum, Rawson's Retreat is in a pleasant easy-drinking style — warm with soft tannins and long fruity blackcurrant flavours touched with spice and pepper. It has good length. Try it with sweet and sour pork or rich meat dishes.
Findlaters

Cranswick Estate Shiraz/Merlot 99 £7–£8
The grape varieties in this blend were crushed, fermented and matured separately prior to blending. It's a delicious, well priced wine with huge concentration of spicy blackcurrant fruits and hints of vanilla giving quite a creamy texture to the finish. Serve it with red meat or spicy dishes.
MacCormaic

McWilliams' Inheritance Shiraz/Cabernet 99 £7–£8
Founded by Samuel McWilliams from Northern Ireland, this is Australia's largest family-owned firm, and has been making wine for five generations. Inheritance Shiraz/Cabernet is a delicious fruit-driven style with ripe, baked bramble flavours and a touch of spiciness. It's a good match for red meat dishes and Italian style food.
TDL

Wakefield Clare Valley Shiraz/Cabernet 98 £7–£8
Made from grapes grown on a single estate in the Clare
Valley, this Shiraz/Cabernet blend is instantly appealing with
its rich, ripe black fruit. A peppery edge adds interest. It's a
good match for meaty dishes: beef, pasta with a meat sauce or
shepherd's pie.
Koala

Penfolds Bin 2 Shiraz/Mourvèdre 97 £9–£10
Mourvèdre, originally from the Rhône, is better known in the
New World as Mataro but the Old World name carries more
cachet. This Shiraz/Mourvèdre blend, from grapes from a
number of regions, has summer pudding aromas and
complex, dark spicy fruit flavours with a long spicy finish. Try
it with beef casserole or pot roast.
Findlaters

Wolf Blass Red Label Shiraz/Cabernet Sauvignon 97 £9–£10
With a super, concentrated nose of blackcurrant and spice this
is a big mouthwatering wine with excellent body. Rich and
ripe, packed with baked blackcurrant fruits and laden with
cinnamon and nutmeg flavours, it has a deliciously long finish.
Try it with grilled or roast lamb and plenty of herbs.
Dillons

Bethany Schrapel Family Vineyards Barossa Valley Shiraz/Cabernet 97 £10–£11
Here's a mouthfilling robust blend of Shiraz and Cabernet
with fig, pepper and spice aromas. The flavours are of
concentrated and ripe blackcurrant, spicy and smoky with a
hint of cigarbox. Try keeping it for a year or two and see how
it develops. It's a good match for roast beef.
O'Briens

Ironstone Shiraz/Grenache 97 £11–£12
The reddish brown soil coloured by iron oxides in South-West
Australia gives this wine its name. Vinified at the Cape
Mentelle winery, the grapes come from all over the region.
This nicely rounded blend of Shiraz and Grenache has a good
weight of dense black fruit, with a touch of pepper, gentle,
undemanding tannins and a good, spicy finish.
Findlaters

Xanadu Secession Shiraz/Cabernet 99 £11–£12
The Chateau Xanadu Winery/Vineyard was established in 1977 which makes it very young in wine terms. Their Secession blend has youthful ripe blackberry fruit aromas with spice and some mint touches. Redcurrant and cough sweet flavours with a hint of black chocolate lead to a balanced chewy finish.
Mitchell

Tyrrell's Winemakers Selection Vat 8 Shiraz/Cabernet Sauvignon 96 £17–£18
Vat 8 follows an Australian wine style first developed in the 1940s and 1950s by such renowned winemakers as Colin Preece and Roger Warren. It is a blend of Hunter Valley Shiraz, from Tyrrell's Brokenback Vineyard, and Coonawarra Cabernet Sauvignon, supplied by Leconfield. The wine was matured for 10 months in new and one-year-old French and American small oak. It is very seductive with delicious mouthwatering blackberries and cherry and chocolate flavours exploding on the palate with bitter chocolate on the finish.
Maxxium

Lindemans Limestone Ridge Coonawarra Shiraz /Cabernet 96 £18–£19
A gorgeous wine, this classic blend of Shiraz and Cabernet has chocolate, vanilla, spice and blackcurrant aromas. Wonderful flavours of ripe red fruits and vanilla in complex layers are aided by softening tannins. An appealing lengthy finish adds to the pleasure.
Gilbeys

Chile

Errazuriz Don Maximiano Estate Aconcagua Valley Syrah Reserva 98 £15–£16
Errazuriz has been producing this Syrah reserve since 1996. It is a powerful wine and often has a little Cabernet Sauvignon added. The intensity of the wine is due to late harvesting the grapes just before shrivelling and then ageing in French and American oak barrels for ten months. The result is a smooth wine with blackberry and red fruits, pepper and cinnamon spices. It also has vanilla, leather and toasty notes. It's a special wine for special occasions.
Allied Drinks

South Africa

Simonsig Stellenbosch Shiraz 97 £8–£9
The Malan family of Stellenbosch own the Simonsig Estate,
one of the leading companies in South Africa, which made this
easy-drinking Shiraz. It has warm, mellow, comforting aromas
and flavours of spicy blackberry fruit with a long-lasting, spicy
finish. It's a good accompaniment for red meats.
United Beverages

USA – California

**Ironstone Vineyards Sierra Foothills California Shiraz 97
£11–£12**
Not much Shiraz is grown in California, so this wine, made by
the Kautz family, is something of a rarity. It is in a full-bodied,
classic style, with very ripe spiced blackberry flavours and an
intriguing smokiness adding an overall complexity. It will keep
for two or three years. Try it with lamb and aubergines.
Gilbeys

Zinfandel

USA – California

Originally from Italy, where it is called the Primitivo, Zinfandel
has been grown in California since the early 19th century. The
wines tend to be dry, sturdy and unsubtle with wild blackberry flavours and chewy, robust textures. The alcohol can be
pretty fiery.

Garnet Point Zinfandel/Barbera 96 £6–£7
Zinfandel has been teamed here with another, more recently
arrived, Italian variety. This is an excellent fruit-laden wine
with brambles on the nose and spicy fruit cake flavours. An
easy-drinking wine, it has lots of body and a very fruity — yet
dry — finish. It's excellent value. Match it with pasta and a
sundried tomatoes and black olive sauce.
Irish Distillers

Stowells Ruby Cabernet/Zinfandel nv £6–£7
Ruby Cabernet, a Californian crossing of Carignan and
Cabernet Sauvignon, has been teamed with another
Californian variety, Zinfandel. The result is a beautifully
crafted, well-structured, fruity wine that is tremendous value
for money and has much complexity and a classic style.
Allied Drinks

Vendange California Zinfandel 98 £6-£7
Zinfandel's strength lies in its huge versatility — it makes wines
from sweetish blush lightweights to flavour-packed alcoholic
blockbusters. If you like slightly sweet wines, this one is for
you! Stewed blackberries and bubble gum flavours abound
with a welcome bit of white pepper on the nice finish. It's
good with hamburgers or ribs from a barbecue.
Barry & Fitzwilliam

Pepperwood Grove Zinfandel 97 £8-£9
In 1985 Don Sebastiani and his brother-in-law Roy Ceccheti
established their own brand — Ceccheti Sebastiani Cellars. This
Zinfandel is one of their excellent wines. Winemaker Bob
Broman has produced a wine with full, lush, brambly fruit,
deliciously concentrated. The tannins are just peeking through
the fruit as a framework to hold the wine together.
Gleeson

Stratford California Zinfandel 97 £8-£9
Stratford began life as a négociant company in 1982, buying in
Chardonnay wine and blending it to produce inexpensive
wines that were highly rated. It has progressed since then and
now has its own winery. Previous vintages of Stratford
Zinfandel have won awards and critical acclaim. Certainly, for
sweet-toothed wine lovers this scores well — juicy, stewed,
sweetened blackberries with soft vanilla. The delicious sun-
ripened fruit is abundant on both the nose and the palate and
it has good length. Try it with mustard glazed steaks or beef
stirfry.
Barry & Fitzwilliam

Fetzer Home Ranch Zinfandel 96 £9-£10
Mendocino and Amador counties supply the grapes for this
classic Zinfandel. The wine is aged in 90% American and 10%
French oak. Appealing autumn fruits and vanilla on the nose
are followed by lovely sweet figs, sultanas and cake mixture
with a well-measured sprinkling of cake spice. A delicious,
well-balanced wine with or without food, it will improve for
two years plus.
Dillons

Francis Coppola Presents Rosso 95 £9-£10
Film director Francis Ford Coppola comes from a winemaking
family and goes back to his roots with this wine. Mainly
Zinfandel, the inclusion of Syrah and Cabernet Sauvignon
makes it rather unusual. It's easy, soft, pleasant, everyday

wine — nice and gentle with lots of fruit and spice, plenty of
character and some elegance for a Zinfandel. It should hold for
two years.
Molloy's

Pedroncelli Mother Clone Dry Creek Valley Zinfandel 97 £11–£12

The older the vine, the more delicious the wine. The grapes for
this wine came from old vines in Dry Creek Valley in Sonoma,
where the Pedroncellis have been growing grapes since 1927.
This is a lovely wine, with an oaky, vanilla, plum jam nose. Big
and mouthfilling with great length and flavours that linger on
and on, it has firm tannins and excellent weight of ripe
bramble fruit. Moist tobacco leaf and plum jam also come
through. On the finish there is some spice lingering on the
palate with good weight in the mouth. Age this one for two
years or more.
Dunnes Stores

Sebastiani Sonoma Cask Sonoma County Old Vines Zinfandel 98 £11–£12

Sebastiani is regarded as a producer of sound, reasonably
priced wines. This Zinfandel is certainly good value, with its
mulberry and bramble fruit aromas followed by powerful and
brash super-ripe opulent black fruits. It has a long, peppery
finish and isn't in the least subtle, but very seductive and
definitely a crowd-pleaser. It will mature for four years or
more.
Barry & Fitzwilliam

Beringer Appellation Collection North Coast Zinfandel 97 £12–£13

Zinfandel, California's very own grape variety, changes its
personality depending on where it is grown and the age of the
vines. Flavours can be berry fruit or plums — even raisins and
prunes. This example has cherry tomato aromas and a velvety
smooth texture with sweet roasted plums and baby corn. An
excellent example of very good Californian Zinfandel, it has
flair and style, but needs some more time to mature. It would
make a good partner for roast lamb with rosemary and will
improve over the next two years.
Allied Drinks

Bonterra Mendocino County Organic Zinfandel 96 £12–£13
The hot northern Californian climate of Mendocino produces black grapes with strong flavours. Add to that the extra care and attention lavished on organic grapes and you have a great wine. A tempting nose of juicy plums is only a teaser compared to the rich palate of flavours thereafter — Turkish Delight, ripe blackcurrants, a hint of rubber, some mint, white pepper — a stunner! A very good food wine, it will mature for two years. Try it with a robust highly flavoured pizza e.g. with aubergine and goats' cheese.
Dillons

Ernest & Julio Gallo Sonoma Frei Ranch Vineyard Zinfandel 95 £15–£16
Gallo, the biggest wine company in the world, bought the Frei Brothers Winery in 1977 as part of their move into Sonoma. This single-vineyard Zinfandel is a big, powerful, spicy, toasty wine with a lovely mature nose and a marvellous return on the palate. It's bursting with flavour — blackberries, black pepper, cake spice, cake mixture, orange peel and fabulous length.
Irish Distillers

Geyser Peak Sonoma County Zinfandel 96 £18–£19
Some of the best Zinfandels come from Sonoma, especially from older vines. This one is a heavyweight, almost port-like, liquefied black fruits and spicy oak ignite the palate in a haze of alcohol. Very strong and very long, it will only get better for the next four years.
Maxxium

Other red

Argentina

Santa Julia Mendoza Sangiovese 99 £6–£7
In Italy, Sangiovese is the mainstay of Chianti. Like some of the lightest Chiantis, this Argentinian wine, although not very striking, is a good and straightforward wine. On the nose it has tar and spice, with rich black fruits with a hint of damson and fig on the palate, and soft well-rounded tannins. It is good value and would suit any pasta dish.
Taserra

Santa Julia Mendoza Tempranillo 99 £6–£7
Tempranillo is widely planted in Spain and is the mainstay of
Rioja. In Argentina, it is an important grape variety with
widespread plantings. This wine from Mendoza has ripe black
cherries layered with vanilla and oak, giving a long, warm and
slightly smoky finish.
Taserra

Santa Julia Mendoza Oak Aged Tempranillo 97 £8–£9
Another Tempranillo from Santa Julia, this one is oak-aged. It
has lots of fruit character on the nose—black cherries and
bramble berries followed through on the palate together with
figs and raisins, and hints of spice and chocolate. It has a nice
long finish.
Taserra

Australia

Jacob's Creek Grenache/Shiraz 98 £6–£7
This is a pleasant, very drinkable wine, with soft juicy summer
berry fruits and a sprinkling of white pepper on the finish. A
good wine to drink on its own, it doesn't need food.
Irish Distillers

Yaldara Whitmore Old Vineyard Reserve Grenache 98 £8–£9
Very appealing and mouth-filling with warm spicy fruit, this
wine's soft ripe tannins add to the lush impression. The finish
is gentle. Try it with spicy lentils or dahl.
Barry & Fitzwilliam

Brown Brothers King Valley Barbera 96 £10–£11
Australia has a number of well-established Italian grape
varieties, dating back to the first Italian immigrants. Barbera is
native to Piedmont, and is a variety that loves to be aged in
wood which gives the wines their vanilla and spicy flavours.
This Barbera is a delicious big, rich wine laden with luscious,
soft blackcurrant and ripe damson fruits. Dense and serious
with earthy tones, it is drinking well now. Try it for a taste of
something different from Australia.
Woodford Bourne

d'Arenberg d'Arry's Original Grenache/Shiraz 98 £10–£11
Named after d'Arenberg's principal Francis d'Arenberg
Osborn, d'Arry's Original has always been made from
Grenache and Shiraz grown on d'Arenberg's low yielding

19th-century vineyards. The final blend varies from year to year. The 98 is 53% Grenache, 47% Shiraz. It has a rubbery nose with touches of sandalwood and concentrated fruit tart flavours, with spicy overtones and a long lingering finish. Try it with game.
Taserra

Rosemount GSM McLaren Vale Grenache/Syrah/Mourvèdre 97 £14–£15

An excellent example of Australian blending *à la* the Southern Rhône. Lots of forward ripe fruit and a lovely, complex array of flavours from super-fruity to savoury. Once the tannins subside, there are waves of juicy black and red currant fruits and oaky taste sensations. Delicious now but wait for another few years until all the elements meld and the tannins soften.
Grants

Chile

Mont Gras Carmenère Reserva 98 £9–£10

Carmenère was originally brought to Chile from France in the 1800s. Until recently it was confused with Merlot but it is now making a name for itself in its own right. Not for everyone, this is the type of wine which grows on you. It is rich, robust and savoury with very intense black fruits, a hint of tar, green peppers and menthol and is drinking well now.
Maxxium

Santa Rita Carmenère Reserva 97 £9–£10

With blackcurrant and bramble berries, wood and a touch of leather this interesting wine also has a herbal quality which is a characteristic of Carmenère. It has a firm structure, is drinking well now and may develop further.
Gilbeys

Miguel Torres Manso de Velasco 95 £20–£21

Made from very old, low-yielding vines on a single estate, this wine has depth and elegance persisting throughout with a complexity of flavours — cassis, raspberry, cedar and white pepper. There is, of course, a price to be paid for this level of refinement. It is drinking well now and will continue for another two years. Try it with rack of lamb with herbs.
Woodford Bourne

Miguel Torres Cordillera 98 £14–£15
With roasted red peppers, tar, stewed fruit and molasses, this
is a serious, full-bodied wine. It is made from 60% Cariñena
grapes plus 30% Syrah and 10% Merlot (which will be replaced
in future vintages by 10% Grenache) and is a super example of
the revolution that has taken place in Chilean winemaking.
With its complexity and balance, it is a worthy rival to
Châteauneuf-du-Pape, for example, at the same price. Drink it
over the next two years.
Woodford Bourne

Mexico

L.A. Cetto Barbera 97 £6–£7
With its aromas of roses and crushed strawberries, this is a
delicious and fresh Beaujolais-like fruity wine. Strawberry fruit
dominates, while easy tannins flatter the fruit. It is a little
peppery on the finish. Try it with salamis.
Grants

L.A. Cetto Petite Sirah 96 £6–£7
Confusingly, Petite Sirah is no relation to the noble Syrah.
Grown mainly in North and South America, in Mexico it
produces a good rustic red. L. A. Cetto's Petite Sirah 96 is
warming and earthy but not rough. It's an interesting wine,
nearing maturity, though good for another year at least, with
blackskinned fruit flavours and firm ripe tannins. Try it with
sauteed liver and onions.
Grants

South Africa

Arniston Bay Ruby Cabernet/Merlot 99 £6–£7
Ruby Cabernet is not the classic Cabernet but is a grape
derived from a crossing of Cabernet Sauvignon and Carignan.
It works well when blended with other classic Bordeaux
varieties such as Merlot. A very appealing wine, this 99 blend
is soft and fruity and great value for casual drinking with or
without food. For drinking young.
Findlaters

Robert's Rock Cinsault/Ruby Cabernet 98 £6–£7
Light and very fruity, with a good concentration of tinned
strawberries, this wine is easy drinking and very fresh with a
soft, fruity finish. Serve it with ham, poultry or roast
vegetables
TDL

Other Wine Styles

Rosé

In this section the wines are listed by
- country
- price

Australia

Mount Hurtle Rosé 99 £6–£7
Deep rose in colour, this wine was made with extended skin
contact for 48 hours, followed by a cool, controlled fermentation of the red juice. It has a very appealing aroma of toffee
and fresh strawberries with some boiled sweets in the background. Sweet strawberry jam tastes come through on the
palate and the jammy and juicy soft red fruits persist all the
way through to the finish.
United Beverages

France – Bordeaux

In the past, red and white wines were blended to create rosé
wines, called 'clairet'. The practice is now banned and today
rosé wines are made by leaving the red grape skins in contact
with the juice for about 24 hours to colour it pink. Rosés are
generally best drunk young, before they change colour from
pink to onion skin orange.

AC Bordeaux-Clairet Ch. Thieuley 99 £8–£9
This Clairet has raspberry and boiled sweet aromas. The red
soft fruits theme continues on the palate with ripe strawberries and raspberry fruits. It has a good depth of plummy fruit
with the crisp acidity adding balance.
Wines Direct

France – South (Languedoc-Roussillon)

**AC Coteaux du Languedoc Bergerie de l'Hortus Pic St Loup
Rosé de Saignée 99 £7–£8**
This large wine area in southern France between Nîmes and
Beziers was upgraded from VDQS to AC in 1985. This crisp,
refreshing rosé is made from Grenache in the stunning setting
of Pic St Loup. It has a great weight of fruit compote and
raspberry fruit on the palate and finishes in the same red
fruity style. Partner it with summer salads and picnics.
Wines Direct

Portugal

VR Ribatejo Casaleiro Colheita Seleccionada 98 £4–£5
This regional wine has an amazing concentration of strawberries with freshly milled black pepper on the nose. The
palate is bone dry and the peppered strawberries continue on
to the palate. This is a simple and easy-drinking rosé.
WineOnline

Spain

DO Navarra Alma Garnacha 99 £6–£7
Two decades ago the rosé wines of Navarra were typically
high in alcohol — up to 15% — and made in an oxidised style.
Today the region has revolutionised itself in the vinyard and in
the winery. The styles are now fresh, fruity and lighter in
alcohol. This rosé has very pleasant ripe strawberries and
raspberries on the nose, followed by a decent weight of red
berry fruits on the palate, with a pleasing finish. This is a
summer barbecue-style wine.
Approach Trade

DO Navarra Chivite Gran Feudo 99 £6–£7
This enjoyable wine is made from the Garnacha, Spain's most
widely planted grape variety, by the *saignée* method where
the juice has minimal contact with the grape skins. It has
perfumed aromas of ripe strawberries and blackcurrant fruits,
and an amazing palate of solid dark strawberry and blackcurrant fruit, combined with a balanced zippy acidity, to produce
a wine of quality at a very good price. There is a lovely
lingering finish. Good food matches with this versatile rosé
would be pasta, risotto, vegetables, fish and white meat.
TDL

Sparkling

In this section the wines are listed by
* country
* price

Australia

Australia has its own style of sparkling wine, usually made
from a mix of grapes and usually other than the classic
Champagne blend of Pinot Noir and Chardonnay. The style
ranges from crisp and fresh wines, made from prematurely
harvested grapes to preserve the fresh acidity in the fruit, to
soft and ripe wines, sometimes opulent and fruit laden.

Orlando Carrington Extra Brut nv £9–£10
This is a tasty Aussie non-vintage sparkler with ample weight
of green apple fruit and a classy minerally edge. It is refreshingly crisp on the finish and is well made and well bred.
Irish Distillers

Hardys Nottage Hill Chardonnay Brut 98 £11–£12
Named in honour of Thomas Nottage who, for 60 years,
managed Hardys Tintara winery in McLaren Vale, this is a nice
zippy young fizz with plenty of Chardonnay fruit character.
Honeysuckle and citrus aromas subtly lift from the glass. The
palate is quite powerful with assertive tangerine and nectarine
fruits. It's a well-made, uncomplicated wine at an attractive
price. Try it with light canapés or Chinese dim sum.
Allied Drinks

Seppelt Salinger Brut 93 £12–£13
Salinger is Seppelt's top of the range sparkling wine. It is made
in the traditional method used for Champagne from top-
quality Chardonnay and Pinot Noir from some of Australia's
coolest regions, sometimes with the addition of a little Pinot
Meunier, another traditional Champagne grape. The wines
rest on their lees for up to three years. The style is usually rich,
buttery and honeyed, producing ripe fruity sparkling wines
with a very creamy mouse. Tasting this 93 immediately lifts
the spirits. The mousse fizzes on the palate and lasts, with lots
of fruity flavours intermingling with pleasant biscuit tones. It's
ideal for those who don't like the steely dryness of Champagne but enjoy a glass of quality bubbly. This wine will
benefit from a further year's ageing.
Dunnes Stores

☆ ☆

Seaview Pinot Noir/Chardonnay Brut 95 £13–£14
The Seaview Winery was established in the McLaren Vale of
South Australia in 1850 and has been making sparkling wines
since 1919. The classic Champagne grape varieties, Pinot Noir
and Chardonnay, give strength and finesse to the wines. This
95 was made in a traditional very dry style. It has a yeasty,
mature, mushroomy bouquet, signalling the Pinot in the
blend, and is full and savoury on the palate with earthy
mushroom flavours and almond nuttiness and apricots from
the Chardonnay. This sparkler has lots of personality and a
very long finish. Try it with lightly spiced Oriental dishes.
Findlaters

France – Champagne

Champagne is France's most northerly wine producing
region, lying at the northern limits of the vine-growing
latitudes. The chalky soil provides, paradoxically, good
drainage, yet moisture retention when required, and heat
retention to help boost the ripening of the grapes in this cool
climate. The conditions are ideal for producing the light, crisp
wines, high in acidity and low in alcohol, used as the base for
the sparkling wine. Three grape varieties are permitted: the
white Chardonnay and the black Pinot Noir and Pinot
Meunier. The second fermentation, which produces the
bubbles, takes place in the bottle.

In this section the wines are listed by
- non-vintage
- vintage
- rosé
and by price in each category.

NON-VINTAGE

Non-vintage wines, blends from several years' vintages, are
the mainstay of Champagne's sparkling wine industry. The
various Champagne houses produce a consistent style of non-
vintage wines through careful selection and blending of the
three authorised grape varieties from the three subregions in
the region and from a number of different years.

Charles de Villiers Brut nv £20–£21
An elegant and lively Champagne, this has good concentration of lemons, limes and apple purée on the palate. The
delicate, lightweight fruit flavours are well integrated with the
fresh and crisp acidity and they follow through to the finish.
Bacchus

Montaudon Brut nv £22–£23

Founded in Epernay in 1891 by 19-year-old Auguste-Eugène
Montaudon, the house remains in family ownership. It
produces well-balanced wines with a good depth of flavour.
The blend is 50% Pinot Noir with the balance equally made up
of Chardonnay and Pinot Meunier. This non-vintage Brut has
a pleasant mousse which plays on the palate with freshly
baked brioche flavours and a long, lemony tangy finish. Its
elegant and delicate style makes it easy to enjoy.
Mitchells

Joseph Perrier Cuvée Royale Brut nv £24–£25

Made from an equal blend of Chardonnay, Pinot Noir and
Pinot Meunier, this is an easily approachable, elegant and
fruity wine, often undervalued. It has a steady flow of tiny
bubbles forming a mousse which cleanses the palate. It is
intensely fruity, yet subtle, with an added cream and biscuit
flavour. The wine finishes long with a balanced complexity of
integrated tastes from the three grape varieties.
United Beverages

Delbeck Brut Heritage nv £24–£25

The small house of Delbeck was reborn in 1991. A high
proportion of the black Pinot Noir is used in the blends,
providing backbone and giving breadth and depth of fruit and
a sometimes meaty, savoury aroma. Fine beads of bubbles
dance in the glass, inviting that 'feel good factor' promised by
a glass of Champagne. The wine is subtle and elegant with
lemon fruit flavours emerging from the mousse. The baked
biscuity flavours are as subtle, but linger longer.
Mitchells

Mumm Cordon Rouge Brut nv £25–£26

Mumm's leading brand, the Cordon Rouge, was launched in
1876 with the idea of boosting sales by putting the sash of the
Légion d'Honneur on the label. (This patriotic gesture did not
prevent the Mumm family, who had German origins, from
being treated as enemy aliens during the First World War.) The
house style is for light fruity wines which tend to be less dry
than most of the other Champagne houses. The blend tends to
be 45% Pinot Noir, 25% Pinot Meunier, 20% Chardonnay and
10% reserve wines from older vintages to add interest. This
Cordon Rouge is in the classic style. It is well-made with
bready aromas of toast and yeast and hints of green apples
and pears. The palate is zingy with citrus fruit flavours and a
suggestion of nuts and freshly baked bread. The very crisp
acidity gives a clean finish — definitely a crowd-pleaser
Barry & Fitzwilliam

Moët et Chandon Brut Impérial nv £25–£26

This company was founded in 1743 by the Moët family, of Dutch origin — so the 't' is pronounced. Pierre-Gabriel Chandon married into the family business in 1832 and the name changed to embrace his. Brut Impérial maintains the house style of well-made, firm and fruity wines. While the blend varies each year, it is typically 50% Pinot Noir, 30% Chardonnay and 20% Pinot Meunier. This wine has class and style and is an elegant, crisp, well made Champagne. The delicate citrussy and nutty bouquet is followed on the mid-palate by lively and flavoursome ripe Pinot fruit and lovely clean length.

Dillons

Pommery Brut Royal nv £25–£26

In 1856 Louis Pommery joined the company founded in 1836 by Narcisse Greno. When he died two years later, his widow, Louise, one of the legendary Champagne widows, took charge. The house was bought by the LVMH group in 1990, and annual production has grown to nearly six million bottles. Pommery's winemaker is Prince Alain de Polignac. The house style is light but with a burst of flavour, displaying great depth and length. The blend for Brut Royal is 40% Pinot Meunier, 30% Pinot Noir and 30% Chardonnay. Substantial proportions of older reserve wines add complexity and depth of flavour. The wine has fine yeasty, toasty aromas with ripe fruits, limes, kiwi and green apples. The palate has a biscuity character with pronounced stewed fruit.

Grants

Perrier-Jouët Grand Brut nv £25–£30

As there were a number of Perrier Houses in Champagne in the early years of the 1800s, Pierre Perrier, the founder of the house in 1811, added his wife's maiden name Jouët to the company. The wine was a favourite with Queen Victoria, King Edward VII and Napoleon III. Sold in 1959 to Mumm and the Seagram group, it maintains remarkable independence with its distinctive house style, producing beautifully aromatic wines, delicate and light, but with depth. The Grand Brut blend is 40% Pinot Noir, 30% Pinot Meunier and 30% Chardonnay. It has a mature, complex and individualistic bouquet of damp undergrowth, wet wood and truffles, and a rounded palate with flavours of red and green orchard fruits, finishing with lemony freshness.

Irish Distillers

Taittinger Brut nv £29–£30

Although Taittinger can trace its roots back to the early part of the 18th century it was only after Pierre Taittinger bought the

house in 1930, and the vineyard holdings were greatly expanded, that its present proud reputation was established. It is one of the few remaining family-controlled houses in Champagne. The wines are matured in the cellars originally excavated by the Romans and later enlarged by Benedictine monks. A large proportion of Chardonnay grapes are used in the blend to produce finesse and the familiar Taittinger flowery nose. This example is true to the house style and is an easy, fruit-driven fizz with green apples and citrus flavours. Dry in style, it has great acidity and good length.
Febvre

> The term **Extra Dry** applied to Champagne means off-dry, rather than dry. **Brut** is a drier style.

Pol Roger Extra Dry White Foil nv £25–£30

The 18-year-old Pol Roger founded this house in 1849 and it is still a family-owned company. The house style is for wines of great longevity with freshness and elegance. White Foil is a blend in equal parts of the three authorised grape varieties and is primarily for the British market. This one is a lovely, smooth and elegantly textured Champagne, with defined yeasty toasty aromas. It has an excellent integration of balanced structure and flavours and a soft mousse. Acidity, though high, is in balance with the yellow-fleshed soft fruit character. The wine finishes long and off-dry.
Oddbins

> The three Champagne houses sharing the name **Heidsieck — Charles Heidsieck, Piper-Heidsieck and Heidsieck & Co. Monopole** are often confused. The original founder in 1785 was Florenz-Louis Heidsieck and the three Heidsieck houses are descended from his three nephews. Charles, a great-nephew of the foder, known as 'Champagne Charlie' for his high-flying lifestyle, established his own house in 1851. Since it was acquired by the Remy group in 1985 the quality of Charles Heidsieck wines has noticeably improved. The innovative house is the first to display the year in which the blend and second fermentation took place and the bottles were laid down in the cellar for ageing — *mis en cave.*

Charles Heidsieck Brut Réserve nv (*mis en cave* 1996) £25–£30

The Brut Réserve from Charles Heidsieck is bottle-aged for a minimum of three years, more than twice the minimum 15 months prescribed for non-vintage wines. The extended ageing develops the aromas and flavours over time. This golden wine, cellared in 96, has a rich concentration of citrus

apple fruit and distinct notes of ripe peach and a hint of vanilla. The acidity is kept in check by the vibrant ripe fruit. It's a stunner..
Maxxium

Veuve Clicquot Ponsardin Brut nv £25–£30
Although Jean Clicquot founded this house in 1772, it owes its reputation to his widowed daughter-in-law, Nicole-Barbe Ponsardin. She renamed the company Veuve Clicquot Ponsardin. A born innovater and businesswoman, she was the first to export Champagne and she invented the method of clarifying the wines. The house style is rich, classy and mature from a high proportion of black grapes, 56% Pinot Noir, 16% Pinot Meunier and 28% Chardonnay. 'The Widow' is always a favourite. The nose is complex, showing delicious shortbread/buttery notes complemented by firm fruits. Richness and generousity characterise the palate with a long nutty and minerally finish. This is a true delight.
Findlaters

Ruinart Champagne Brut nv £30 – £35
Light, elegant and full of finesse, this non-vintage is from Ruinart, the oldest Champagne house. Made from 70% Pinot Noir and Pinot Meunier and 30% Chardonnay it is dry in style with grassy, floral aromas and refreshing lemon and lime acidity. On the palate, ripe full-flavoured citrus fruit is complemented by toasted brioche — the subtle flavours linger long after the last delicious drop has been swallowed. Beautifully expressing the Ruinart house style, this Champagne is consistently excellent and good value.
Taserra

VINTAGE

The marginal, cool climate in Champagne makes it difficult for the grapes to ripen fully each year. The rare wine produced from a single year owes its first allegiance to the characteristics of that particular year. Vintage Champagnes benefit from at least ten years ageing. Most houses declared 90 a vintage; very few declared 91 or 93 vintages; 92 was a reasonable vintage and 95 was good.

André Beaufort Brut 92 £27–£28
Nuts, baked apples, honey and even sherry appearing on the complex nose of this very aromatic Champagne. On the palate it is rich and mouthfilling with mature brioche flavours fanning over the palate and again there is a hint of sherry that

denotes ageing. This is an unusual, but correct style, techni-
cally slightly oxidized. Some people will love it but it is
definitely an acquired taste. Because this is a rich wine it can
handle some rich and assertive food tastes — lobster terrine,
smoked oysters or a fish carpaccio. It will drink well from 2001
over four years.
Bubble Brothers

Piper-Heidsieck Brut 95 £25–£30
In 1989 Piper-Heidsieck was taken over by the Remy
Cointreau group. The wines have gained in richness and
ripeness since then. Because they do not undergo malolactic
fermentation (the natural conversion of the crisper citric acids
to softer, milkier acids) the wines need greater ageing to
soften their initial austerity. This 95 is still youthful and is only
just beginning to mature, So resist until 2005. Very smooth
and dry, it has toast crumbs and broken biscuit aromas.
Creamy yeasty flavours coat the palate, with a finish of
delicious nectarines.
Maxxium

Joseph Perrier Cuvée Royale Brut 90 £25–£30
This elegant complex, vintage Champagne is a 50/50 blend of
black and white grapes and is only just starting its mature

phase. The crisp acidity is integrated and not as marked as expected because lots of berry and ripe tropical fruit flavours intermingle on the palate with a long and creamy biscuity finish. Keep it for at least another two years before popping the cork.
United Beverages

De Venoge Brut 91 £30–£35
Founded in 1837 by Henri-Marc de Venoge, this house was bought by the Troillard Champagne house in 1958. There was a noticeable improvement in quality and image when Thierry Mantoux took over as Managing Director in 1986. The house style is for easy drinking and fruity styles with a certain creaminess. De Venoge 91 is for the lover of mature Champagne who likes it in a slightly oxidising style. Pinot Noir accounts for 66% of this blend with the balance made up in equal measure by Pinot Meunier and Chardonnay. There is a very obvious mature bouquet of nuts and red fruits on the nose. Deeply concentrated biscuit flavours emerge on the palate and there is a long lingering finish. It will drink well for several years.
Bacchus

Laurent-Perrier Brut 93 £30 – £35
A few houses, including Laurent-Perrier, declared 93 a vintage. The wine has creamy and yeasty aromas. Rich tea biscuit flavours are enhanced by citrus and green apple fruit, fresh pineapple and grapefruit. The flavours unite to form a long and tangy finish.
Gilbeys

ROSÉ

Pink or rosé Champagne is made by either the maceration or the addition method. The maceration method leaves the skins of the crushed black grapes in contact with the fermenting grape juice, for one to two days to stain the juice with a pink colour. This method gives the winemaker very little control over the consistency in colour. Using the addition method, a small amount of still red wine from the Champagne region, AC Coteaux Champenois, is added during the blending before the second fermentation in bottle. Demand for pink fizz moves in cycles — it seems to gain in popularity during times of prosperity.

Montaudon Grand Rosé Brut nv £24–£25
Montaudon's pink Champagne is a fun bubbly, made from 38% Pinot Noir, 50% Chardonnay and 12% Pinot Noir red wine from Bouzy. Aromas of fresh strawberries and digestive biscuits levitate from the glass. Fruit flavours dominate the

palate—red berries with a strawberry cheesecake combination of creamy mousse with the biscuity base. It is a very refreshing glass of Champagne, leaving a long tingling finish.
Mitchells

Delbeck Brut Heritage Rosé nv £25–£26
This pink Champagne, with its beautiful onion skin colour, is a serious rosé. Aromas of redcurrants and strawberry fruit lift out of the glass. The palate is dry and rich with strawberry and cream flavours.
Mitchells

J. Dumangin Fils Brut Rosé nv £25–£26
This light and fruity pink Champagne has a delightful salmon pink colour and lovely strawberry aromas. On the palate it is crisp and clean with hints of citrus and green apple fruit. It finishes well with fresh raspberry fruit. Keep the food you serve with this rosé delicate and light, just like the wine.
Bubble Brothers

Billecart-Salmon Brut Rosé nv £30–£35
This fine Champagne house has had mixed fortunes since its foundation in 1818. Its Brut Rosé nv, which dates from 1830, is the mainstay of the house. It is made from 60% Pinot Noir and 40% Chardonnay. The pink colour is achieved by adding 8% of red Pinot Noir wine from the house's own vineyards. Elegant and stylish, with great finesse, the wine has lovely biscuity flavours, and excellent lively mousse. A very, clean, length is the finishing touch to this beautifully smooth, well-integrated and memorable pink Champagne.
Oddbins

Laurent-Perrier Brut Rosé nv £30–£35
Laurent-Perrier was founded in 1812 by Eugène Laurent. In 1887 when Eugène's son died, and his widow took over, her name, Perrier, was added to the company name. This house takes its rosé Champagne very seriously. It one of the few houses to produce a genuinely rosé still wine from macerating the skins of black grapes for a day or two in the fermentation vessels. Made from 100% Pinot Noir grapes, the Champagne has a lovely salmon pink colour with pronounced fruity and toasty aromas. It is dry on the palate, with a depth of flavour and elements of melons and redcurrant fruit. The wine is rich enough to partner with light food.
Gilbeys

France – Loire

AC Saumur Gratien & Meyer Cuvée de Minuit Brut 96 £14–£15
The tufa soils of the Saumur region in France's Loire Valley
add definition and focus to the fruit in their wines. Chenin
Blanc reigns supreme and sometimes a little Chardonnay is
added to give a fuller flavour. This Cuvée de Minuit has been
matured for two years in cool, chalky stone cellars. It has delicate,
nutty aromas against a floral background. The steady mousse
lifts the palate with a bready, yeasty character accompanied by
smooth citrus fruits. The finish is long and lingering. Drink over
two years and try it with oysters and other delicate shellfish.
Gilbeys

Germany

**Hessische Bergstrasse Schloss Starkenburg Heppenheimer
Schlossberg Riesling Extra Trocken 98 £13–£14**
A light, subtle sparkler made in a dry (trocken) style, this German
Riesling has subtle fruity and floral scents of hot-house flowers
and a gentle suggestion of yeast. Orchard fruits evolve on the
palate with ripe red apples and honey following through to the
finish. It is an interesting and quite different style of bubbly.
Classic

Italy

Italy's popular sparkler Asti Spumante is made by suppressing
and filtering out the yeast half-way through the first fermentation. The natural carbon dioxide gas is trapped and the
remaining unfermented sugars add sweetness to the wine.
The Muscat grape contributes a perfumed and grapey character.

DOCG Asti Tesco Sweet Asti nv £6–£7
Asti Spumante should be drunk young and fresh and this
great-value wine certainly displays its youth. It has a vibrant,
youthful floral nose of spring flowers and apple blossom. Very
ripe pear, apple and peach flavours dance on the palate. It's
slightly sweet but not cloying and makes a refreshing end to a
meal, matched with fresh fruit salad or strawberries and
cream.
Tesco

DOCG Asti Spumante Mondoro Asti nv £10–£11
This Asti Spumante is a typical light, medium-sweet sparkling
wine with scents of apple blossom, rose petals and peaches. It
is fresh, frothy and frivolous, a garden party in a glass.
Grants

New Zealand

The combination of a cool climate and mineral-rich volcanic soils in New Zealand has the potential to produce sparkling wines with elegance and concentration of flavour, especially when the two classic Champagne grapes Pinot Noir and Chardonnay are used.

Lindauer Special Reserve Brut nv £13–£14
Made by Alister McIntosh and Jamie Marfell in the cooler South Island, this terrific New Zealand sparkler, with its tiny bubbles, is fantastic value for money. The Pinot Noir gives the wine a pinkish hue and added richness. A lovely enticing nose of strawberry shortcake, with a hint of boiled sweets, leads to a fruit-laden palate of summer fruits with a toasty and nutty fullness.
Oddbins

> The **Marlborough** region on the north-eastern tip of South Island is an ideal vine-growing location for white varieties. It has the highest number of sunshine hours and the lowest rainfall in the important months of January to March preceding the harvest. The flat river-bed plains are protected from the rain-bearing clouds by the jagged Richmond mountains to the west.

Deutz Marlborough Cuvée Brut nv £14–£15
The Marlborough wine company Montana and the Champagne house Deutz came together to produce this refreshing, typical, zippy New Zealand sparkler. It's fruit-driven but with crisp acidity — the ripe fruit flavours hide under the greener, sharper gooseberry and lime initial attack. It has a long, clean finish.
Oddbins

Pelorus 95 £21–£22
Pelorus is owned by Cloudy Bay with the Champagne house Veuve Clicquot as its principal shareholder. Two classic Champagne grapes are used in this mature bubbly — the black Pinot Noir and the white Chardonnay. The maturity of this 95 vintage shows in the complex nose with its lovely scent of baked apples and warm toast. The mature palate offers a profusion of flavours — fruit, toast and mushrooms. Dry and full-bodied, it has crisp, clean acidity and good length. It will continue to drink well over the next two years.
Findlaters

Spain

Cava is Spain's traditional sparkling wine. It is made using the traditional, or Champagne method, with the second fermentation in bottle. The DO rules specify that only the first portion of free-run juice (the finest quality juice when the grapes are pressed) may be used. Non-vintage wines must rest on their lees in bottle for at least nine months (as opposed to fifteen months in Champagne). As a result most non-vintage Cavas do not have a yeasty character. Vintage Cava must be aged on the lees for three years.

DO Cava Brut Reserva Segura Viudas nv £10–£11

Segura Viudas has been making quality sparkling Cava wines since the 1950s in Penedès, north-east Spain. The Reserva wine spends three years ageing on its lees, which gives it a nutty quality. This example is an easy-drinking, everyday sparkling wine, well made in a modern style, and good value. Its lively mousse has citrus fruit, pear drop and nettle aromas, while the palate has balanced flavours of orchard fruit. Drink it with almonds, tapas and light canapés.
Oddbins

DO Cava Brut Codorníu Cuvée Raventós nv £11–£12

Produced by Codorniú, a family company, winemaking since 1551, this Cava has a predominance of Chardonnay, giving it a less typical Cava character and more international appeal. The wonderfully complex nose is backed by ripe fruit. It is creamy on the palate, with a good mousse, and stewed apples flavour on the mid-palate, ending with a lemony finish.
Grants

DO Cava René Barbier Brut Reserva nv £11–£12

This non-vintage Cava uses three of the native grape varieties: the Macabeo (white Rioja's Viura grape) provides freshness and fruitiness when young; the Xarel-lo gives the alcohol a boost and the Parellada benefits the wine with a flowery aromatic scent. It is a very well-made, lively and crisp young Cava with lots of melon and tropical fruits and a clean, crisp finish. Chill it well for a summer aperitif and try it with some light creamy vegetable terrine.
Febvre

ROSÉ

DO Cava Rosado Brut Natural Reserva Gran Caus 97 £14–£15

A pink Cava is uncommon on the Irish market. This one comes from the Can Rafols dels Caus estate in the Penedès near Barcelona, which is one of the few estates in this region to bottle its own wines. Traditionally, Garnacha and Monastrell

are used to make rosé Cava, but Pinot Noir is used here. The wine is a pale salmon colour with an elegant lively mousse. Complex, multi-layered aromas follow through on the palate, giving delicious mouthfilling satisfaction The wine finishes long with some spice underneath — delicious. This dry Cava is versatile enough to drink with light summer fare. Celebrate in style over the next two years.
Approach Trade

USA – California

The French Champagne House Mumm is one of several Champagne makers to buy vineyards in California. Initially, in these hotter climates their problem was how to achieve the crisp acidity so easily attained in the cooler climes of northern France's Champagne region. When picked early, the immature grapes offered crisp acidity but partnered it with unripe green and sour tastes because the grapes had not developed. The key was to blend grapes harvested at different stages of ripeness and to let them rest for sufficient time on the lees to ensure a creamy, yeasty character.

Mumm Cuvée Napa Brut nv £16–£17
Mumm used the classic Champagne blend of Pinot Noir, Chardonnay and Pinot Meunier, aged for 18 months on the lees, to produce this uncomplicated and straightforward sparkler. Lots of lively bubbles when first poured lead to nice, honest aromas of firm fruits and honey. Dry, smooth and yeasty, with tons of crunchy green apple acidity to give it a bit of bite, the wine ends with a clean finish.
Barry & Fitzwilliam

> **Blanc de Blancs** (white of whites) indicates that a white sparkling wine was made from white grapes only.
> **Blanc de Noirs** (white of blacks) indicates that the white sparkler was made from black grapes.

Mumm Cuvée Napa Blanc de Blancs Brut nv £21–£22
Unusually, Pinot Gris, a grape not included in Champagne, has been used here by Mumm to produce a sparkling wine with a difference. The nose is complex, with nice yeasty, appley aromas and toasty notes. The palate has tons of fruit — pears with hints of melon, crisp digestive biscuit flavours and good supporting acidity. It has a decent long finish. This is an elegant, well-made sparkler, offering value for money. Good food matches would be lightly smoked fish dishes — try kedgeree for a posh Sunday brunch.
Barry & Fitzwilliam

Sweet

In this section the wines are listed by
- country
- price

Australia

Miranda The Pioneers Raisined Muscat 98 £6–£7 (½ bottle)
Delicious is the only word for this sweet wine made from
dried (or raisined) Muscat grapes. It has super-fresh aromas of
tangy, juicy soft-fleshed fruit which are echoed on the palate
and lifted with refreshing acidity. In no way cloying, this
dessert wine is great value for money. It would make a great
substitute for afternoon tea with moist fruit cake. Treat
yourself over the next two years.
Taserra

Miranda Golden Botyritis 93 £10–£11 (½ bottle)
Honeyed, fat, rich and sweet this botrycic wine is made from
an eclectic blend of 65% Semillon (the grape used for Sauternes) and 35% Riesling. It has a lovely nose, redolent of
honey, figgy golden syrup, with some controlled and deliberate oxidation. The palate is deep and concentrated with lush
fruit flavours, with shy acidity
Taserra

d'Arenberg The Noble Riesling 97 £14–£15 (½ bottle)
As a grape variety, the Riesling makes excellent dessert wines
due to its extraordinary ability to maintain high acidity levels
in even the ripest of late harvested grapes.This counterbalancing freshness and crisp fruit adds balance to the lusciousness of
the honeyed fruit. D'Arenberg's Noble Riesling has an
extraordinarily spicy nose which is also mirrored on the palate
in a strong and forthright manner. While the fruits are a bit
burnt they come though to the end with a good gingery
finish. Drink it over the next two years.
Taserra

**De Bortoli Noble One Botrytis Semillon 95 £18–£19 (½
bottle)**
Established in 1928 in New South Wales De Bortoli produces
some of Australia's best Sauternes-like rich dessert wines. This
fine example displays a wide spectrum of intense luscious

honey and apricot jam aromas. Delicious, mouthwatering
honeyed and caramelised apricot flavours have an infusion of
lime fruits infused to sharpen the senses. All in all, it is a beautifully poised and balanced wine. Enjoy it over the next four years.
Febvre

France – Bordeaux

Sauternes produces some of the finest sweet wines in
the world. The Semillon and Sauvignon Blanc grapes
must be affected by **botrytitis** or **noble rot** which
appears at harvest time in those vineyards with high
humidity caused by a nearby river, stream or lake. The
less viscous water content in the grapes' juice drains
away from the pricked grape skins, leaving concentrated sugary pulp. The abundant sugar is too much for
the yeast to gorge on and convert into alcohol. A
residue of natural sugar remains in the wine after
fermentation.

Ch. La Bouade AC Sauternes 95 £15–£16
This 95 Sauternes has amazing rich orange peel, marmalade
and lemon zest aromas. Light in style, the wine is full of sweet
orange fruit flavours, combined with honey and finishing with
sweet spiciness. It is good value but should be resisted until
the end of 2001, when it will drink well for about two years.
Dunnes Stores

Ch. Lafaurie-Peyraguey AC Sauternes 95 £28–£30 (½ bottle)
One of Sauterne's classed growths (from the 1855 classification),
this château, owned by Cordier, is a very high achiever. The small
vineyard covers 49 acres in Bomme, one of Sauterne's five
communes. The 95 is a complex, rich, layered, textured and
luscious wine, combining everyhing you'd expect from a dessert
wine – honey, nutty, dried fruit flavours with weight, body and
long length. It will drink well for at least five years.
United Beverages

Germany

The QmP classification for the finest quality German wines has
six sub-sections determined by the ripeness levels of the
grapes and this Auslese is one of them

Hessische Bergstrasse Heppenheimer Stemmler
Gewürtztraminer Auslese QmP 99 £12–£13
The Gewurztraminer for this Auslese was late harvested from
specially selected extra-ripe bunches of grapes, some of which
might even have been affected by noble rot. The aromas are

quite assertive and very musky but the cool elegance of the mouthfeel is lovely — rose petal and gentle Turkish Delight. The fruit is deliciously sweet but nicely balanced and there is a long, lingering finish of floral and honeyed fruit.
Classic

Greece

'Achaia' Clauss Imperial Mavrodaphne of Patras   £7–£8
The black Mavrodaphne is grown around Patras in the Peloponnese. It produces lightly fortified wines, dark and sweet and Port-like.The wine usually benefits from a few years bottle age. This example was aged in oak barrels for added layers of flavour — it is a real adventure of a wine. On the nose, it has quintessential toffee apple covered in highly roasted hazelnuts with just enough acidity and freshness to carry it off. The wine will drink well over the next four years.
Taserra

'Achaia' Clauss Muscat de Patras £7–£8
This is a most intriguing, interesting wine. While the nose is a little confected, it is nonetheless strong and distinctive. The dominant texture on the palate is a very unctuous mouthfeel, oily and almost nutty. Overall, it is a very distinctive wine.
Taserra

Hungary

Some of the world's finest dessert wines come from the Tokaji-Hegyalja region in the extreme north-eastern part of Hungary. Two grape varieties make up the blend. The Furmint, the dominant grape, has very high acidity and high alcohol levels with a susceptibility to noble rot. The Harslevelu ('lime leaf') is an aromatic and spicy grape. The number of 'puttonyos' denotes the level of sweetness. The higher the number of 'putts.' the sweeter the wine.

Royal Tokaji Tokaji Aszú 5 Puttonyos 93 £11–£12 (250 ml bottle)
This Tokaji has a sherry, nutty, oxidised quality but it's restricted to the aromas. The palate is dominated by honey and apricot jam and ends with a caramel and nutty finish. The counterbalancing fresh acidity disciplines all the rich flavours. Remarkable value for money it will drink well over the next four years.
Findlaters

Choices

Tasters' choices

We invited the members of our tasting panel to recommend favourite wines (from firms other than their own, if they work in the wine trade) and these are what they came up with. There was no limit to the price, and the tasters were encouraged to select wines other than those they had blind-tasted for the main section of the book. Not all of the tasters felt able to recommend wines under these conditions, but those who did, came up with a remarkable selection for you to explore.

In this section the wines are listed by
* style
* price

Sherry

Tony Cleary
Lustau Manzanilla Sherry (Spain) £7–£8 (half bottle)
Manzanilla could be termed 'the wine merchants' dry sherry'.

Many prefer it to the more usual Fino. It is made by law exclusively in Sanlúcar de Barrameida, in solera systems housed in bodegas with doors opened towards the sea. The sea air wafting through gives a slight salty tang to the sherry. This, together with high chalk (*albariza*) content soil makes the wine so appealing. A little tip here. Manzanilla and Fino should be drunk as young as possible. In Sanlúcar they drink it straight from the barrel. Look at the back label. You will see something like L9261. Ignore the letter. The first figure represents the year of bottling. The next figures (261) tell you that the sherry was bottled 261 days into the year, i.e. 25 September. Try to drink it at less than one year and definitely not over two years old.
Mitchells

White

Maureen O'Hara
DO Penedès Torres Viña Esmeralda 1999 (Spain) £6–£7
Estate bottled, the wine is a blend of 85% Moscatel and 15% Gewurztraminer. Cold fermented in stainless steel vats, it's made by the fourth generation of the Torres family to be involved in winemaking. An attractive bouquet of lychees, Turkish delight and honeysuckle is followed by a slightly off-dry palate with lots of aromatic-type flavours — gooseberries, lychees and pineapple. Rather low in alcohol, it's very easy to drink a lot of it! Unusual

and satisfying—perhaps not everyone's cup of tea but certainly
worth a try.
Oddbins

Julie Martin
**VdP Maurel Vedeau La Cessane Marsanne Viognier 1999
(France) £6–£7**
A delightfully vibrant wine, this offers generous heady aromas
of orange blossom, fresh lime and ripe honeyed nectarine. Full
bodied and dry with a luscious palate of ripe apricot tones and
mildly zesty acidity, this is an unusual glint in an ocean of
mediocrity. It has good fruit structure and is well balanced
with a long, tasty, lingering finish. This is a super aperitif and
would also be a great match for salmon hollandaise.
WineOnline

Anne Mullin
**DO Penedès Santa Digna Barrel Fermented Chardonnay
Miguel Torres 1998 (Spain) £9–£10**
Miguel Torres was the man responsible for putting Spain on
the wine map of today and it was he who introduced all the
new techniques such as stainless steel temperature-controlled
fermentation, which has made it possible for such a warm
country to produce such subtle wines. His family is now
making wine not only in Spain, but in California and Chile.
This 98 from Spain is a superb example of a well-made
Chardonnay at a reasonable price, with classy use of new oak.
Many cheap Chardonnays are made using oak chips, which
not only colours the wine but gives it the overpowering oak
flavours that so many people have come to dislike. This wine
has warm, buttery aromas with lots of tropical fruits—mango
and guava and a hint of toast. On the palate it's dry, with
balanced acidity and excellent weight of ripe tropical fruits
with hints of vanilla, lemon grass and toasty, buttery fruit. A
delicious wine, it's round and mouthfilling with a lingering
spicy finish and great length. Excellent value for money.
Woodford Bourne

Canice McCarthy
**AC Alsace Gewurztraminer Trimbach
1998 (France) £12–£13**
Trimbach, a respected Alsace grower
and merchant, produces remarkably
elegant, subtle, slightly reserved wines.
This Gewurztraminer's intense bouquet
is spicy and floral with honey and
apricot undertones. The taste is fresh
and crisp with deliciously appealing
spiciness combined with beautiful honeyed flavours of
apricots and tropical fruit. A dry wine that has so much to
offer, the bouquet and palate hint at sweetness.
Gilbeys

Niamh Boylan
AC Alsace Léon Beyer Riesling 1999 (France) £12–13

Riesling is beginning an overdue revival in popularity, but I'd hate to think that this wonderful classic grape would become merely fashionable. Wines produced from Riesling run the style gamut from light and floral to steely, intense, luscious and long-lived. One of my favourites is from Alsace, produced by Léon Beyer, a very long-established family firm based in the delightful village of Eguisheim. Alsacien Rieslings tend to be much fuller bodied than their German neighbours and more elegant than those from Australia. The Beyer 99 Riesling has delicious, fresh, tangy grapefruit and green apple flavours with hints of just-cut grass and lots of racy acidity. I love to drink it with seafood terrine, quiche or even a dish of mild smoked pork sausages.
James Adams

David Lonergan
Ch. Tahbilk Marsanne Victoria 1992 (Australia) £15–£16
A somewhat obscure grape variety, originally from the Rhône Valley, Marsanne is rarely seen on its own. It was brought to Tahbilk in the 19th century and now 10 % of Marsanne plantings in the world come from Tahbilk. The wine develops well with age, becoming deeper in colour and more intense and complex on the nose and palate, but always dry. The 92 has a deep gold colour with rich, tangy citrus fruits and again complex honeyed flavours, giving a long, lingering finish. Very interesting stuff indeed. A serious white wine, almost unique in character, it must be tried at least once. A good accompaniment for pork dishes cooked in citrus sauces or a rich smoked salmon dish.
United Beverages

Carly Ptashnick
Riesling Spätlese, Forster Krischenstuck 1996 (Germany) £17–£18
The-I-Am-A-Clever-Little-Minx-Wine You've been up to something deliciously sneaky — and it's worked. Or maybe you've made a life-affirming decision, and it's a biggie. Like you are off to Morocco to eat all your future meals out of twenty little coloured bowls and sleep in a bed with a veil like in *The English Patient*. Celebrate your brilliance in a giant bubble bath with enough candles to burn down the house. Quick! Pour yourself another glass of Forster Krischenstuck Riesling Spätlese. Oh God, the heady aromas of beautiful, beautiful green jelly, honey and juicy orchard fruit. The palate shows perfect acidity, going from sweetness to pleasing tartness, with fabulous

flavours of kiwi and even blood oranges. Excellent balance and body, alive and spritzy, it's far too easy to drink the entire bottle yourself.
Fields

Evelyn Jones
Trimbach Riesling Cuvée Frédéric Émile 1995 (France) £17–£18

I often have this wine with spicy, but not too hot, Indian or Malaysian food. It's a rich wine with lovely weight in the mouth that particularly appeals to the red wine drinker, even though it's a white wine. Although it's a 95 vintage, it's still quite young in terms of maturity. Its mildly floral influence is backed up by a tangy lime fruit character that complements the flavours of ginger, coriander, lemon grass, etc. that one finds in Asian-style food, while refreshing and cleansing the palate with its long yet zippy finish.
Gilbeys

Alison Gallagher
AC Chablis 1er Cru Côte de Lechet La Chablisienne 1998 (France) £19–£20
Chablis is my favourite style of white wine — dry, crisp and refreshing. This one is classic Chablis, from its pale colour with a greenish tinge to the complex nose which is minerally with lemony citrus notes and slightly scented in the background. It has distinctive acidity, beautifully crisp and refreshing. A lovely blend of lemony flavours, green scented melons and a wonderful mineral element gives structure to the wine. The rich fullness of flavours lingers, producing a lovely crisp finish. A full-bodied, steely, elegant wine, it's delicious to drink now and will improve. If you want to taste classic wines, this one will not disappoint.
Mitchells

Pat Carroll
AC Condrieu Guigal 1998 (France) £30–£31
With subtle aromas of flowers, tropical fruits and a bit of toasty background from the oak, this is a really inviting and delicate wine. Made from 100% Viognier grapes, it's dry, rich and smooth, but with enough acidity to keep it interesting. On the palate there are oranges, peaches and toasted hazelnuts. There is quite a punch of alcohol and the finish is nutty and very

long. This wine is still maturing and will develop over the next two to three years. The producer, Marcel Guigal, is one of the best winemakers in the Rhône. He uses organic methods as far as possible. The grapes are grown on steep hillsides so all the grapes are hand harvested. The wine is fermented in stainless steel vats and matured in oak, but the oak flavour is subtle, enhancing the flavour of the wine without overpowering it. If you're looking for something a little bit different (and special), this Condrieu is well worth a try.
Syrah Wines

Martina Delaney
AC Beaune Clos des Mouches Joseph Drouhin 1997 (France) £45

The Beaune Clos des Mouches is the flagship white wine of Joseph Drouhin, a very well-known négociant house. It's one of the most stunning white wines I've ever tasted. The nose displays some earthy, minerally, zippy, zesty aromas which are heaven on the palate — subtle and elegant with toasty almond, lemon and lime juice, ripe melons and vanilla pods beautifully integrated with great structure and balance. Quite seductive and classy.
Drink now and up to 2005. I recommend decanting this wine about half an hour before drinking, which will allow it to open up and develop. It would go well with monkfish or scallops in a rich sauce, or with veal.
Gilbeys

Red

Canice McCarthy
Correas Syrah 1997 (Argentina) £7–£8
This is a big, fruity wine with an attractive bouquet of spicy, ripe-berried fruit with hints of vanilla. The palate is full and warm with characteristic Syrah/Shiraz flavours of spice, pepper and delicious fruit. The tannins are evident but don't overshadow the flavour.
Gilbeys

Maureen O'Hara
Tyrrell's Long Flat Shiraz 1999 (Australia) £7–£8
The Tyrrell family has been producing wines in the Hunter Valley since 1858. The company is headed by Murray Tyrrell, winemaker for over forty years, and his son Bruce. This wine is very fruity on the nose (blackberries, damsons, etc.), the

same fruit follows through on the palate, where it is matched
by intense black pepper. It's a great value-for-money wine
that goes very well with peppered steak, barbecues or grills.
Maxxium

Carly Ptashnick
AC Minervois Comté de Mérinville 1997 (France) £7–£8
The-Classic-Friends-Come-Round-For-A-Really-Great-Meal-And-
We-All-Wind-Up-In-Knots-Laughing-About-The-Stupid-Things-
We-Did-When-We-Didn't-Know-Better-Wine It's going to go
down in history as a legendary night—everybody can just feel
it. The food was unreal (and could have been roast pork with a
redcurrant and rosemary stuffing with baked squash and
parsnips) and now the air is punctuated with laughter that
could set off car alarms. What's the empty bottle on the table?
It's got to be Comté de Mérinville Minervois. This wine has
the most infatuating flavours of zippy cranberry, redcurrant,
and raspberry you've ever tasted, with whiffs of spice box on
the layered, expansive palate. The finish goes on for ages—far
longer even, than Oisín's joke about the priest, the bartender
and the cashew nut . . .
Bubble Brothers

Simon Keegan
AC Coteaux de Languedoc Bergerie de l'Hortus Pic St Loup
Classique 1998 (France) £8–£9
A blend of Syrah, Mourvèdre and Grenache, this wine is made
by Jean Orliac, who is becoming a reference point in this
region for quality. With some oak, this opens with a clean
smoky nose with lots of fruit, thyme and white pepper spice.
The fruit is succulent and moreish. Tannins are soft and easy
on the palate with an elegant finish. It will continue to improve
for another three years at least.
Wines Direct

Carly Ptashnick
VdP de l'Hérault Moulin de Gassac Elise 1998 (France) £8–£9
The-Great-Seduction-In-Front-Of-A-Roaring-Fire-Wine It's a
crisp, starry night, the kind where on the walk home you can
see ghosts of breath escape your mouth and sink into the inky
sky. The light from the fire is fracturing in her hair like
splinters of gold. The last time you saw a man with such a
perfect nose was in the room full of marble statues in the
Louvre. Quick! What are you drinking? It has to be Moulin de
Gassac Elise, of course. Slinky and intense, this wine has a
superb bouquet of crushed berries and a sublime palate of
strawberries dipped in pure Swiss chocolate, with slight
eucalyptus notes and a gorgeous lingering finish.
O'Briens

David Lonergan
DO Costers del Segre Gotim Bru Castell del Remei 1997 (Spain) £9–£10
Best of Wine in Ireland 2001 Wine of the Year
The quality of this wine is very striking, but so is the price—it's quite the best value I've come across for a long time. Had it been twice the price, I wouldn't have been surprised. This wine comes from Costers del Segre, a small DO within Penedès in Catalonia in north-eastern Spain. It's one of the few wineries there, the biggest and best known being Raïmat of Codorníu fame. Made from a blend of Cabernet Sauvignon, Merlot and Tempranillo, it has intense, complex aromas of sweet vanillin oak, ripe currants, cherries and black fruits with hints of spice and coffee. On the palate it's dry and full bodied with rich, chewy black fruits and complex, spicy tobacco flavours. A good tannic background offers excellent ageing potential over the next four to five years and beyond, though it's a pleasure to drink now. A classic red meat wine.
Searsons

Kate Barrett
VR Alentejo Cortes de Cima Chamine 1999 (Portugal) £9–£10
Alentejo, east of the Lisbon coast, land of olive and cork trees, is the largest region in Portugal and has ideal conditions for vine growing. Until recently production was dominated by co-ops, but there are now over forty individual producers raising standards. Cortes de Cima is a family-owned estate in the southern part of Alentejo making wines from traditional local varieties Aragonez, Trincadeira and Periquita. Their Chamine has a very ripe dark fruit nose with lots of ripe redcurrants and blackcurrants in the mouth with a fantastic lick of spice. The finish is extremely tasty with oodles of fruit and spice and very easy-drinking tannins—one bottle won't be enough. A real testament to some of the great quality coming out of Portugal!
James Nicholson

Evelyn Jones
Arnaldo B. Etchart Cafayate 1996 (Argentina) £11–£12
For me this wine typifies all that Argentina is capable of and encapsulates the best of the old and the new wine styles produced in the New World. Argentina has a micro-climate that is rich in trace elements and benefits from high altitude and cooling mountain breezes. This is a wine of structure and concentration with elegant, ripe fruit in the classic Bordeaux style, yet it offers excellent value. A food wine in the classic sense.
Irish Distillers

Tony Cleary
AC Fronsac Ch. de la Rivière 94 (France) £12–£13
Fronsac is not usually mentioned as a great area for wine. Truth
is, it is not! However, one property stands out above the mediocre—Ch. de la Rivière. Jacques Borie, the winemaker, returned
from West Africa, having sold his coffee plantation, about thirty
years ago. He bought one of the most imposing châteaux in all of
Bordeaux, built on a tufa-type soil that was originally the site of a
Charlemagne fortress. Later an order of monks quarried out an
amazing labyrinth of corridors and rooms. The dining room
contains a table and chairs, large enough for the whole congrega-
tion, carved out of solid rock. These amazing workings now
house the cellars. There is even a small waterway carved out to
maintain an even temperature. The château is open to visitors by
appointment and should be on everybody's itinerary when
touring Bordeaux. Having bought the estate, M. Borie immediately planted more Merlot to soften the rather harsh traditional
style of these wines. Acutely aware of the fanatical following his
neighbour Ch. Pétrus enjoys, he spared no expense in upgrading
the vineyard. This is a wine to drink when tired of fruit-driven,
blowsy wines. Definitely a food wine, it's a good companion for
game and hard cheese.
Irish Distillers

Niamh Boylan
AC Sancerre Fournier 1997 (France) £12–13
Mention Sancerre and one immediately thinks of a gorgeous
Loire white with tingling fresh acidity. Right! But also wrong.
Sancerre also produces a red wine from the Pinot Noir grape and
this lovely example is from the house of Fournier. Pour a glass
and you will see a vibrant ruby jewel colour with a fresh bright
hue. The bouquet gives rich aromas of rhubarb and ripe red
berries—redcurrants and loganberries—with a slight whiff of
farmyard. This is a 97—a great year for the Loire. I love the
refreshing acidity, the purity of the fruit and the mild smoky
tannins—altogether a very harmonious wine with lots of class.
Red Sancerre of this quality is a real alternative to a more
expensive village Burgundy and is a good wine to drink with fish.
Salmon would be an excellent choice and so too would monkfish
wrapped in Parma ham served with a light herby wine *jus*.
TDL

Canice McCarthy
Wolf Blass President's Selection Cabernet Sauvignon 1996 (Australia) £13–£14
A complex wine, this Cabernet Sauvignon has a very attractive
bouquet of cassis with minty and buttery oak nuances. The
palate is full and rich—chewable—with mouthfilling ripe
blackcurrants and nicely balanced tannins.
Dillons

Brian Brady

IGT Rosso di Salento Candido Duca d'Aragona Apuglia 1994 (Italy) £14–£15

A blend of the grapes Negroamaro and Montepulciano, this is the finest wine to come from the Salice Salentino area. At six years old, it is mature and balanced, exhibiting dark chocolate and summer pudding traits.

Findlaters

Alison Gallagher

WO Stellenbosch Thelema Cabernet Sauvignon 1996 (South Africa) Vaughan Johnson £14–£15

With its warm black berry fruits on the nose with eucalyptus and leather aromas, this luscious red wine from home promises much and delivers plenty. Smooth and velvety in the mouth, crammed with blackcurrants and blackberries, plus a dash of liquorice, this wine is bursting with flavour. Full-bodied and rounded, it has a delicious long finish. This is a wine to stimulate all the senses with its rich colour, lovely aromas, delicious flavours, velvety feel and the sound as it flows from bottle to glass! Rich, warming, satisfying — Cape sunshine in a bottle!

Vaughan Johnson

Tony Cleary

Bethany Shiraz 1996 (Australia) £14–£15

Despite tasting over two hundred wines blind for this year's *Best of Wine in Ireland*, finding a favourite was no problem. Bethany Shiraz 96 is one of those wines that make you sit up immediately. At the price it's not everybody's daily drinking wine, but it should be a weekend treat. Tasting notes include cassis, cedar, freshly ground pepper and black cherries plus velvet-smooth texture and long aftertaste. The vineyard has been in the possession of the same family since 1844. The grapes used to make this wine come from the old 'home blocks' using some of the oldest vines. It was a hot year in 1996, so picking started early to ensure good acidity levels. You will find slight variations from bottle to bottle, but this just makes the wine more interesting.

O'Briens

Anne Mullin

Bonny Doon Il Fiasco 1998 (USA) £15–£16

An unusual wine, this is made by an unusual gentleman — Randall Grahm, who is often referred to in California as the 'Rhône ranger' for his pioneering work in the popularisation of Rhône varieties in California. He bought vineyards in the

Santa Cruz mountains in an area aptly named Bonny Doon, where, unusually for California, the main grape variety is Sangiovese, the Italian Chianti grape, along with some Syrah, the northern Rhône variety. The wine, a blend of 77% Sangiovese, 12% Syrah and 11% Mourvèdre, is full-bodied with an abundance of very ripe baked black cherry fruits on the nose with hints of chocolate and spice. On the palate it's dry, with well-balanced acidity and well-structured tannins. There is an excellent weight of rich, ripe bramble fruits laced with dark chocolate and the oak is nicely integrated. The palate is very spicy. It's a delicious, elegant, mouthfilling, rich wine, with layers and layers of fruit with a long, lingering finish and drinking beautifully now, with or without food.
James Nicholson

Pat Carroll
AC Chinon Réserve Privée Marc Brédif 1996 (France) £15–£16
I love Chinon. It's so different. Red Loire wines aren't very popular in Ireland, but they deserve to be drunk a lot more. Made from the Cabernet Franc grape grown on chalk and flinty clay, this wine is very complex. There are aromas of blackcurrant leaf, rubber and cherry. On the palate the wine is dry, with lots of acidity and concentrated cranberry fruit, bitter cherries and blackcurrants. Tannins are quite firm and there is a wonderful long finish with a mineral note. Expect the wine to mature and improve for three to four years. The first time I drank this Chinon was at a dinner with friends. We all thought it was a super wine. When I retasted it for this book on a Sunday afternoon on its own, however, it seemed more astringent and tannic — it clearly needed food (a bit of cheese made all the difference). The wine should be opened and preferably decanted for at least three hours before drinking — it was perfectly delicious the day after the tasting, as it had softened even more. (Yes, there was some left — but not much!)
Morgans

Colm Conaty
St Hallett Old Block Barossa Shiraz 1995 (Australia) £16–£17
Aromas of spice and chocolate are followed by lots of very ripe blackcurrant fruit. The tannins are still quite firm, but they're balanced with crisp acidity. The wine is drinking well now but will develop over the next ten years. Excellent with roast beef.
Dunnes Stores

Anne Mullin
DO Brolo di Campofiorin Masi 1996 (Italy) £16–£17
This is one of the nicest wines I've tasted this year. It's made with two grape varieties and fermented in the normal way. However, it is then given a second fermentation on the

Amarone lees. Then, to add additional flavour, semi-dried grapes are added. The wine is aged in small oak casks for two years and for six months in bottle. On the nose there are complex aromas of spice, blackcurrants, damsons and rich Christmas cake. A dry wine, with balanced acidity and firm tannins, there is huge weight of ripe, sweet blackcurrant fruits on the palate. Big, full, rich, ripe and robust with excellent mouthfeel, this is a delicious, elegant, velvety wine with layer upon layer of fruit, giving a long finish with great length and flavours that go on and on and on. It has plenty of time to go so treat yourself.

Grants

Evelyn Jones
DOC Rioja Marqués de Murrieta Ygay Reserva Especial 1991 (Spain) £17–£18
This is a lovely traditional style of Rioja, which still manages to retain its fruit while having a lot of wood ageing. The barrels used are not new, which gives the wine a lovely nutty character and this, coupled with succulent sun-dried fruits and crisp acidity, goes so well with traditional roast meats that you can almost imagine you are in northern Spain.

Gilbeys

Julie Martin
Terrungo Carmenère 1998 (Chile) £18–£19

This is one of the aristocrats of Chilean wines — opulent, noble and round with a rich and ripe cedar-scented bouquet. It has a seductive, silky smooth texture with wood smoke, brambles and cassis touched with pepper and a heavy slash of *goût de terroir*, weighty and gorgeous. The well-integrated flavours are in layers of baked fruit with notes of mulled wine spice. Try it on its own, with Christmas dinner, or with a selection of fine cheeses.

Findlaters

Martina Delaney
DO Estremadura Quinta de Pancas Touriga Naçional Special Selection 1997 (Portugal) £20–£21
Quinta de Pancas is situated 45 km north-east of Lisbon in an area abounding with old manors and estates, most of them devoted to grapes. Quinta de Pancas is one of the oldest estates, dating back to the 15th century. This wine is produced from 100% Touriga Naçional, using traditional maceration. It's then aged in small oak barrels, one-third being new. I was very taken with its wonderful aromas of stewed black cherries and Christmas cake — spices and figs leap out of the glass. The palate is as exciting and pleasurable as the nose suggests. Well-

focused flavours of blackcurrants, aniseed, cassis and cherries intermingle with spice and are supported by fleshy tannins. The overall impression is one of elegance and youthful vitality — a real eye-opener. The wine will happily age for five to ten years. Good food accompaniments include lamb, osso bucco, duck or goats' cheese.
Terroirs

Simon Keegan
DOC Rioja La Rioja Alta Viña Ardanza 1993 (Spain) £20–£21
La Rioja Alta is one of the foremost producers of traditional-style Rioja. This is one of their range of sublime wines. Released ready to drink, the 93 has a lovely leather and prune nose. On the palate it has warm red berries with an elegant oakiness and smooth tannins. It's delicious now and will carry on improving for another three years.
Woodford Bourne

Willie Dardis
DO Douro Duas Quintas Reserva 1995 (Portugal) £22–£23
Made from the same grape varieties used to make Port, this wonderful wine has developed aromas of spicy figs and blackcurrants with chocolate nuances. On the palate there are big and bold flavours of ripe black fruit, vanilla, dark chocolate and spicy berries. Big, complex, balanced and well structured, long and delicious, this wine still has plenty of life in it.
Searsons

Simon Keegan
VdP l'Herault Dom. de la Grange de Peres 1997 (France) £26–£27
From the Cévennes foothills in the Languedoc, this wine was recently tasted by an Australian winemaker in that excellent wine bar Ely in Dublin. He has taken a bottle back home to show them what elegant finesse Syrah wines can have. Since this is a big wine, it's best to decant it to help the wine open up. It has lots of dark brambly fruit with pepper, spice and sumptuous tannins, yet it's yielding with a long, intense fruit finish. Still quite youthful, it has great ageing potential — four years or more.
Wines Direct

Mary O'Callaghan
DOCG Amarone della Valpolicella Classico Masi 1997 (Italy) £25
Deep, dark, dense ruby in colour — almost opaque — with orange/russet hues, the wine has very good viscosity. Clean,

pronounced, mature, complex and multi-layered, the bouquet is of very dark plums, nutmeg, chocolate and violets, with herbs, smoke and spice under the well-integrated layers. Excellent high acidity and very firm, almost robust tannin, balance a huge weight of hot, spicy, very ripe dark cherry and mulberry fruits, with spicy truffle, black olive and a 'mossy' complexity underneath. The big,

smooth chocolate texture is full bodied with a very long length that eventually finishes with a black cherry, almost bitter, twist that oozes Italian style and character. At 15%, it has very high alcohol. This Amarone is still very young. It will improve over six to eight years and will last at least ten to twelve. Serve it at warm room temperature with roast game — venison or wild boar — accompanied by piquant sauces.
Grants

Martina Delaney
AC Nuits St George Robert Chevillon Les Pruliers 1997 (France) £25–£26
Robert Chevillon owns about eight hectares of vines and his domaine is regarded as one of the most outstanding in Burgundy. He uses one-third new oak barrels and filters his wines lightly. This one has a wonderful array of juicy, soft berry fruit, strawberries, raspberries, bubble gum and mint leaf. Then comes a dense concentration of fruit compote, soft summer berries and minerally notes, broad and rich — it's a velvety, textured wine with a good backbone and structure, delicate yet very approachable when young. The 97 is the one I've tasted, but the 98 is due in soon — reviews say it surpasses the 97 — I can't wait! Try it with veal, lamb, quail or cheese.
Burgundy Direct

Willie Dardis
AC St Julien Ch. Gloria 1995 (France) £26–£27
On the nose there are pronounced aromas of plum and soft bramble fruit with spicy oak. There is great depth and weight in this mouthfilling and highly complex wine with layers of flavours of blackcurrant, plums and soft bramble fruit, with some damsons and cassis, all well integrated. This is a superbly balanced wine, delicious now and potentially classic.
Grants

Pat Carroll

DO Priorat Alvaro Palacios Finca Dofi 1996 (Spain) £26–£27

Winemaking in Priorat goes back at least 500 years, but until
the mid-1980s most wines were produced by co-ops using
traditional methods. A group of young winemakers recog-
nised the potential of the area and invested jointly in eight
well-sited vineyards, where they produced high-quality wine
by keeping yields very low and using modern methods. One
of these pioneers was Alvaro Palacios, whose family has been
making Rioja for generations. Finca Dofi takes no prisoners.
Made from 60% Garnacha, 20% Cabernet Sauvignon, 10%
Merlot, 5% Cariñena and 5% Syrah, it's a deep, dense, dark
ruby, with a concentrated nose of prunes, figs, Christmas cake,
loganberries and cherries. There are more rich and complex
dark fruits on the palate — blackberries and blackcurrants, as
well as figs, chocolate and spices. Alcohol at 13.5% is quite high
and the finish is extremely long. This is superbly made wine —
think Supertuscan at a bargain price. It's expensive, but worth
it. Buy two and keep the other one for ten years.
Approach

Mary O'Callaghan

**Marimar Torres Green Valley Sonoma Pinot Noir 1996
(USA — California) £30**

Beautifully clear, bright mid-ruby in colour with a sheen and
tawny pink rim, this wine has a complex, clean nose that is
initially very perfumed and fragrant, with evolving layers
underneath of rosemary and gorse with some liquorice
nuances complementing the soft ripe and mellow blackberry
fruit aromas. On the palate excellent acidity balances the ripe
firm tannin and refined elegant weight of ripe red summer
berry fruits — strawberries, raspberries and redcurrants — with
evolving vegetal flavours, tar, spice and rhubarb. An elegant,
silky smooth, velvety-rich texture with long flavoursome
length, there's a touch of just crushed black pepper on the
finish. This is a beautifully crafted, well-made wine of excellent
quality, beginning to show some developmental characteristics
as it moves into its second phase. Drinking very well now, it
will improve for up to three years and should last for about
eight years. It shows that excellent Pinot Noir can be made
outside Burgundy. Serve it at room temperature with roast
rack of lamb or roast duck.
Woodford Bourne

Liam Campbell

AC St Julien Ch. Gruaud Larose 1988 (France) £50–£55

Ch. Gruaud Larose is one of the largest and most popular
second growths (1855 classification), with 77 hectares. Smooth,
rich and cedary in style, this wine needs at least a decade to
mature and can sustain another two decades quite easily. Of the

three glorious vintages of 88, 89 and 90 the 88 shows the most promise in the long term It was tannic and austere in youth, but is beginning to open up wonderful sandalwood aromas infused with herbs. On the palate, it's supple and velvety textured. Cassis and damsons, tobacco leaf and dried herbs add complexity to the wine, which is atypically ripe for an 88.

O'Briens

Conor Richardson

DOC Barbaresco Angelo Gaja 1996 (Italy) £55–£60

Angelo Gaja has elevated his long-established family reputation for the best Barbarescos around. Toughness and tannins are the hallmark of Nebbiolo, but Gaja's Barbaresco is deliciously soft with hints of smoke, herbs and pine. It finishes with nuances of chocolate raisins, prunes and tobacco. Remarkable. Wonderful with red meat dishes.

Best Cellars

Niamh Boylan

AC Morey-St-Denis Grand Cru Clos de Tart 1986 (current vintage available 1995) (France) £70

I bought this in the cellars of Clos de Tart in Burgundy and carried it home as a precious cargo. Every so often I checked it as it matured slowly and gracefully on my rack, waiting for the optimum time to drink it. A chilly Saturday night with three winey friends was the occasion. The colour was a gorgeous amalgam of garnet and old brick with a pronounced bouquet of ripe red fruits and mature undergrowth. The palate was silky and soft with a great depth of elegant and subtle flavours—a true classic from a classic region. This was Pinot Noir at its seductive best. A generous wine, it gave us pleasure right through to the last drop. And yes! We drank it with breast of guinea fowl served with a Marsala and redcurrant sauce. Sublime!

United Beverages

Monica Murphy

AC St Estèphe Ch. Cos d'Estournel (France) 1970 £65–£85 depending on vintage

Elegant, silky, so intense, with clearly defined fruit and great length—this was the first serious Bordeaux Cru Classé I ever tasted and I realised the difference! Cos is available—in younger vintages, of course—from specialist outlets and off-licences, such as O'Briens.

Monica Murphy
**AC Morey-St-Denis Grand Cru Clos de la Roche Dom. Dujac
1986 (France)**
Tasted on cold cellar steps in November 1989 — all I could say
was 'Wow!' Alas this vinage is no longer available, but try a
later one. Available from wine merchants such as Findlaters.

Sparkling

Colm Conaty
Huia Marlborough Sparkling nv (New Zealand) £19–£20
This is an excellent sparkler, with very fine long-lasting
mousse. It has a complex nose, with aromas of yeast and
green fruit and a touch of honey. It has great weight of fruit
on the palate. Balanced with crisp acidity giving a long finish,
like all non-vintage sparklers this is made for drinking as soon
as it's made. Be sure to buy it from an outlet with a fast
turnover so that you will get a fresh rather than a tired bottle.
Searsons

David Lonergan
Pelorus Marlborough 1995 (New Zealand) £22
From the famous Cloudy Bay vineyards comes this delicious
'serious' sparkler. A really good alternative to Champagne
(except the best ones), it's made from a blend of Pinot Noir
and Chardonnay, bottle-fermented and aged on its lees for
thee years. It has a developed nose of honeyed tropical fruits
with an underlying oily yeastiness. Dry on the palate with lots
of creamy vanilla with passion fruit, butter and toasted
almonds, it's a big wine with loads of concentration, yet it's
elegant and fresh. No sharpness here. An ideal way to spend
some time in good company or any morning.
Findlaters

Alison Gallagher

Champagne Veuve Clicquot Ponsardin Yellow Label Brut nv (France) £29–£30

For Christmas, New Year, birthdays or any other celebration, my choice is always my favourite Champagne — Veuve Clicquot Ponsardin. Just watching the tiny even stream of bubbles fizzing up through the glass sets my tastebuds tingling with anticipation. On the nose it's fresh apples and citrus, slightly yeasty with a hint of caramel. It has wonderful, crisp, refreshing acidity balanced with full fruity flavours of apples and citrus. This is a full-bodied and elegant wine, with a long finish and almost spicy caramel. It has a lovely creamy mousse and feels as good as it tastes. Utterly delicious!
Findlaters

Liam Campbell

Champagne Grande Cuvée Krug (multi-vintage) (France) £86

Krug makes remarkably long-lived wines. They can be austere in youth, but gain great complexity, balance and depth with age. There are two reasons for this. First, all wines undergo their first fermentation in small oak barrels. Second, the wines used for blending, which are six to ten years old, are very mature and complex. The blend will include up to fifty of these wines. The varieties' proportions are 45–55% Pinot Noir, 25–35% Chardonnay and quite a high 15–20% Pinot Meunier. The deep straw colour indicates the maturity of the wine. In the glass there is a volcanic eruption of tiny bubbles with great persistence — microscopic strings of pearls. There are aromas of hazelnuts, marzipan and a savouriness from the Pinot Noir. On the palate, the wine is dry, rich and mellow, with lively but balanced acidity fine-tuned by an earthy fruitiness.
Findlaters

Sweet

Colm Conaty

AC Sauternes Ch. Rieussec 1996 (France)

Deep yellow in colour, this wine has a pronounced nose with layers of honeyed botrytis aromas, apricots and burnt sugar. The palate is very complex with apricot marmalade orange fruit, lots of acidity and a long, clean finish. It goes well with blue cheese and has a further life of at least four years.

Willie Dardis

AC Vouvray M. Brédif Nectar Vin Moelleux 1990 (France) £22–£23 (35 cl)

A sensational wine. It's liquid gold in colour, with wonderful aromas of honey and Seville oranges. It has a weighty mouthfeel with a luscious honey and marmalade palate in a classic, well-integrated style showing great elegance but still

with a youthful edge. It has a long and impressive finish. This is a wine that will last for sixty years. Wonderful for after Christmas dinner.
Morgans

Des Drumm
DOC Breganze Maculan Torcolato 1996 (Italy) £25–£26 (75 cl)
As a lover of dessert wine this took my fancy as something very different. It's made by brother and sister Fausto and Franco Maculan in the little-known northern region of Breganze. The wine has been compared by some writers with some much more expensive Sauternes. It has a flowery aroma, with underlying honey, vanilla essence and very lush raisin-like fruit, held in check with marked acids and a touch of oak. Its finish is markedly clean. It's unusual, well made and makes a refreshing change.

Oddbins

Mary O'Callaghan
AC Bonnezeaux Ch. de Fesles 1997 (France) £33 (50 cl)
This wine is deep lemon, of great clarity, with gold lights and a glossy sheen. It has excellent viscosity. The nose is very clean and honeyed with an abundance of ripe, luscious, yellow fruit — apricots and peaches with some citrus (tangerine) aromas and very subtle hints of botrytis (noble rot). Excellent, fresh, lively, well-integrated acidity balances an elegant weight of ripe, honeyed yellow fruit as on the nose, with some floral and citrus notes underneath. The luscious, silky smooth texture is very classic, with an elegant restraint and delicious long length that has a very clean finish. This is a top-quality, very well-made sweet wine that is understated in style. Although luscious, it's very fresh and is not at all heavy or cloying, due to the lovely, racy, zippy, lively acidity. An elegant wine with much class and restraint, rarely found in Vins Liquoreux. Serve slightly chilled — not too cold — with fresh fruit, dessert or blue cheese for a stunning taste sensation.
Febvre

Monica Murphy
Max Ferdinand Richter Eiswein 1988 (Germany)
This Eiswein is the most intense, high-toned, racy pure nectar I have ever tasted. It was saved for me in a baby Power bottle when I missed a tasting and it was mind-blowing.

The production of **Eiswein** (ice wine) is high risk. One of Germany's rarest sweet wines, its structure is different from Beerenauslese and Trockenbeeren-auslese wines affected by noble rot. Eiswein is made from grapes gathered at a temperature of –8 °C. The frozen grapes are crushed and the water content of the juice is discarded, leaving a high proportion of sugar in the juice. The risk lies in the lateness of the harvest, sometimes as late as mid-December or even the following January, as there is no guarantee that the temperature will drop low enough and the crop may be lost.

Liam Campbell
Riesling Eiswein Winkeler Hasensprung Wegeler Deinhard Rheingau 1983 (Germany) £95
In 1997 the Wegeler family sold the two-hundred-year-old merchant house of Deinhard, but kept their three magnificent estates. The 83 vintage in the Rheingau was excellent. The deep amber colour reveals the wine's age. There are milky, creamy aromas with no sign of a mature Riesling petrolly bouquet. On the palate there is crème brûlée richness and beautiful harmony and integration between the fresh acidity and the luscious fruit, which has hints of apricots.
Mitchells

Money no object

We invited the importers of the wines included in The Best of Wine in Ireland *to recommend some of their more expensive wines for that special occasion.*

In this section the wines are listed by
- style
- price

White

Maxxium
AC Pouilly-Fumé La Grande Cuvée Pascal Jolivet 1998 (France) £25
This muscular white wine offers ripe flavours of melon and apple with notes of herb and almond. Not a show-off, it's a well-made traditional wine that achieves power without oak and verve without tart acidity. It will last for another ten years at least. Serve it with snapper, crab or smoked salmon.

Gleeson
AC Meursault Meursault du Château 1997 (France) £29
Soft and ripe, with gentle acidity, this delicious vintage shows unaccustomed hints of tropical fruit flavours. In an ideal world, this wine should be enjoyed before the 96. Perfect dining accompaniments would be organic roast chicken stuffed with fresh rosemary and lemon or steamed lobster with clarified butter and baby asparagus tips.

Grants
Roxburgh Chardonnay Rosemount 96/97 (Australia) £27
Complex aromas, with concentrated peach fruit supported by subtle soft oak. Exprressive rich fruit on the palate supported by fine natural acidity. Its long, rich, fruit-driven finish goes on for ever. The wine will repay long-term cellaring — ten to 15 years.

Bacchus Wines
IGT Toscana Batar 1997 (Italy) £40 (limited availability)
Batar is produced by the 25 hectare Querciabella estate in Tuscany and is a blend of 50% Chardonnay and 50% Pinot Bianco, fermented and aged in 100% new oak. The *Gambero Rosso* wine guide 1999 refers to Querciabella as 'the best Chianti Classico estate of the year' and voted Batar 'the best Tuscan white'. Pale golden in colour, the wine has a pronounced nose of ripe fruit and crème caramel that follows through on the palate. Medium-bodied, with attractive balancing acidity and a long finish, it will improve over two to three years.

Febvre
AC Le Montrachet Grand Cru Dom. Jacques Prieur Antonin Rodet 1997 (France) £250
This wine is incredibly concentrated, with smooth, luscious fruit and rich, nutty, buttery texture and flavour. With its intense, many-layered aromas of all sorts of delicious fruit and flowers, it lingers forever. To partner this full-bodied classic wine, serve Poulet de Bresse.

Red

Gleeson
DOC Amarone della Valpolicella Giama 1995 (Italy) £18
A stunning, luxurious wine, made for seduction! The decadent palate of baked fruit flavours, cinnamon, black cherries, toasted tobacco and expansive blackcurrant fill the mouth and taper into an exceptionally lengthy finish. This wine will complement traditional grilled Italian sausage, tomato sauces with pancetta over fresh pasta, fine Italian cheeseboards or even rich, chocolate-loaded desserts.

O'Briens
WO Stellenbosch Rust-en-Vrede Estate Wine 1997 (South Africa) £19
Rust-en-Vrede is one of South Africa's greatest assets. This boutique winery, owned and operated by the Engelbracht family in the Stellenbosch region, produces only 12,000 cases from its premium vineyards. This wine has just been awarded a double gold medal at the 2000 Veritas awards in South Africa. This Cabernet/Shiraz blend has a wonderful deep colour. On the nose there are black fruits, spice and toast. On the palate it's elegant, complex and concentrated. Made in a traditional style, this wine has great structure and will evolve over the next five to seven years. It would go well with roast meat or wood pigeon.

Bubble Brothers
AC Cahors Prince Probus 1997 (France) £24
Over the past few decades Prince Probus has earned a reputa-tion as the uncrowned king of South-West France. This outstanding wine has a superb deep black colour coming from the best local grape (Auxerrois) produced with low yields. On the nose there is an intense concentration of black fruit (blueberry, blackcurrant), leather and vanilla. The Auxerrois brings firm but elegant and fine tannins. A big, massive Cahors perfect for autumn and winter, this wine will improve for twenty years or more in your cellar or can be enjoyed now

with game and forest mushrooms.

Dunnes Stores
AC Corton Grand Cru Clos du Roi Dom. Pierre Ponnelle 1997 (France) £25
This is a medium-bodied classic wine. The intense vegetal bouquet with its whiff of farmyard aromas is intriguing. An immediate attack of sweet fruit is followed by savoury complexity. With its firm tannins and high acidity, it's ready to drink now, but has plenty of potential for long-term cellaring for at least four years. Try it with game or ripe soft cheese.

Select Wines
DOCG Barolo Riserva Marchesi di Barolo 1993 (Italy) £26
A full-bodied classic wine with very complex aromas and flavours, this wine has chocolate and truffle aromas with an edge of rubber and a mouthfilling concentration of dark fruit flavours to balance firm tannin and acidity. Complex and well structured with a long finish, it goes well with red meats, especially beef braised in wine. It will last for at least another three years.

Findlaters
Don Melchor Private Reserve Cabernet Sauvignon Concha y Toro 1996 (Chile) £26
Dark ruby and opaque in the glass, the nose shows classic Old World *goût de terroir* or earthiness, but is overlaid with a typical Maipo Valley mintiness. The palate is rich with ripe blackcurrants and subtle vanilla, with highlights of cedar, tobacco, leather and spice, all of which finish long and slow on the palate. It will keep for at least four years. Try it with fillet steak au poivre or daube of beef.

Gilbeys
Wolf Blass Black Label Cabernet/Shiraz 96 (Australia) £27
This is a rich red wine with an aroma of ripe fruit and mint chocolate and vanilla complexity. On the palate it's full bodied with intense blackberry fruit and strong vanilla overtones.

Burgundy Direct
AC Nuits-St-Georges 1er Cru Vaucrains Dom. Robert Chevillon 1998 (France) £27
Robert Chevillon flies the flag for the older generation of Burgundy's top growers. The estate produces seven Premiers Crus, each one as individual as the soil from which it comes. Chevillon produces consistent wine; impressively so, even in mediocre vintages. This is a full, robust, rich, powerful red

Burgundy. Though a 'sleeper', this Vaucrains has a smoky, earthy, full character and a marked *goût de terroir*. It needs at least another five years' maturation.

Grants
Balmoral Syrah Rosemount 96/97 (Australia) £27
This classic Australian wine has excellent deep purple-red colour showing intense concentrated plum and blackberry fruit with underlying, well-integrated American oak. It has intense, long fruit flavours and a rich velvety texture on the finish. It needs at least five years' maturation and achieves its full potential at ten to fifteen years. A great match for strongly flavoured meat dishes.

Cana Wines
DOC Amarone della Valpolicella Classico Brunelli 96 (Italy) £28
Luigi Brunelli is the third generation in this family of wine producers, who are based in Cariano, which lies in the Classico area of Valpolicella. The superb quality of his wines is the result of the perfect marriage between the old passion and the most modern oenological technologies, selection during vintage after careful thinning out of the grapes and the utmost care during refinement. On the nose there are intense aromas of blackcurrant jam and walnuts. Christmas cake comes to mind. The wine is dry, velvety and warm. Sit in front of the fire and enjoy it or serve it with game, guinea fowl or as a digestif. It will age happily for another four or more years.

Findlaters
AC Beaune 1er Cru Grèves Dom. Bouchard Père et Fils 1996 (France) £29
The nose shows a restrained bouquet of soft raspberries, lulling the taster into a safe, secure sensation, then wow! The palate explodes in glorious complexity, revealing more summer fruit, sweet vanilla and soft spiciness, tamed by earthier characteristics such as well-worn leather, vegetal flavours and mocha. A heavenly wine. Try it with game. It will keep for at least four years.

Dillons
DOC Rioja Gran Reserva Montecillo 85 (Spain) £29
An elegant, mature Rioja with dry strawberries with oaky vanilla overtones.

Grants
Tignanello Piero Antinori 1997 (Italy) £30
The first of the Supertuscans (wines made outside the normal
DOC rules, using international grape varieties such as
Cabernet Sauvignon), Tignanello had its first vintage in 71. It's
a rich, highly concentrated, fruit-driven wine. Complex cassis
flavours on the nose follow through on the palate. It's full
bodied with firm tannins and has a very long, lingering finish.
It requires a long maturation period, so the 97 vintage should
be kept for at least ten years before drinking. The wine has
tremendous ageing ability — up to twenty years. It's a good
match for meat dishes.

Koala Wines
**St Andrews Cabernet Sauvignon Wakefield 1996 (Australia)
£25–£30**
The Taylor family, who live in the Clare Valley in South
Australia, bought an old dairy farm adjoining their property
and, to their delight, discovered the disused winery of St
Andrews, which had produced wines of excellence in the
1890s. This wine was matured in American and French oak
hogsheads for 18 months. Deep garnet in colour with brick-
red hues, the wine has a nose of pine nuts, nutmeg and spice
initially, followed by a sweet liqueured cassis lift with complex
characters of leather and forest floor earthiness. The taste is
rich, with powerful flavours and supple tannins. Medium to
full bodied, it has a herbal, savoury finish. Persistent in length
with a pleasant drying astringency, it will improve for up to
ten years or more. An absolute cracker with fillet steak and
lashings of garlic.

Koala Wines
St Andrews Shiraz Wakefield 1996 (Australia) £25–£30
This wine is an intense inky colour. On the nose there are
fennel, vanilla, coffee bean and an intense berried lift with
underlying biscuity oak. It tastes fleshy, supple and velvety
throughout the palate. Oak tannins enhance the fruit flavours,
giving depth and structure. The palate is tight with firm
astringency. The 96 vintage, like the Cabernet Sauvignon,
reflects an excellent year from the Clare Valley. This Shiraz
was matured in oak for 18 months and was given a further 18
months' bottle maturation. Its ageing potential is 15 years
plus. Get your hands on some venison and give yourself a
treat.

Koala Wines
1904 Block Shiraz Baileys of Glenrowan 1996 (Australia) £30
Baileys of Glenrowan is a winery rich in heritage and cel-
ebrates 130 years of winemaking in Glenrowan, north-eastern
Victoria (known as Ned Kelly country). The 1904 Block
exhibits all the characteristics of Shiraz vines that are nearly a
century old, with extraordinary depth and complexity of fruit
as its hallmark. The wine has been made in traditional slate
open fermenters and matured in a combination of new and
seasoned French and American oak. Vintage conditions in 98
were near perfect and for that reason this vintage is a must for
anyone who loves old-vine Shiraz. The wine is rich and
complex in the traditional Baileys style, while relying on ripe,
soft tannins to give it suppleness in youth as well as the ability
to age comfortably for twenty years. There is very little
available, but it's well worth seeking out to accompany
venison.

Select Wines
**DOCG Brunello di Montalcino Fattoria dei Barbi 1995 (Italy)
£30**
This is a top example of Brunello?Tuscany's most important
wine. It has earthy fruit aromas and strikes a fine balance
between fruit, tannins, acidity and alcohol. It will develop
more complexity in time, and will last at least four years. Serve
it with red meats, especially game or venison.

Findlaters
**DOC Rioja Reserva Barón de Chirel Marqués de Riscal 1995
(Spain) £32**
Here we have a very classic and traditional nose, with vegetal
and strawberry/raspberry aromas. The wine opens up when
decanted and left open for a while. The palate is subtle, yet the
flavours are complex and intertwined?savoury, almost smoky,
nuances with developing vegetal flavours (slight mushroom
note?very attractive), lots of strawberry fruit and some spice.
Ravishing! It will keep for at least four years. Serve it with beef
Wellington or strong game.

Fields
Elderton Command Shiraz 1995 (Australia) £35
A tensely textured *vin de garde* with a world-wide reputation,
this wine spends three years in American oak and a further
year in bottle before release to ensure layers of rich flavours
and fine tannins. Vines on this 28 hectare estate are between
forty and eighty years old. Full bodied and classic, it's rich,
creamy and voluptuous. Try it with turkey.

O'Briens
Shiraz Bethany 1995 (Australia) £35 (limited availability)
Bin GR is made only when the vintage is outstanding and only
333 cases of this wine were made. It is oak aged for two years.
Bethany is an outstanding boutique winery located in the
Barossa Valley. This fifth-generation family-owned winery sets
the benchmark for quality wine production. Geoff Schrapel
and his brother Rob, as the proud owners of 30 hectares of
premium aged vines at the foot of the Barossa ranges, are the
envy of all and sundry.
This is an extraordinarily intense and complex wine. Huge,
packed with black fruits, spice, leather and chocolate, the wine
just explodes on the palate, offering an intense profusion of
ripe fruits, vanilla and spice. It has huge length. This is a classic
collector's wine that shows the true majesty of well-made
Shiraz.

Gilbeys
Viña Tarapaca Millennium 1996 (Chile) £36
This is a superb example of how Chilean winecraft can reach
and match heights previously exclusive to select châteaux.
With intensely concentrated aromas of blackcurrants, cloves
and damsons, the palate unfolds into a rich tapestry of crushed
berries, orchard plums, cigar box spices and a seductive
chocolate finish. This sophisticated, luscious wine blossoms
with food and would be ideal with grilled filet mignon, classic
cheese fondues or Austrian-style meats enveloped in herbs
and breadcrumbs.

Maxxium
Geyser Peak Shiraz Reserve 1995 (USA) £36
Daryl Groom, an Australian winemaker (ex-Penfolds), has
established the winery's pre-eminence since joining Geyser
Peak in 1989. It shows in this classic Shiraz. Spice, chocolate
and raspberry emerge on the nose; on the palate it is luscious
and velvety with cigar and pepper tones. Drink it from now
until 2010 with beef, venison or well-hung game.

O'Briens
AC Margaux Grand Cru Classé Ch. Kirwan 1996 (France) £39
Ch. Kirwan is one of the truly majestic Wine Geese châteaux of
Bordeaux. Classed as a third growth in Margaux, this château
has been identified as one of the sleeping giants of Margaux,
and year on year attracts more attention and accolades due to
the genius of winemaker Jean Marc Troussard and the
château's outstanding terroir. This is a classic Margaux.
Although extremely youthful and in need of significant
cellaring, it shows all the classic signs of a truly thoroughbred
Margaux. The nose shows intense, elegant black fruit, with a

hint of toast and cedar. On the palate it's big and concentrated, with a firm tannic structure and good acidity. This wine is truly worthy of laying down. It would be a good match for rack of lamb or grilled meats.

Burgundy Direct
AC Gevrey-Chambertin 1er Cru Champeux Dom. Denis Mortet 1998 (France) £39
'The new kid on the Gevrey block', according to Hugh Johnson. Denis Mortet part acquired his father's estate in 1992 and has since gone on to make wines that have become the source of considerable international acclaim. Every bottle produced is sold in advance. His wines are among the most magnificent in Burgundy today. This Premier Cru Champeux is dark, elegant, powerful and opulent. It's very concentrated — dense, cassis-like hedonistic Burgundy. It will take three years to mature.

Dunnes Stores
The Armagh Shiraz Jim Barry 1996 (Australia) £40
From Clare Valley, this is considered one of Australia's great red wines and is often described as 'the black essence of Shiraz'. It's ready to drink now and will improve for at least another four years. Full bodied and fruit driven, this would be good with food — rare beef, venison or mature cheese. This is an enormously impressive wine with great concentration of rich spice and cassis berry fruit. The finish is never-ending. What is amazing is how enjoyable the wine is while it's still young, even though it's capable of long-term cellaring.

Bacchus Wines
DOC Rioja Reserva Marqués de Vargas Private Reserve 1996 (Spain) £40
This is a single-estate Rioja made with organically grown grapes, although this is not stated on the label. The estate produces only Reserva quality wines. A blend of Tempranillo, Mazuelo, Garnacha and other varieties, the wine is aged for approximately 23 months in 100 % Russian oak. Michel Rolland acts as technical adviser. In September 1999 *Decanter* magazine highlighted the 96 as one of the best wines they had tasted. Dark ruby in colour with a pronounced rich nose of spicy dark berry fruit, the wine is medium to full bodied with loads of intense berry fruit, subtle vanilla character and a long finish. Definitely one to lay down for a few years — three or more years from the vintage.

Greenhills
AC Margaux Grand Cru Classé Ch. Lascombes 1996 (France) £42–£43

If money's no object, it has to be Margaux! The château takes its name from Chevalier Antoine de Lascombe, the seventeenth-century owner. Now a modern vineyard with a new winery built in 1986, grapes are harvested by hand to ensure quality. Ch. Lascombes blends Cabernet Sauvignon, Cabernet Franc (to give body and a solid cassis fruit bouquet and brilliant colour) and Merlot (to provide vitality and softness). This is a good vintage and will improve with age.

Burgundy Direct
AC Chambolle-Musigny Dom. Comte Georges de Vogüé 1996 (France) £54

Together with Dom. de la Romanée-Conti, this is Burgundy's most legendary estate. It's an impeccable source, producing glorious wines with a capacity to age for many years. Since 1990 the wines have been textbook. Though youthful, this Chambolle-Musigny is extremely fine, elegant and rich. It has an almost exotic finish that seems to go on forever. 'The iron fist in the velvet glove!' It will be at its peak in three years' time—try to leave it till then.

Cana Wines
AC Corton Grand Cru Clos du Roi Dom. Remoissenet Père et Fils 1992 (France) £55

This wine is made by Christian Remoissenet, a young producer from a well-known family. Christian's wines have soft, rich fruit, complexity and balance as well as *goût de terroir*. This is a rich, powerful wine. The nose is port-like. A wine to drink slowly and savour, it has a long, rich finish. Serve it with guinea fowl.

Gilbeys
AC Hermitage La Chapelle Paul Jaboulet Aîné 97/98 (France) £55

Made from 100 per cent Syrah grapes grown on the hill of Hermitage, the wine is matured for 12 to 18 months in oak barrels. Full bodied and classic, this is an absolute blockbuster and lives up to its legendary reputation. Intensity and complexity are the two words that sum it up, from the dark, almost opaque, colour through the rich, spicy and berried nose to the palate, which is powerful and well rounded with great delicacy. It will age for ten years from the vintage. Try it with braised steak or most game dishes.

Gilbeys
AC Corton-Charlemagne Grand Cru Louis Latour 1997 (France) £65
The vineyard of Corton-Charlemagne is situated in the prime area of the legendary hill of Corton. The wines are vinified and aged in 100 per cent new oak in Latour's cellars at the foot of the hill in Corton-Grancey. It is Louis Latour's flagship wine and legend has it that in the ninth century Charles the Great (Charlemagne) used to stop off at the village of Aloxe-Corton and stock up on their 'honeyed, nutty wine'. A full-bodied classic, it will age for up to twenty years. This wine has a powerful nose with toasty and creamy floral tones. It fills the mouth with a multiplicity of flavours and has a long, silky finish.

Febvre
DOC Rioja Reserva Artadi Grandes Añadas 1994 (Spain) £85
Artadi is making stunning wines such as Viñas de Gain, Pagos Viejos and Viña el Pison, but their Grandes Añadas is made only in top vintages and the 94 is certainly that. A huge, concentrated wine full of deep red fruit, subtle oak and great complexity, it's good for another four years at least. Serve it with rack of lamb with rosemary.

Gilbeys
DOC Rioja Gran Reserva Especial Castillo de Ygay Marqués de Murrieta 1970 (Spain) £95
This huge wine is made only in very good vintages in Rioja and has rightly earned its reputation as one of Spain's finest wines. It is made by Bodegas Marqués de Murrieta, the oldest bodega in Rioja, and is aged in oak barrels coated with tartrate crystals, so that the oak affects the wine very slowly. It will age for decades—the 70 is good for another twenty years. Full bodied and classic, the nose on this wine fills you full of anticipation with its powerful, complex aromas. The palate has delicious dried fruit flavours and a remarkable balance of tannin and acidity right to the finish. Very special. Try it with beef the Cantabrian way, i.e. you let it see the grill for five seconds.

Mitchells
Vega Sicilia Unico Reserva 1981 (Spain) £110
Vega Sicilia is considered Spain's most important wine by most wine writers. Planted in 1864, the vineyards in the Ribera del Duero region produce complex and outstanding wines. Aged in American and French oak for up to eight years, this is the heart of Vega Sicilia style and uniqueness. Pablo Alvarer is the

winemaker. On the nose this wine has wonderful lead pencil and smoky notes that follow through on the palate. Hints of classic Médoc (e.g. Ch. Lafite-Rothschild) come through and the finish is extraordinary, with beautiful fruit, smoke, black-currant and weedy tobacco notes, long and fresh in the finish. A delight!

Champagne

Greenhills
Champagne Bricout Carte Noir nv (France) £25
A stylish blend of Chardonnay, Pinot Noir and Pinot Meunier gives the finesse that we expect from good Champagne. With its lovely toasty nose, good mousse and good body, it's best enjoyed with delicious food, friends and any celebration. Try it with smoked salmon or strawberries and cream in summer.

Bubble Brothers
Champagne Jacques Beaufort 1990 (France) £34
Organically produced and aged in oak casks for 8–10 months, this stunning Champagne is produced in minuscule quantities by the Beaufort family at their Grand Cru domaine in Ambonnay. Made predominantly from Pinot Noir with a sprinkling of Chardonnay, the wine shows a beautiful pale golden yellow 'robe'. The bubbles are tiny and fine, reflecting a wine of this age and quality from a great vintage. The aromas are exquisite — lively apple, some vegetal fruit with subtle mineral notes. In the mouth the taste is amplified — very pronounced, slightly toffeed apple with hints of apricots and figs. There is a truly lovely balance of fruit and crispness going on here! The finish is long, complex, intense and delicious with almonds and a touch of the wood in the finale. A Champagne to savour, not to be quaffed! For the full-on Beaufort experience, enjoy it at 7–8 °C.

Maxxium
Champagne Charles Heidsieck Brut Grande Marque 1985 (France) £58
Gold in colour, this stunning champagne has a clear sparkle with a bouquet of dried flowers, then more powerful aromas of glacé fruits and dried apricots combined with nuances of almond, brioche and hazelnuts. It will keep on improving and will go with almost everything!

Febvre
Champagne Deutz Cuvée William Deutz 1990 (France) £70
This house, now owned by the Louis Roederer group, is making headlines at comparative tastings for its elegant, intense character, persistent fine mousse and toasty length. Cuvée William is the house's prestige Champagne, along with

Amour de Deutz Blanc de Blancs 95. Try it with fish dishes in rich cream sauce.

Dillons
Champagne Dom Pérignon Moët et Chandon 92/93 (France) £80
The world-famous luxury cuvée from Moët et Chandon has rich, full, biscuity aromas followed by a depth of mature buttery style.

Fields
Champagne Cristal Louis Roederer 1993 (France) £120
This is one of the most sought-after and distinctive prestige cuvées, created especially for Tsar Alexander II in 1876. It is made to extremely high standards and even in small uneven vintages the quality cannot be questioned. The wine has an enticing nose of toast and spice matched by a rich, creamy palate. A fabulous vintage with a very fine mousse, it goes with everything — even cornflakes.

Sweet

Bubble Brothers
AC Maury Mas Amiel 1980 (France) £34
Twenty years old and still young! Mas Amiel makes some of the best red dessert wines in the world and the 80 vintage was bottled early to allow this nectar to evolve slowly in the bottle. The wine, which is made from 100% Grenache grapes, has an amazing tawny brown colour. On the nose it develops superb and complex aromas of Havana cigars, grilled coffee, choco-late, jammy red fruit, figs and plums. Well balanced with a nice refreshing acidity, it fills the palate with its rich and sensual sweetness. It would be perfectly complemented by rich chocolate cake, black and red fruit desserts or a very fine Cuban cigar.

Bacchus Wines
Bernkasteler Badstube Riesling Eiswein Dr Pauly Bergweiler 1998 (Germany) £45 (37.5 cl)
Dr Pauly Bergweiler is a long-established producer based in Bernkastel on the Mosel. Dr Peter Pauly owns vineyards in several key sites nearby, including Graacher Himmelreich, Erdener Treppchen and Wehlener Sonnenuhr. The Badstube (bath-house) vineyards lie directly above the town and Eiswein is the pinnacle of what Riesling can achieve. The frozen grapes are harvested from vineyards half-way up the slopes. Pale lemon in colour with a very delicate apple/citrus character, the wine is light bodied with an amazing balance between delicate sweetness and crisp acidity. It would be a shame to drink this wine now, although it is very tempting. It

should be kept for as many years as possible to allow the real Riesling character to develop, at least fifteen years from the vintage.

Fields

AC Sauternes 1er Cru Supérieur Ch. d'Yquem 1989 (France) £250

The king, or is it queen, of all Sauternes. It was very hot in 89 with a near-perfect growing season and a high level of botrytis infection. Among the best wines of the decade, this is a blockbuster with an intensely perfumed nose. Full bodied with rich botrytis fruit, it has a luxuriously rich palate and the ability to age for decades. If we consider this wine as the sauce, it will accompany your foie gras perfectly.

Where to buy the recommended wines

Wine is imported into Ireland by over a hundred separate importers, ranging from multi-million pound businesses to one-person operations. For most of these importers wine sold through restaurants (the 'on-trade') is as important as that sold retail (the 'off-trade') — most wine is, after all, designed to be consumed with food. As a result, some wines are deliberately given a low retail profile because they are popular in restaurants, and restaurant proprietors prefer that their customers shouldn't find it too easy to calculate the mark-up.

The picture is further complicated by the fact that for some wines — the so-called 'trophy' or 'allocation' wines — the producers may make only a few dozen cases of that vintage available to the importers, which naturally go to favoured outlets. These are just the wines that receive rave reviews from wine writers. Then again, popular wines styles such as Rioja, Chianti, Australian Chardonnay and Bordeaux are much more widely distributed than less well-known styles.

Perhaps three-quarters of the wine sold in Ireland comes through the top five importers. Much of this is branded wine such as Pedrotti, Blossom Hill and Jacob's Creek. As well as the high-volume brands, all the larger importers also carry a range of fine wines, which is less widely available. So a single importer might have some wines that are available in most convenience stores, and others that can be bought only from a handful of specialist shops. The commonly used term 'widely available' is quite inadequate to describe this situation.

A group of twenty middle-sized importers accounts for a further 20 per cent of the market, with the small operators the remaining 5 per cent. Naturally the coverage of the country varies widely from organisation to organisation. As a result some of the wines listed in this book are readily available across the country, others at a few select outlets, others again in only one outlet, or solely by direct mail.

The key to buying wine in Ireland, however, in every type of outlet is a manager/proprietor who is sufficiently interested in wine to respond to and stimulate local demand. Luckily, there are lots of them around.

Importers sell into seven broad categories of retailer, each with different characteristics. We have confined the use of the term 'widely available' to wines that are stocked in at least five of the seven categories listed.

1. Multiple stores: Dunnes, Roches Stores (which is owned by Musgraves), Superquinn, Tesco: The multiples usually import their own wine as well as selling wine from other importers. Their own wines are available only through their branches. Because of their enormous buying power, they can provide great value for money, but. because they need the volume, they tend not to have the most exclusive wines, though the larger Dunnes and Tescos have an impressive range.

2. SuperValu/Centra (owned by Musgraves) Particular managers can make an enormous difference to the range carried. The combination of this chain and Roches make Musgraves a powerful influence in the market.

3. Symbol groups: e.g. Londis, Mace, Spar. These shops generally stock a smallish range of basic wine. Once again, a particular manager with an interest in wine can make a substantial difference.

4. Pub–off-licence groups: Cheers and Next Door Until these two chains got going, pub off-licences had a dismal reputation. The two chains are run by the Licensed Vintners' Association (Dublin) and the Vintners' Federation (rest of the country) respectively and are changing the image dramatically with the aid of wine consultant Mary O'Callaghan. Both chains are growing rapidly — at the time of going to press Cheers had twenty-three stores and Next Door thirty.

5. NOffLA members There are over three hundred members of the National Off-licence Association who have the triple licence (beer, wine and spirits). Members are encouraged to display the NOffLA logo on the door. NOffLA run an annual awards scheme in conjunction with Gilbeys to encourage exoertise and to raise standards. From the winelover's point of view the best NOffLA stores have several hundred wines in stock, as well as interesting beers and spirits, and will have time and interest to help you personally. They will often be able to order specific wines from the importer.

6. Off-licence groups NOffLA also includes a number of chains of off-licences. Some trade observers believe that this is the way the Irish trade will go, following the British example. Irish examples of this growing sector include O'Donovans (Cork), Galvins (Cork), Fine Wines of Limerick, Molloys (Dublin), O'Briens (Dublin), and of course Oddbins, the one British chain in the south.

7. Specialists A few stores, like the wine merchants of old, sell nothing but wine and wine accessories. Typical examples are Mitchells, Searsons and Berry Brothers & Rudd. They tend also to import and sell their own wines elsewhere, as well as selling wine imported by others.

Importers and stockists

Availability is not only complicated, it changes from week to week. Below is a snapshot of where a specific importer's wines, selected for this book, are likely to be stocked, based on information supplied in October 2000. Because of the complexity of the distribution web, not all importers felt able to provide the information. If you have any difficulty finding a wine, the importer would be happy to identify your nearest stockist.

James Adams Vintners Ltd. 1 Charleston Road, Dublin 6. Tel (01) 496 3866 Fax (01) 496 0186 e-mail adamsvintners@tinet.ie

Allied Drinks Ltd, Windsor Hill House, Glounthaune, Co. Cork. Tel (021) 4353 438 Fax (021) 4354 362, e-mail info @alliedrinks.ie; JFK Road, JFK Industrial Estate, Dublin 12 Tel (01) 450 9777 Fax (01) 450 9699, e-mail anne@allieddrinks.ie

> The Hardy and Errazuriz ranges are widely available, the Villa Maria and Laroche ranges in urban areas only.

Approach Trade Ireland Ltd, South Quay, Carrick-on-Suir, Co. Tipperary. Tel (051) 640 164 Fax (051) 641 580 Mobile (087) 233 2025

> Wines are available direct and also from Egan's (Liscannor, Co. Clare); Karwig Wines (Cork); Mitchells (Dublin), On the Grapevine (Dalkey, Co. Dublin); The Gourmet Gallery (Dublin 6): McCambridges (Galway); The Sky & The Ground (Wexford).

Bacchus Wine & Spirit Merchants Ltd, Unit T, 28 Stillorgan Industrial Park, Blackrock, Co. Dublin. Tel (01) 294 1466 Fax (01) 295 7375; Bacchus Munster, 'Thornbury', Model Farm Rd, Cork, Tel (021) 4874 164 Fax (021) 4874 307 Mobile 086 830 0842

> Wines are available from Roches Stores, SuperValu-Centra, Cheers, Molloys and a few individual off-licences.

Barry & Fitzwilliam Ltd, Ballycurreen Industrial Estate, Airport Rd, Cork. Tel (021) 432 0900 Fax (021) 432 0910; 50 Dartmouth Square, Dublin 6. Tel (01) 667 1755/660 6984 Fax (01) 660 0479

> Some ranges, such as Michel Lynch, Chapel Hill, Vendange and Yaldara are widely available. Specialist stores such as Redmonds (Dublin 6), DeVine Wine (Dublin 15) and On The Grapevine (Co. Dublin) stock most of the list.

Bubble Brothers, 43 Upper John St, Cork. Tel/Fax (021) 455

2252 e-mail: info@bubblebrothers.com Web site: http://
www.bubblebrothers.com

> All the wines are available by mail order or through the
> Bubble Brothers shop in the English Market, Cork.
> Some are also available through Pettits.

Burgundy Direct, 8 Monaloe Way, Blackrock, Co. Dublin. Tel
(01) 289 6615/288 6239 Fax (01) 289 8470

> The wines are available by mail order only.

Cana Wines, 10 Castle St, Mullingar, Co. Westmeath. Tel (044)
42742 Fax (044) 47547

> All the wines are available from the Cana Wine and
> Food Shop (Mullingar); some are also available from
> DeVine Wines (Dublin 15), Vin Wines (Letterkenny),
> Next Door (Longford) Bord Coffee & Wine (Dublin)
> and The Mill Wine Cellar (Maynooth).

Cassidy Wines Ltd, 1B Stillorgan Industrial Park, Stillorgan,
Dublin 18. Tel (01) 295 4157/4632 Fax 295 4477

Classic Wines, 3 Annmount, Glounthane, Co. Cork. Tel (021)
435 4888 Fax (021) 435 1010 Mobile 086 885 7840

> All the wines are available direct. Some are also
> available through O'Donovans (Cork).

Peter A. Dalton Food & Wine, 'Loch Grein', Ballybetagh,
Kilternan, Co. Dublin. Tel/Fax (01) 295 4945 e-mail
padwines@indigo.ie Web site http://www.daltonwines.com

> The wines are available in some SuperValu-Centra
> stores, some symbols, some Cheers (Co. Dublin,
> Roscommon), Deveneys (Dublin), DeVine Wine (Dublin
> 15), Ashford Food & Wine (Wicklow), Cana (Mullingar),
> Cuisine de Vendange (Naas).

Edward Dillon & Company, 25 Mountjoy Square East, Dublin
1. Tel (01) 819 3300 Fax (01) 855 5852

> The larger the importer, the more complex the pic-
> ture — some of Dillon's wines are 'widely available',
> others only through independents and specialists.

Dunnes Stores, Head Office, 67 Upper Stephen St, Dublin 8. Tel
(01) 475 1111 Fax (01) 475 1441

> The wines are available only from branches of Dunnes
> Stores.

Ecock Wines, Unit 6, Riverview Business Park, Nangor Rd,
Dublin 12. Tel (01) 460 0511 Fax (01) 460 0484

Febvre & Co. Ltd, 15–17 Maple Avenue, Stillorgan Industrial Park, Stillorgan, Co. Dublin. Tel (01) 295 9030 Fax (01) 295 9036

Fields Wine Merchants Ltd., 1B Birch Avenue., Stillorgan Industrial Park, Stillorgan, Co. Dublin. Tel (01) 295 4422 Fax (01) 295 4452

> Fields is the wholesale branch of Berry Brothers & Rudd; Berry Brothers' own-label wines are available only through the shop, others are available through NOffLA specialists.

Findlater (Wine Merchants) Ltd The Harcourt Street Vaults, 10 Upper Hatch St, Dublin 2. Tel (01) 475 1699 Fax (01) 475 2530

> Most of the wines are widely available, through Superquinn, Pettits, SuperValu-Centra, the pub off-licence groups, O'Donovans and Molloys, and the top individual independents and specialists. The Ironstone range may be harder to find.

Gilbeys of Ireland, Nangor House, Nangor Road, Western Estate, Dublin 12. Tel (01) 419 4000 Fax (01) 419 4001 (Reception); Tel: (01) 419 4040 Fax: (01) 419 4041 (Sales) e-mail: gilbeys.info@udv.com

> Some of Gilbey's wines are 'widely available', others only through what they call the 'premium off-trade', which includes the Merrion Tesco, Dunnes Cornelscourt, the NOffLA chains and the independent specialists.

M. & J. Gleeson & Co., 15 Cherry Orchard Estate, Ballyfermot, Dublin 10. Tel (01) 626 9787 Fax (01) 626 0652. Greenlawn, Borrisoleigh, Co. Tipperary Tel (0504) 51113 Fax (0504) 51480

> Most of the wines are available through independents and specialists, and through wine-oriented symbols and SuperValu-Centras.

Grants of Ireland Ltd, Kilcarberry Industrial Park, Nangor Rd, Clondalkin, Dublin 22. Tel (01) 630 4156/630 4157/630 4121 Fax (01) 630 4124 (Customer Service) Tel (01) 630 4100 Fax (01) 630 4123 (other departments) e-mail: grants @cantrell.ie

> The wines are aell distributed through the multiples; they are also available from the O'Briens chain and specialists such as McCabes and Redmonds.

Greenhills Wines & Spirits, Aisling House, Shanowen Rd, Santry, Dublin 9. Tel (01) 842 2188 Fax (01) 842 2455

> Look for their wines in Mace, Spar and Superquinn.

Irish Distillers Group, 11–12 Bow Street, Dublin 7. Tel (01) 872 5566 Fax (01) 872 3109 e-mail info@idl.ie

Koala Wines, 25 Seatown, Dundalk, Co Louth. Tel (048) 4175 2804 Fax (048) 4175 2943 e-mail koalawines@ireland1.fsbusiness.co.uk

> The wines are available from Roches, Superquinn, SuperValu-Centra, Londis, Spar, Cheers, Next Door, Pettits, O'Donovans, most NOffLA independents, On the Grapevine.

B. MacCormaic Vintners, 116a Terenure Road North, Dublin 6W. Tel (01) 490 7928 Fax (01) 490 7930 e-mail maccormaicvintners@eircom.net

> The wines are available from SuperValu-Centra and the symbols.

Maxxium, Rembrandt House, 1 Longford Terrace, Monkstown, Co Dublin (01) 280 4341 Fax (01) 2801805

> Try Roches, Londis, SuperValu-Centra or O'Briens.

Mitchell & Son, 21 Kildare St, Dublin 2. Tel (01) 676 0766 Fax (01) 661 1509/54 Glasthule Rd, Sandycove, Co. Dublin. Tel (01) 230 2301 Fax (01) 230 2305 e-mail michkst@indigo.ie, mitchell@indigo.ie web site http://mitchellandson.com

> Available only from Mitchells wine shops — orders can be processed through the web site.

Molloy's Liquor Stores, Head Office, Block 2, Village Green, Tallaght, Dublin 24. Tel (01) 451 5544 Fax (01) 451 5658 e-mail molloys@indigo.ie

> Available only from branches of Molloy's Liquor Stores or through their web site www.liquorstore.ie.

Morgan Wines 20 Clanbrassil Street, Dublin 2 Tel (01) 662 7752 Fax (01) 662 7756

James Nicholson Unit 4, Santry Hall Industrial estate, Dublin 9 Tel 1890 667799 Fax 048 4483 0028

O'Briens Wine Off-Licence Group, Unit 33 Spruce Avenue, Stillorgan Industrial Park, Co. Dublin. Tel (01) 269 3139 Fax (01) 269 7480 e-mail accounts@obriensgroup.ie web site www.obrienswine.ie

> The wines are available only from branches of O'Briens.

Oddbins, 17 Baggot St, Dublin 2. Tel (01) 667 3033 Fax (01) 667 3109. Other Dublin branches in Blackrock, Churchtown and Clontarf.

> Only available from branches of Oddbins.

On The Case Organic Wines, 2 St James Terrace, South
Circular Rd, Dublin 8. Tel/Fax (01) 473 0156 Mob 087 2309173
e-mail info@onthecase.ie web site www.onthecase.ie

> The wines are available direct and also in Dublin from
> McCabes, Laydens, Claudio's, On The Grapevine, For
> Goodness Sake, Mortons, Bird Flanagan, Swiss
> Delicatessan, Quinns, and in Co. Meath from The
> Barrow (Ashbourn).

River Wines, Sandpit House, Termonfeckin, Co. Louth. Tel
1850 794 637, Fax (041) 982 2820 e-mail: rvrwines@indigo.ie

> The wines are available only by mail order.

Searsons Wine Merchants, Monkstown Crescent, Blackrock,
Co. Dublin Tel (01) 280 0405 Fax (01) 280 4771

> Searsons and The Wicklow Wine Co. stock all the wines
> listed; individual wines are also stocked in Dublin by
> DeVine Wine, On the Grapevine, McCabes, The Vintry,
> Michael's Wines, Redmonds, Laydens, and by The Wine
> Centre (Kilkenny), Murtaghs (Enniskerry), The Old
> Stand (Mullingar), O'Donovans (Cork) and The Vine-
> yard (Galway).

Select Wines from Italy Ltd 13 Grattan Court, Gorey, Co.
Wexford. Tel (055) 80955 Fax (055) 80958 e-mail
winesit@indigo.ie

> Most of the wines are available from Mitchells; indi-
> vidual wines are also available from McCambridges
> (Galway), McCabes (Dublin), Bradleys (Cork), and the
> Kilkenny Wine Centre.

SuperValu-Centra, Laurel House, PO Box 929, Robinhood
Industrial Estate, Clondalkin, Dublin 22 Tel (01) 450 1442 Fax
(01) 450 5249 email svcd@musgrave.ie web site http://
www.musgrave.ie

> The wines are available only from SuperValu-Centra
> outlets.

Syrah Wines, 11 Rowanbyrn, Blackrock, Co. Dublin. Tel (01)
289 3670 Fax (01) 289 3306

Taserra Wine Merchants, 17 Rathfarnham Road, Terenure,
Dublin 6W. Tel (01) 490 4047 Fax (01) 490 4052

TDL Distributors, Naas Rd, Clondalkin, Dublin 22. Tel (01) 413
0100 Fax (01) 413 0123 e-mail tdl@tdl.ie

Terroirs Ltd 103 Morehampton Road, Donnybrook, Dublin 4.
Tel (01) 667 1311 Fax 667 1312 e-mail info@terroirs.ie

Tesco Ireland, Gresham House, Marine Rd, Dun Laoghaire, Co. Dublin. Tel (01) 280 8441 Fax (01) 280 0136

The wines are available only from branches of Tesco.

United Beverages, Finches Industrial Park, Long Mile Road, Dublin 12. Tel (01) 450 2000 Fax (01) 450 9004

Vaughan Johnson Wine Shop 11a East Essex St., Dublin 2. Tel (01) 671 5355

WineOnline Unit 8 Hilltop Business Centre, Raheny, Dublin 5. Ireland Tel (01) 851 1205 Fax (01) 851 1206 web site www.wineonline.ie

The wines are available only through the web site.

Wines Direct, Lisamate, Irishtown, Mullingar, Co Westmeath. Tel 1800 579 579 Fax (044) 40015 e-mail winesdirect@wines-direct.com Website http://www.wines-direct.com/

The wines are available only by mail order.

Woodford Bourne (inc. Mitchells Wholesale) 79 Broomhill Road, Tallaght, Dublin 24. Tel (01) 404 7300 Fax (01) 459 9342

Send a gift of wine— www.wineonline.ie

Gilbeys/NOffLA National Off-Licence of the Year 2001

The following off-licences got through the demanding first round of the Gilbeys/NOffLA Off-Licence of the Year Award. They are not, of course, the only good off-licences around, but they certainly represent a good place to start in your area.

CORK
Bradley's Off-Licence, 81/82 North Main Street, Cork
Galvins Wines & Spirits, 37 Bandon Road, Cork
Galvins Wines & Spirits, Claremount, Douglas Road, Cork
Galvins Wines & Spirits, Washington Street, Cork
O'Donovans Wines & Spirits, Bishopstown, Co. Cork
O'Donovans Wines & Spirits, Main Street, Midleton, Co. Cork
O'Donovans Wines & Spirits, Riversdale, Midleton, Co. Cork

DUBLIN
Sweeney's Off-Licence, 20 Lower Dorset Street, Dublin 1
Sweeney's Off-Licence, 117 Philipsburgh Avenue, Fairview, Dublin 3
O'Briens Wine Offlicence Group, 30 Donnybrook Road, Donnybrook, Dublin 4
Kelly's Off-Licence, 25E Malahide Road, Dublin 5
McHugh's Off-Licence, 57 Kilbarrack Road, Dublin 5
O'Briens Wine Offlicence Group, 105 Rathgar Road, Dublin 6
O'Briens Wine Offlicence Group, 149 Upper Rathmines Road, Dublin 6
Redmond's of Ranelagh, 25 Ranelagh, Dublin 6
The Vintry, 102 Rathgar Road, Dublin 6
O'Briens Wine Offlicence Group, Unit 2, New Development, Templeogue Village, Dublin 6W
O'Briens Wine Offlicence Group, Unit 6, The Maple Centre, Navan Road, Dublin 7
Deveney's Off-Licence, 382 South Circular Road, Dublin 8
Ashleaf Off-Licence, Crumlin Cross, Crumlin, Dublin 12
Martha's Vineyard, Rosemount Shopping Centre, Rathfarnham, Dublin 14
Molloy's Liquor Stores, Clonsilla Mall, Clonsilla, Dublin 15
Molloy's Liquor Stores, Main Street, Blanchardstown, Dublin 15
Molloy's Liquor Stores, Nutgrove Shopping Centre, Rathfarnham, Dublin 16

DUBLIN COUNTY
Jus de Vine, Unit 10, Portmarnock Shopping Centre, Co. Dublin
McCabe's Off-Licence, 51/55 Mount Merrion Avenue, Blackrock, Co. Dublin
O'Briens Wine Offlicence Group, 1 Main Street, Malahide, Co. Dublin
O'Briens Wine Offlicence Group, 58 Upper Georges Street, Dun Laoghaire, Co. Dublin
The Pottery Vine Ltd, Pottery Road, Dun Laoghaire, Co. Dublin

GALWAY
Vineyard Off-Licence, 14 Mainguard Street, Galway

KERRY
O'Sullivan's Off-Licence, 29 The Mall, Tralee, Co. Kerry

KILDARE
Next Door Off-Licence, 52 Leinster Street, Athy, Co. Kildare
The Mill Wine Cellar, Mill Street, Maynooth, Co. Kildare

KILKENNY
The Wine Centre, John Street, Kilkenny

LAOIS
Portlaoise Wine Vault, 67 Main Street, Portlaoise, Co. Laois

LIMERICK
Fine Wines Megastore, 42 Roches. Street, Limerick
Mac's Off-Licence, Ennis Road, Limerick

LOUTH
Byrne's Off-Licence-The Off Trade, 10 Hill Street, Dundalk, Co.
    Louth
Callan's Off-Licence, 40 Park Street, Dundalk, Co. Louth
Egan's Off-Licence, 1 Peter Street, Drogheda, Co. Louth

MAYO
Centra, Foxford, Co. Mayo
Fahy's Off-Licence, Teeling Street, Ballina, Co. Mayo

MEATH
Next Door, Main Street, Enfield, Co. Meath
The Ryan Vine Wine Shop & Off-Licence, 22 Trimgate Street,
    Navan, Co. Meath
The Wine Bottle, Dunshaughlin, Co. Meath

TIPPERARY
Eldon's Clonmel Ltd, 13 Dillon Street, Clonmel, Co. Tipperary
Lonergan Off-Licence, O'Connell Street, Clonmel, Co. Tipperary
Mulqueen's Off-Licence, 38/41 Connolly Street, Nenagh, Co.
    Tipperary

WATERFORD
Ardkeen Superstores, Dunmore Road, Waterford

WESTMEATH
SuperValu, Castlemaine Street, Athlone, Co. Westmeath

WICKLOW
O'Briens Wine Offlicence Group, 19 Quinsboro Road, Bray, Co
    Wicklow

Index